PAUL ALLOR
CHRIS EVENHUIS
SJAN WEIJERS

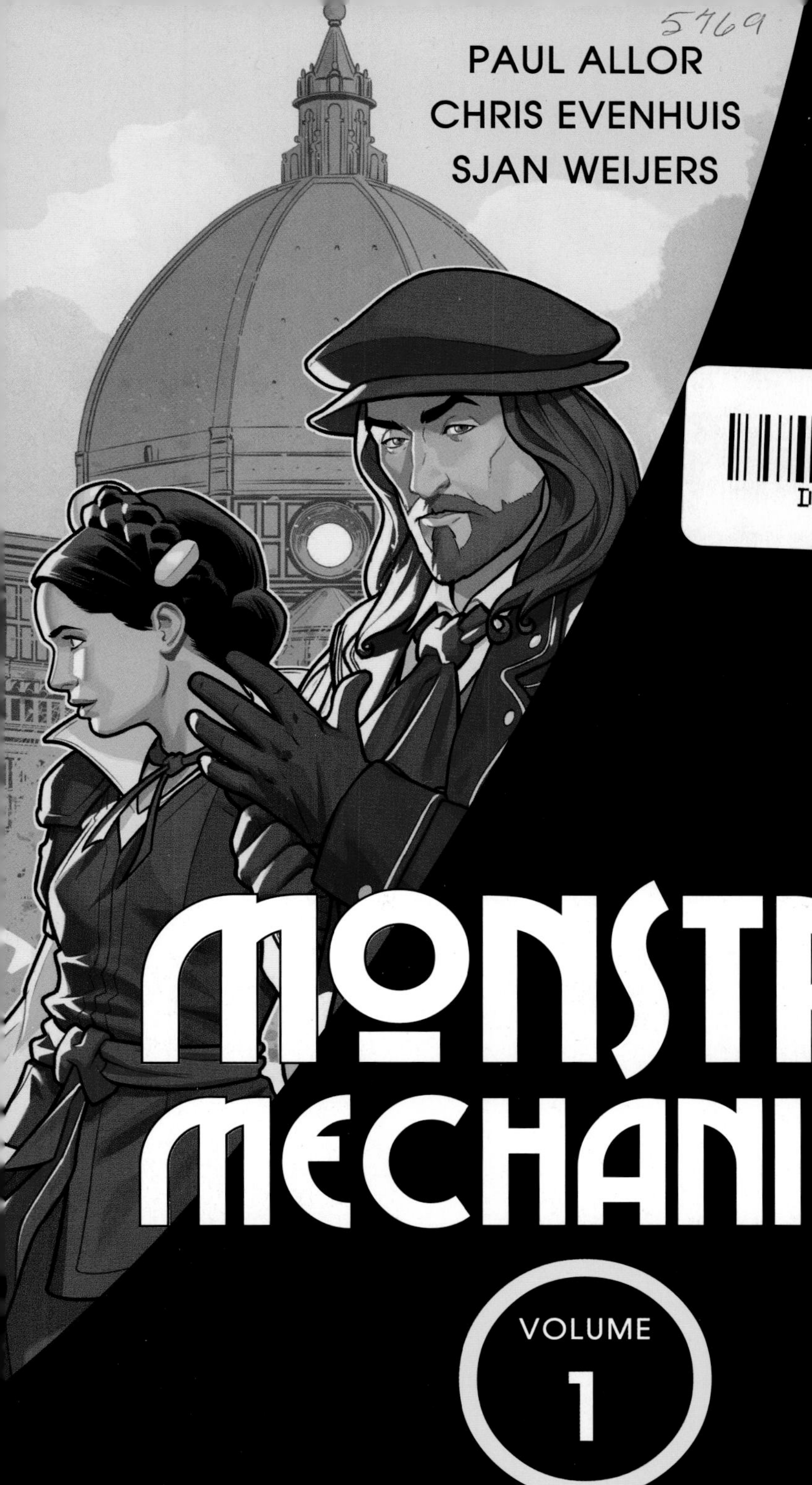

MONSTRO MECHANICA™

VOLUME 1

THE AUTOMATON

AFTERSHOCK™

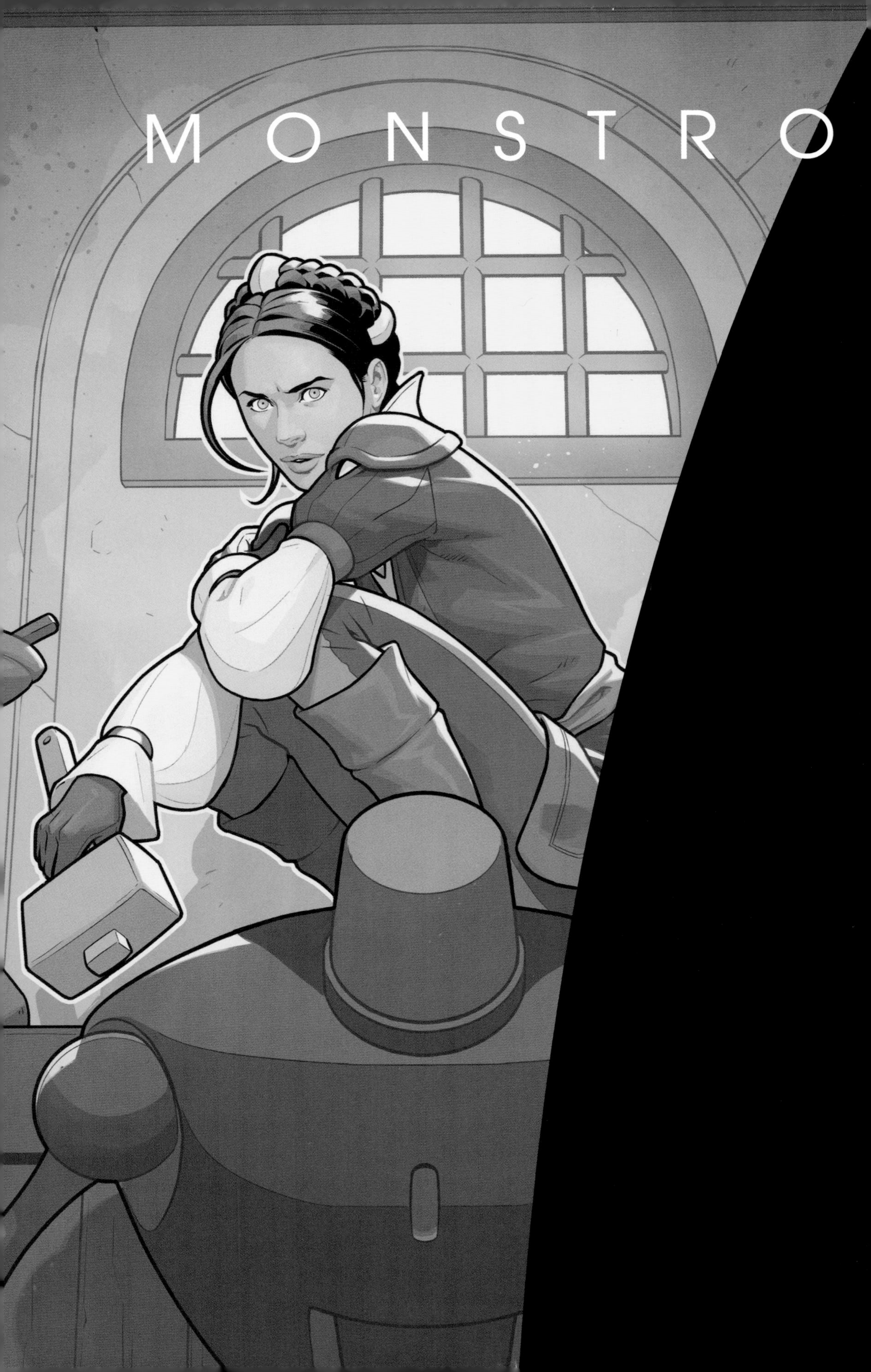
MONSTRO

MECHANICA™
VOLUME 1
THE AUTOMATON

PAUL ALLOR co-creator & writer

CHRIS EVENHUIS co-creator & artist

SJAN WEIJERS colorist

PAUL ALLOR letterer

CHRIS EVENHUIS w/ **SJAN WEIJERS** original covers

ARIELA KRISTANTINA w/ **ANDRE SZYMANOWICZ** variant cover

JOHN J. HILL logo designer

COREY BREEN book designer

MIKE MARTS editor

AFTERSHOCK™

MIKE MARTS - Editor-in-Chief • **JOE PRUETT** - Publisher/ Chief Creative Officer • **LEE KRAMER** - President
JON KRAMER - Chief Executive Officer • **STEVE ROTTERDAM** - SVP, Sales & Marketing • **LISA Y. WU** - Retailer/Fan Relations Manager
CHRISTINA HARRINGTON - Managing Editor • **JAY BEHLING** - Chief Financial Officer • **JAWAD QURESHI** - SVP, Investor Relations
AARON MARION - Publicist • **CHRIS LA TORRE** - Sales Associate • **KIM PAGNOTTA** - Sales Associate • **LISA MOODY** - Finance
CHARLES PRITCHETT - Comics Production • **COREY BREEN** - Collections Production • **TEDDY LEO** - Editorial Assistant

AfterShock Trade Dress by **JOHN J. HILL** • AfterShock Logo Design by **COMICRAFT**
Publicity: contact **AARON MARION** (aaron@publichausagency.com) & **RYAN CROY** (ryan@publichausagency.com) at **PUBLICHAUS**
Special thanks to: **IRA KURGAN, STEPHAN NILSON, JULIE PIFHER** and **SARAH PRUETT**

AFTERSHOCKCOMICS.COM Follow us on social media 🐦 ⓘ f

I N T R O D U C T I O N

MONSTRO MECHANICA is a swashbuckling meditation on the nature of identity.

I've said that a lot over the last several months. Both because it puts a smile on my face, and also because it's true. With this book we aimed to be simultaneously cerebral and kinetic, meditative and action-packed.

But it wasn't always that way. When I first pitched MONSTRO MECHANICA to the extraordinary artist and co-creator Chris Evenhuis (almost exactly five years ago to the day, as I write this), I said that it would be "a rollicking, off-beat adventure story set in Italy during the Renaissance, as our characters get caught up in the spycraft and warfare taking place at that time."

In the next paragraph I got around to mentioning da Vinci, his "butt-kicking apprentice" and "a fully operable A.I. robot that da Vinci creates."

Chris responded with an enthusiastic yes, and then immediately mentioned that the robot should be made of wood—an idea so perfect it made me giggle with anticipation. That was the first of many, many joyful moments during the making of this comic.

So we set out to make our slightly-odd-but-mostly-straightforward action tale. But as I started reading up on da Vinci's life, I was quickly reminded that the Renaissance was the birth of humanism in the Western world—the cradle of our modern belief that all women and men have inherent value as individuals (and not just as a cog in the machine of society).

The connection was obvious: a story about a sci-fi robot slowly gaining sentience during a period of societal upheaval, when the very nature of the self was being reconsidered.

And so MONSTRO MECHANICA became a platform for Chris, colorist Sjan Weijers and I to explore issues of identity and consciousness: how the way we view ourselves is shaped by the way others view us, and vice versa; how our outer appearances belie what's happening beneath the surface; how societal forces impact all of the above. And to wrap it all up in a stylish adventure tale, permeated with panache and filled to the brim with derring-do.

All of which was accomplished largely through Chris Evenhuis and Sjan Weijers' extraordinary work.

Chris' early character designs went a long way to shaping our characters. Da Vinci transitioned from being an aloof, benign mentor into something far more sinister: a man who is aware of his own extraordinary ability to connect the dots between nature, art, science and engineering, and who values himself above all those around him.

Or nearly all. Isabel—our true main character—challenges da Vinci. He respects and appreciates her as one of the few people who sees through his games and is willing to call him on them. She sees da Vinci buildings weapons for both sides of a simmering cold war, and she knows it will end badly for him—even if he's too arrogant to see it for himself.

And just as the story evolved over the years, Chris honed his already-exquisite style, working with Sjan to create a book that looks and feels very much like a product of pop culture, modern but with just a touch of art deco. It's bright, it's fun, it's exquisitely well-designed, and it's all done in a line style so clean you could eat dinner off of it. It's the perfect style for this weird, wonderful, slightly-ridiculous story. The perfect style for a swashbuckling meditation on the nature of identity.

This book was a joy for us to make, and we truly hope it's a joy for you to read. So, get started!

PAUL ALLOR
July 2018

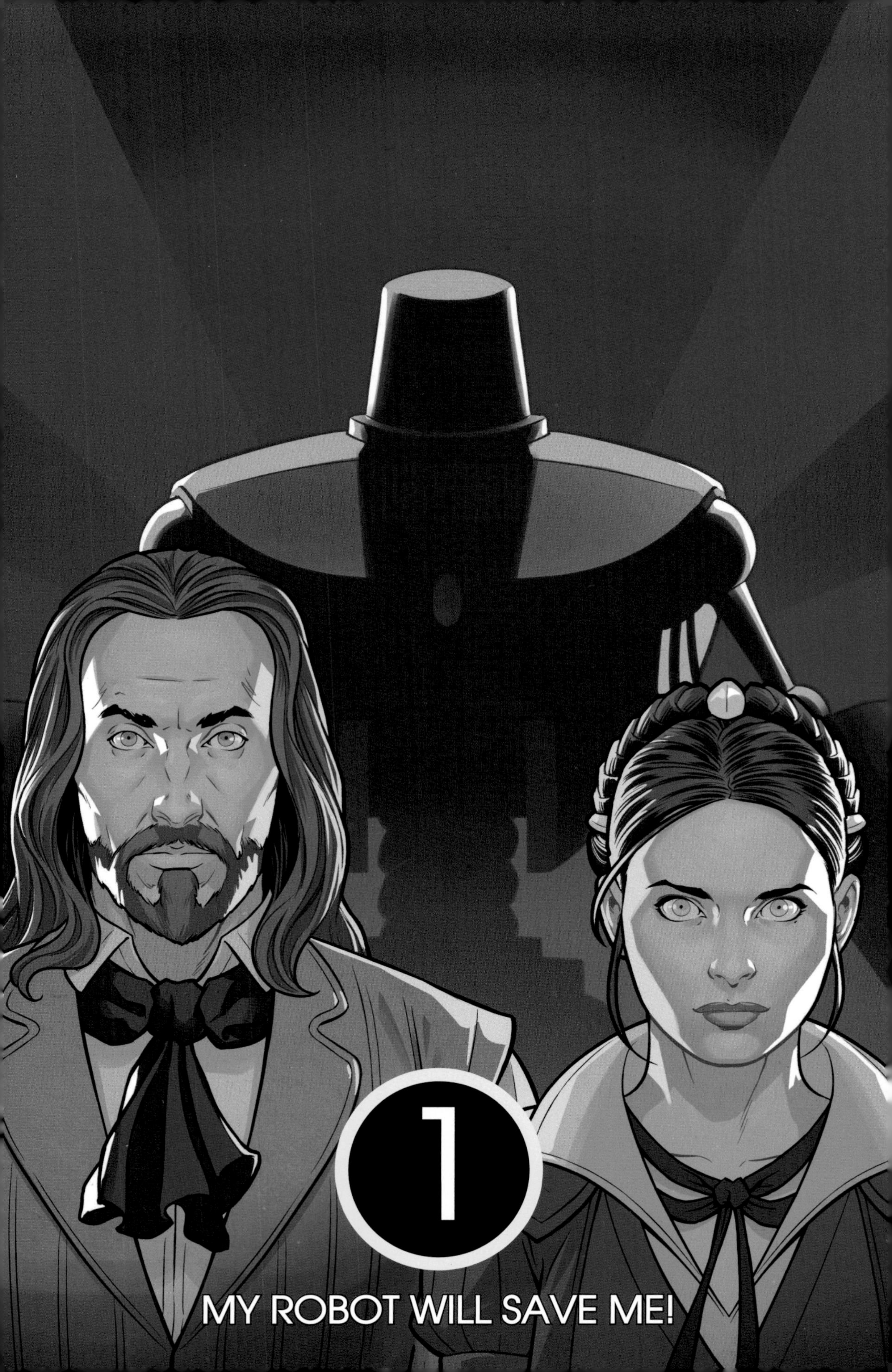
1
MY ROBOT WILL SAVE ME!

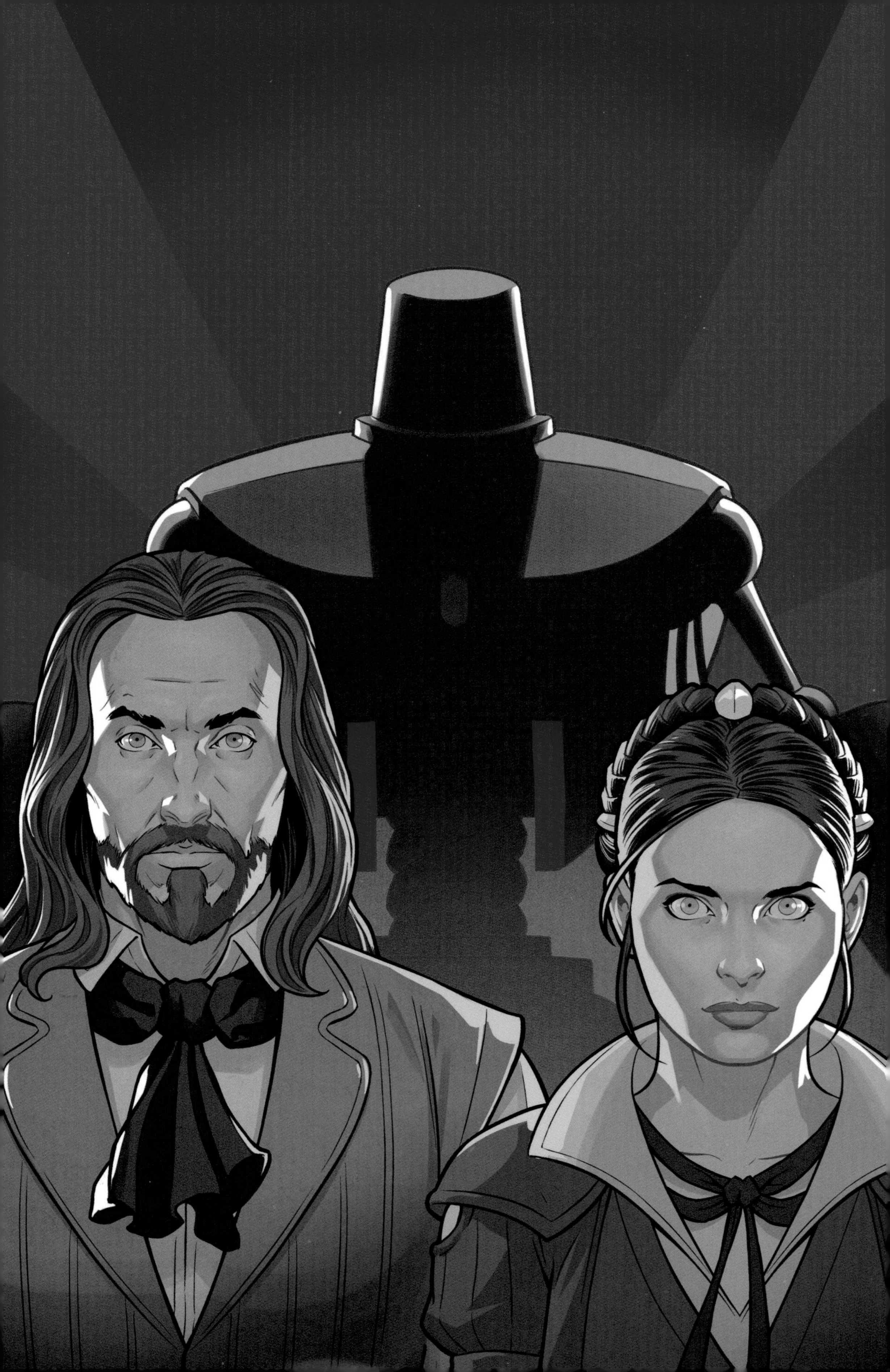

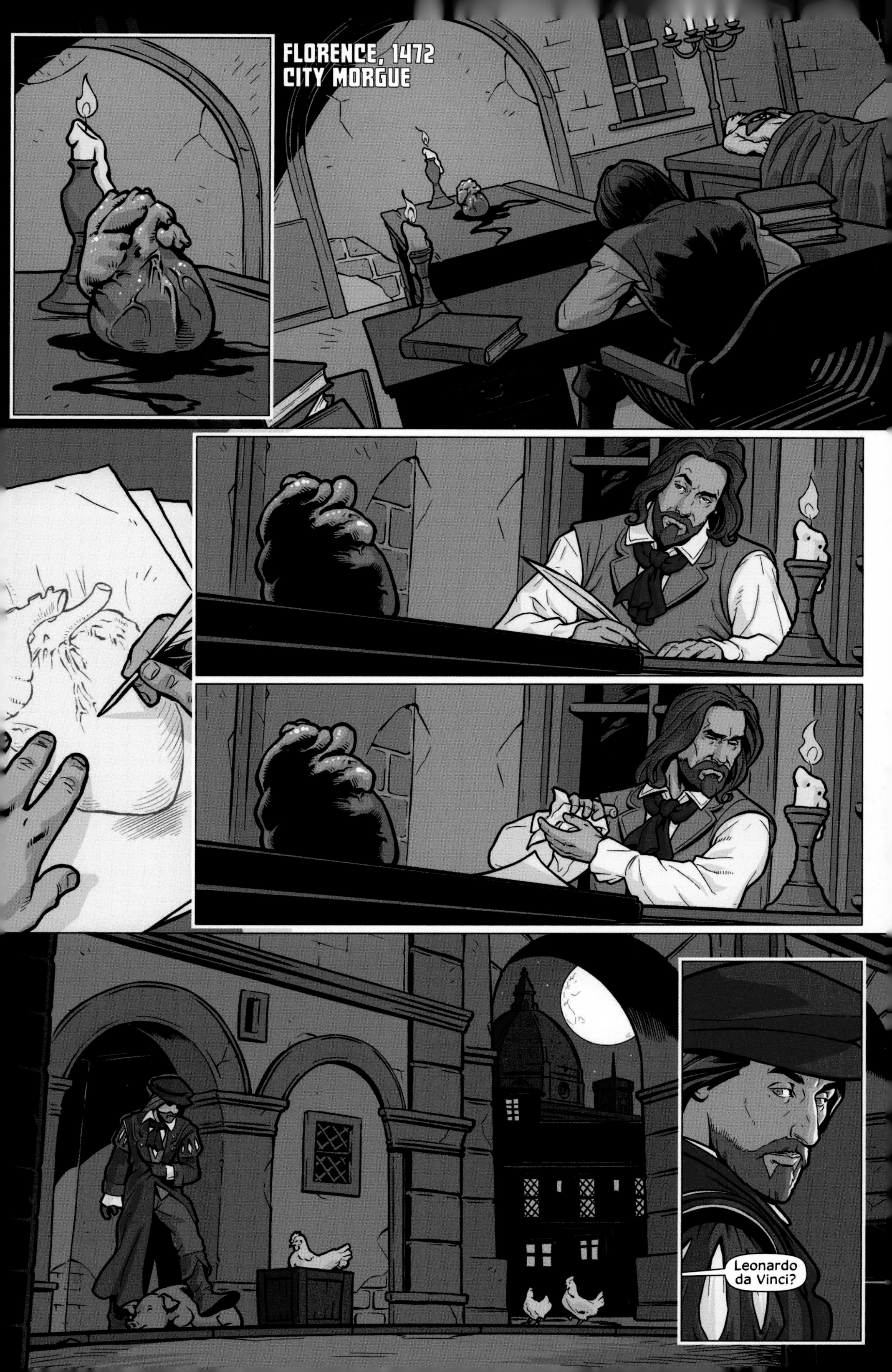
FLORENCE, 1472
CITY MORGUE
Leonardo da Vinci?

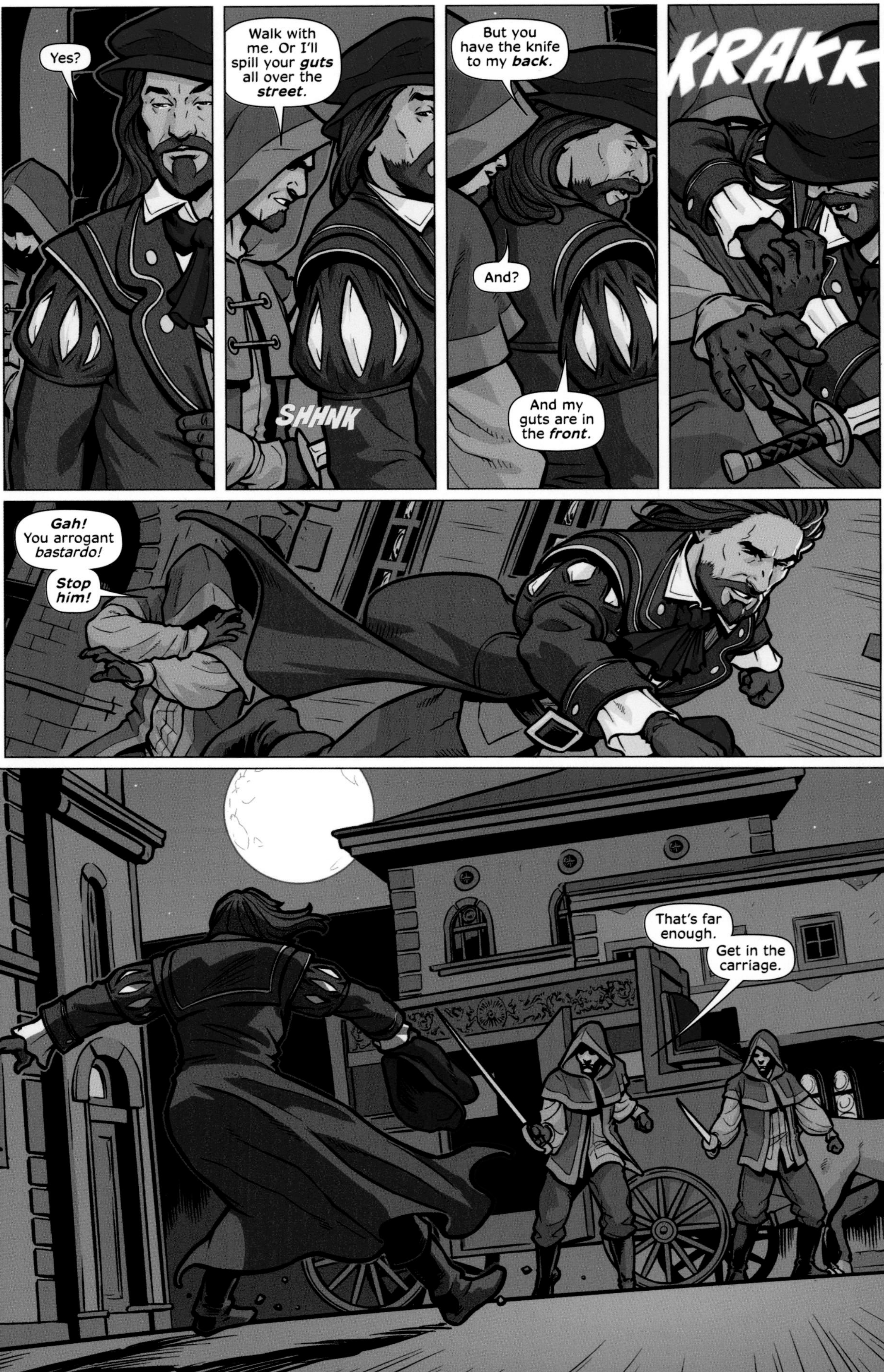
Yes?
Walk with me. Or I'll spill your *guts* all over the *street*.
SHHNK
But you have the knife to my *back*.
And?
And my guts are in the *front*.
KRAKK
Gah! You arrogant *bastardo!*
Stop him!
That's far enough.
Get in the carriage.

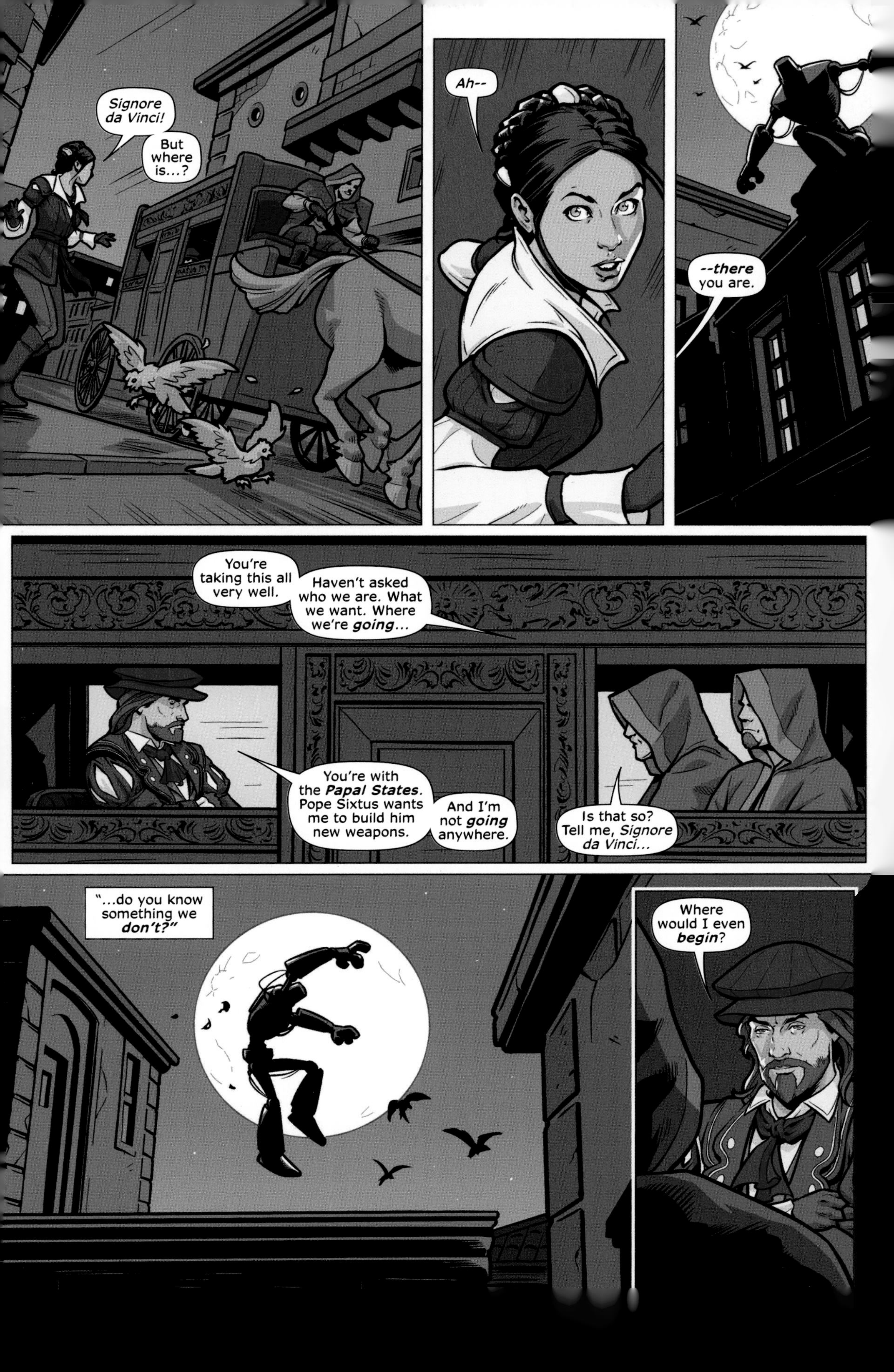
Signore da Vinci!
But where is...?
Ah--
--*there* you are.
You're taking this all very well.
Haven't asked who we are. What we want. Where we're *going*...
You're with the *Papal States*. Pope Sixtus wants me to build him new weapons.
And I'm not *going* anywhere.
Is that so? Tell me, *Signore da Vinci*...
"...do you know something we *don't?*"
Where would I even *begin*?

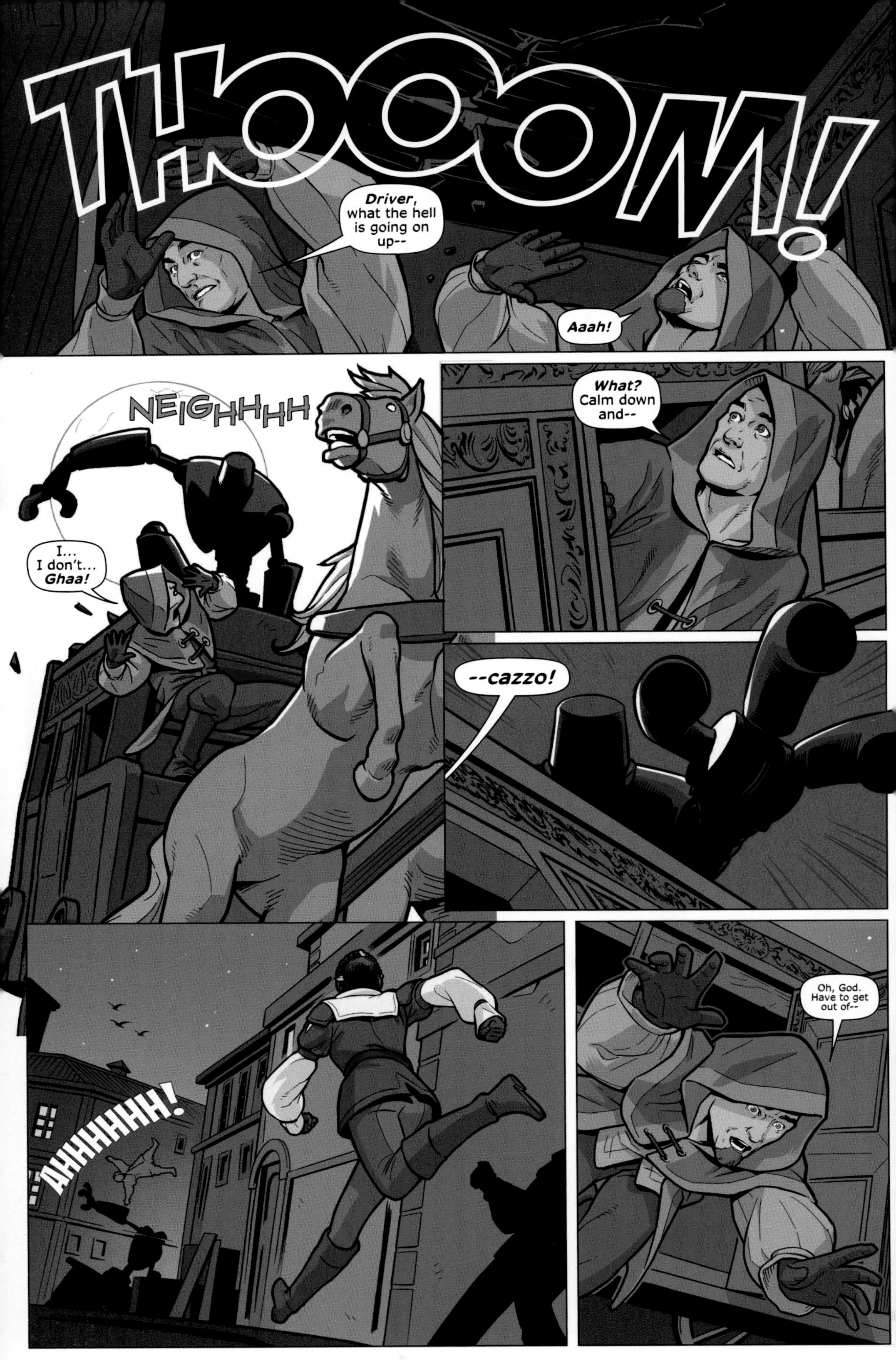
THOOOM!
Driver, what the hell is going on up--
Aaah!
NEIGHHHHH
I... I don't... Ghaa!
What? Calm down and--
--cazzo!
AHHHHHH!
Oh, God. Have to get out of--

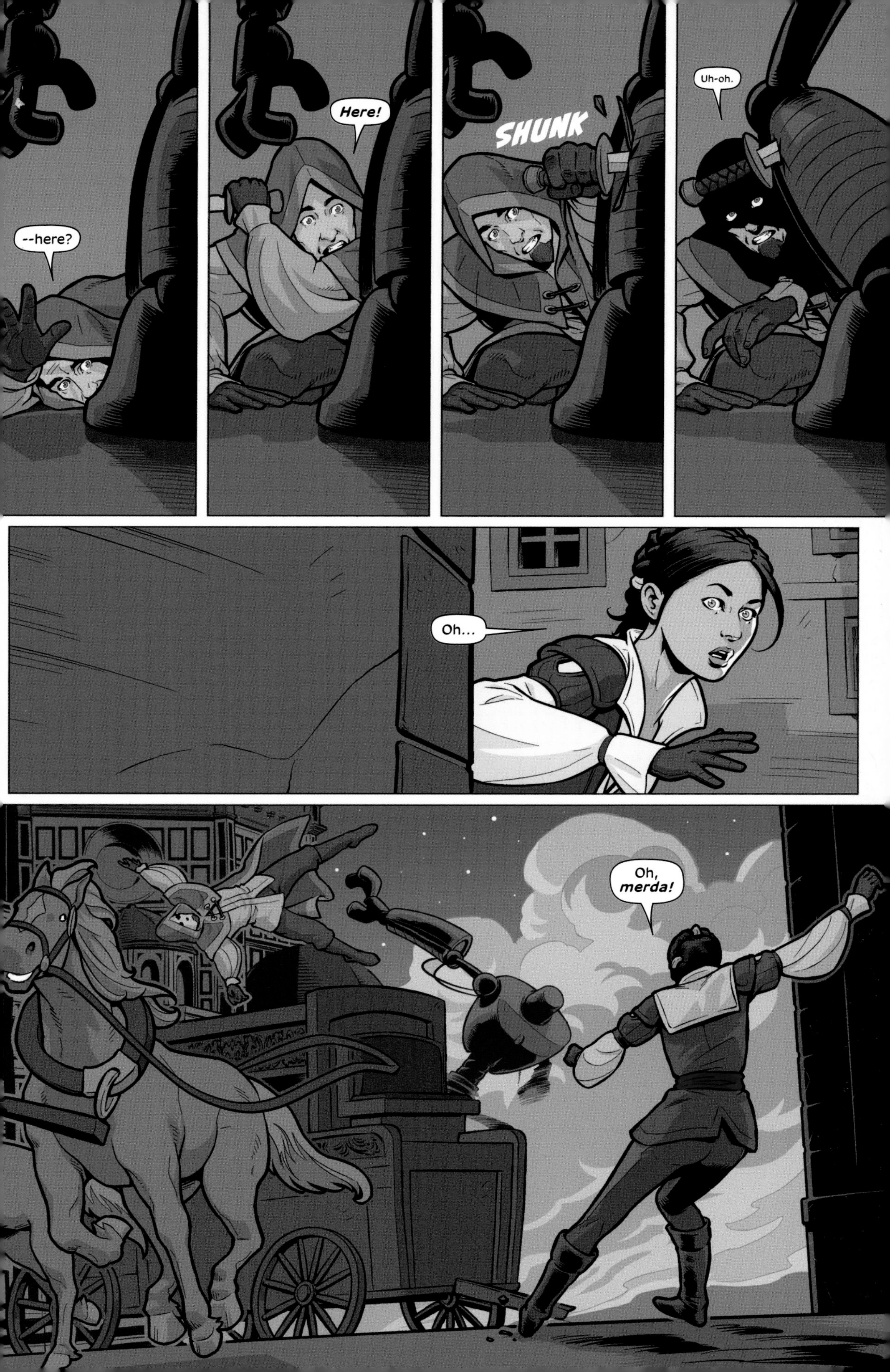
--here?
Here!
SHUNK
Uh-oh.
Oh...
Oh, merda!

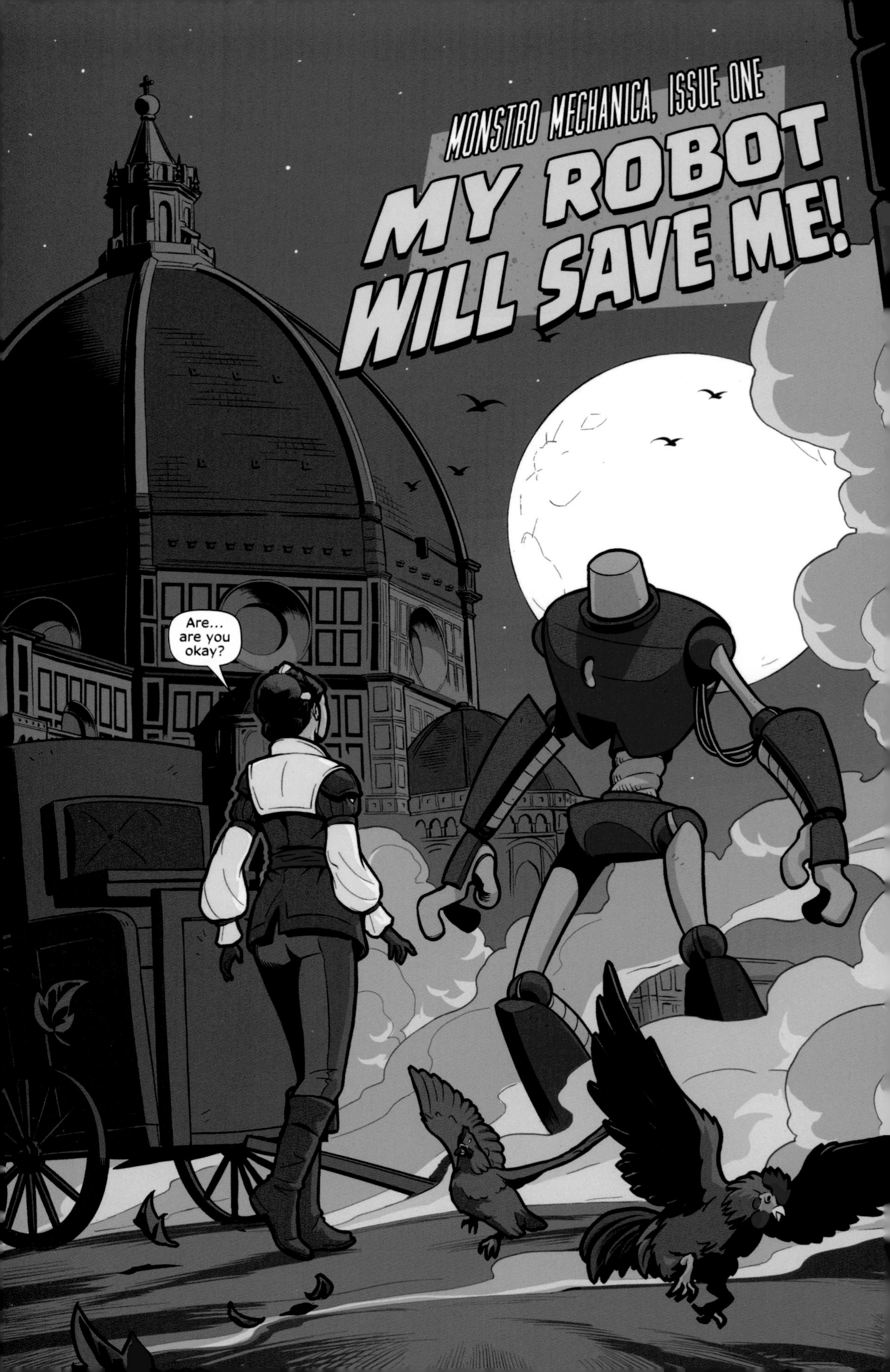

MONSTRO MECHANICA, ISSUE ONE
MY ROBOT WILL SAVE ME!
Are... are you okay?

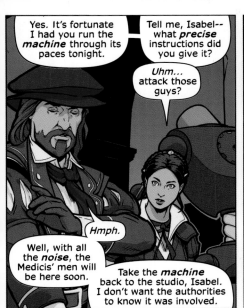

Yes. It's fortunate I had you run the *machine* through its paces tonight.

Tell me, Isabel-- what *precise* instructions did you give it?

Uhm... attack those guys?

Hmph.

Well, with all the *noise*, the Medicis' men will be here soon.

Take the *machine* back to the studio, Isabel. I don't want the authorities to know it was involved.

But--

You're my *apprentice*. Not my *partner*.

Now *go*.

Fine.

≥sigh≤

My Lord...

...I am sorry to have failed you.

Please welcome me into your heavenly kingdom, as I preserve your secrets here on Earth.

Amen.

THUNK

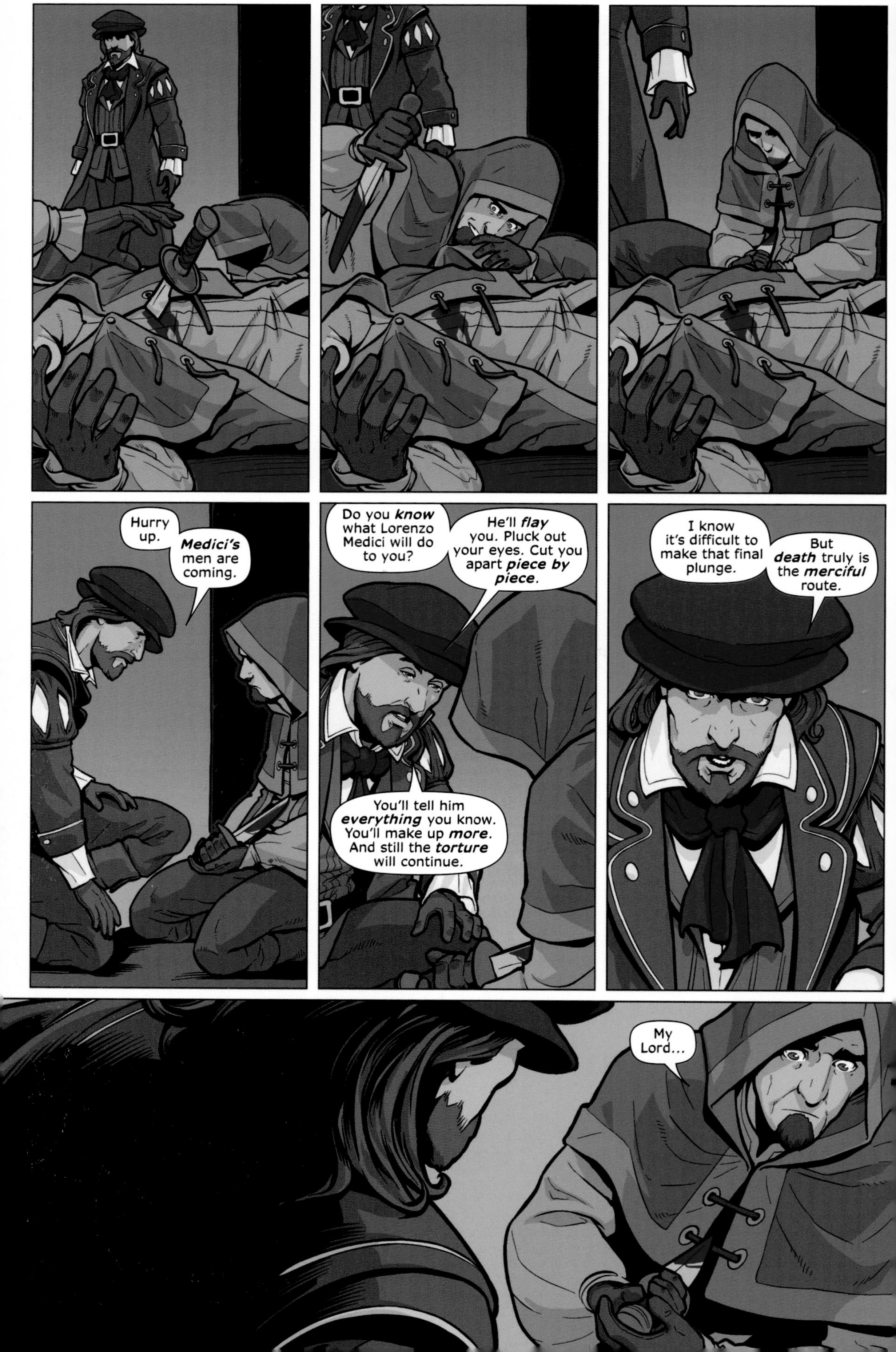

Hurry up.
Medici's men are coming.
Do you know what Lorenzo Medici will do to you?
He'll flay you. Pluck out your eyes. Cut you apart piece by piece.
You'll tell him everything you know. You'll make up more. And still the torture will continue.
I know it's difficult to make that final plunge.
But death truly is the merciful route.
My Lord...

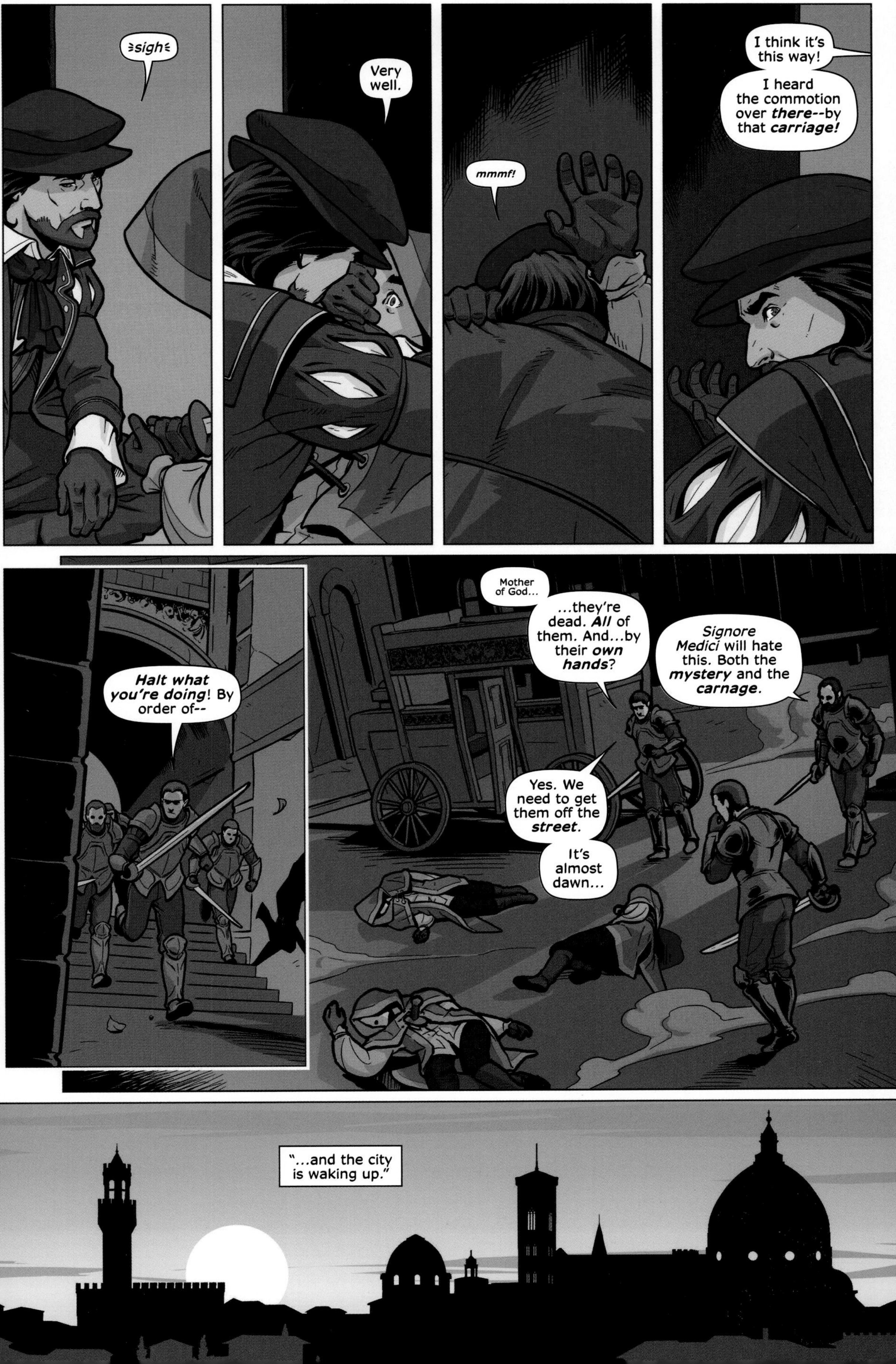

≥sigh≤
Very well.
mmmf!
I think it's this way!
I heard the commotion over *there*--by that *carriage!*
Halt what you're doing! By order of--
Mother of God...
...they're dead. *All* of them. And...by their *own hands*?
Signore Medici will hate this. Both the *mystery* and the *carnage*.
Yes. We need to get them off the *street*.
It's almost dawn...
"...and the city is waking up."

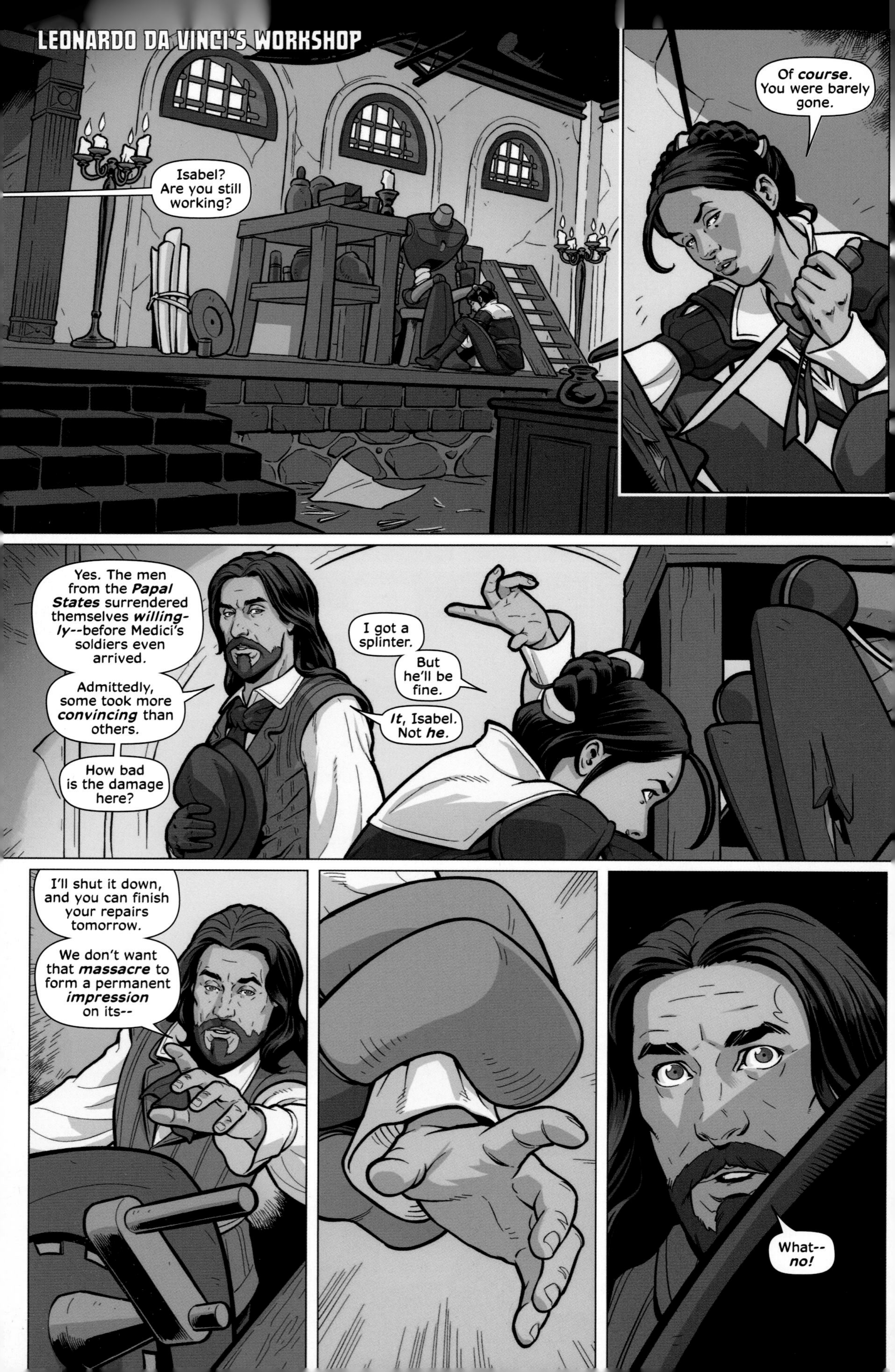
LEONARDO DA VINCI'S WORKSHOP
Isabel? Are you still working?
Of *course*. You were barely gone.
Yes. The men from the *Papal States* surrendered themselves *willing-ly*--before Medici's soldiers even arrived.
Admittedly, some took more *convincing* than others.
How bad is the damage here?
I got a splinter.
But he'll be fine.
It, Isabel. Not *he*.
I'll shut it down, and you can finish your repairs tomorrow.
We don't want that *massacre* to form a permanent *impression* on its--
What-- *no!*

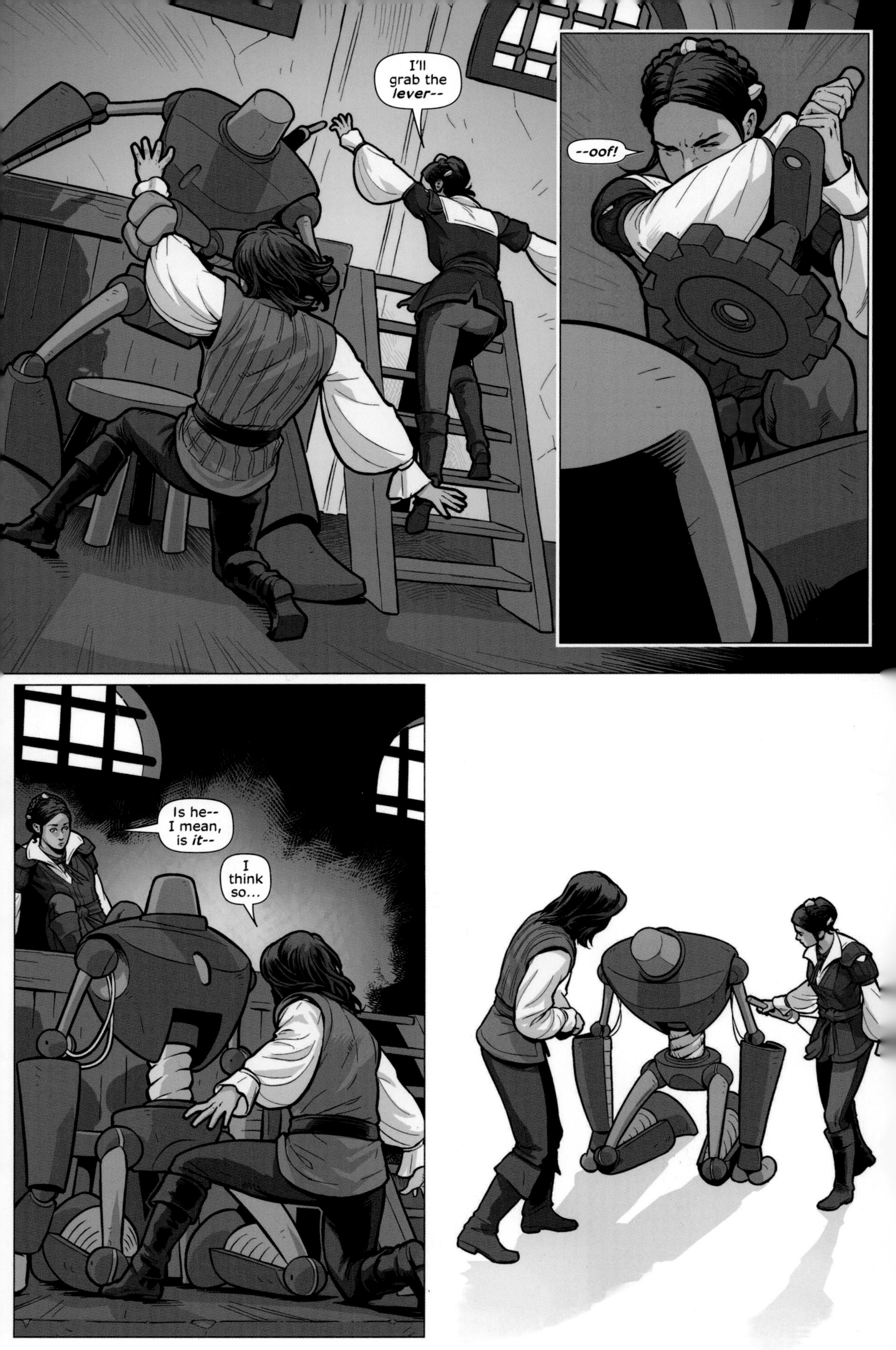
I'll grab the *lever*--
--oof!
Is he-- I mean, is *it*--
I think so...

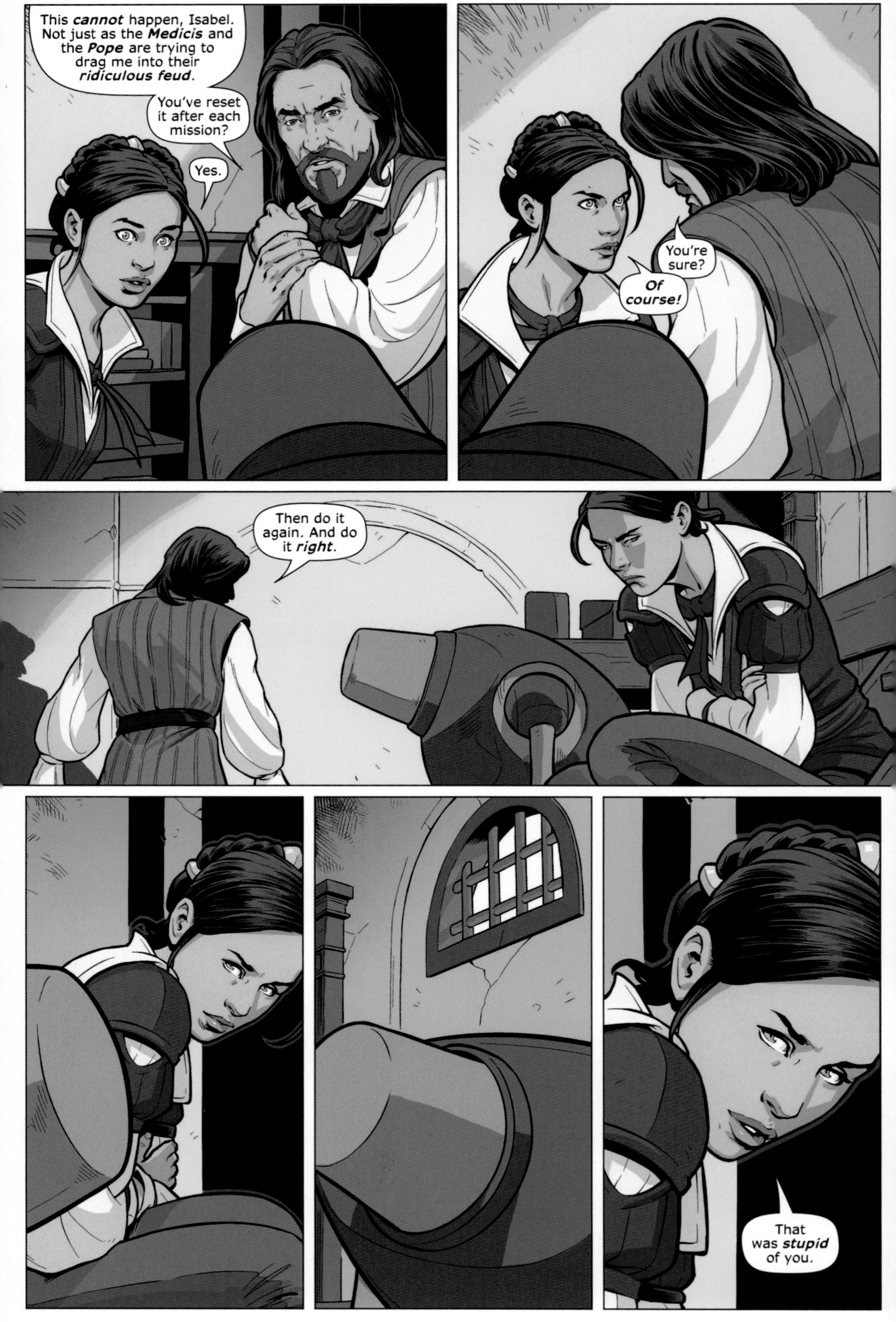

This *cannot* happen, Isabel. Not just as the *Medicis* and the *Pope* are trying to drag me into their *ridiculous feud*.
You've reset it after each mission?
Yes.
You're sure?
Of course!
Then do it again. And do it *right*.
That was *stupid* of you.

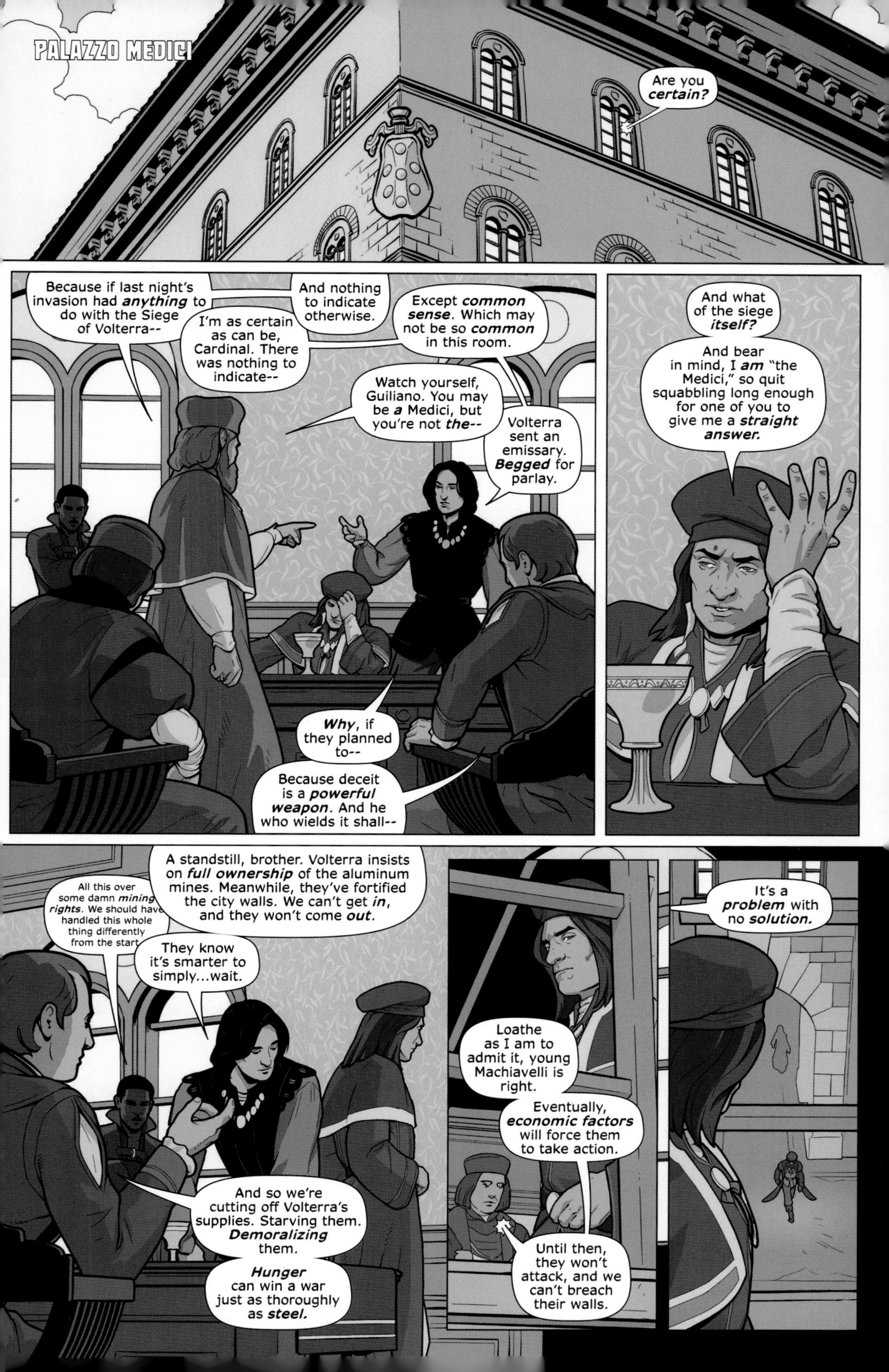
PALAZZO MEDICI
Are you *certain?*
Because if last night's invasion had *anything* to do with the Siege of Volterra--
I'm as certain as can be, Cardinal. There was nothing to indicate--
And nothing to indicate otherwise.
Except *common sense*. Which may not be so *common* in this room.
Watch yourself, Guiliano. You may be *a* Medici, but you're not *the*--
Volterra sent an emissary. *Begged* for parlay.
Why, if they planned to--
Because deceit is a *powerful weapon*. And he who wields it shall--
And what of the siege *itself?*
And bear in mind, I *am* "the Medici," so quit squabbling long enough for one of you to give me a *straight answer.*
A standstill, brother. Volterra insists on *full ownership* of the aluminum mines. Meanwhile, they've fortified the city walls. We can't get *in*, and they won't come *out*.
All this over some damn *mining rights*. We should have handled this whole thing differently from the start.
They know it's smarter to simply...wait.
And so we're cutting off Volterra's supplies. Starving them. *Demoralizing* them.
Hunger can win a war just as thoroughly as *steel.*
Loathe as I am to admit it, young Machiavelli is right.
Eventually, *economic factors* will force them to take action.
Until then, they won't attack, and we can't breach their walls.
It's a *problem* with no *solution.*

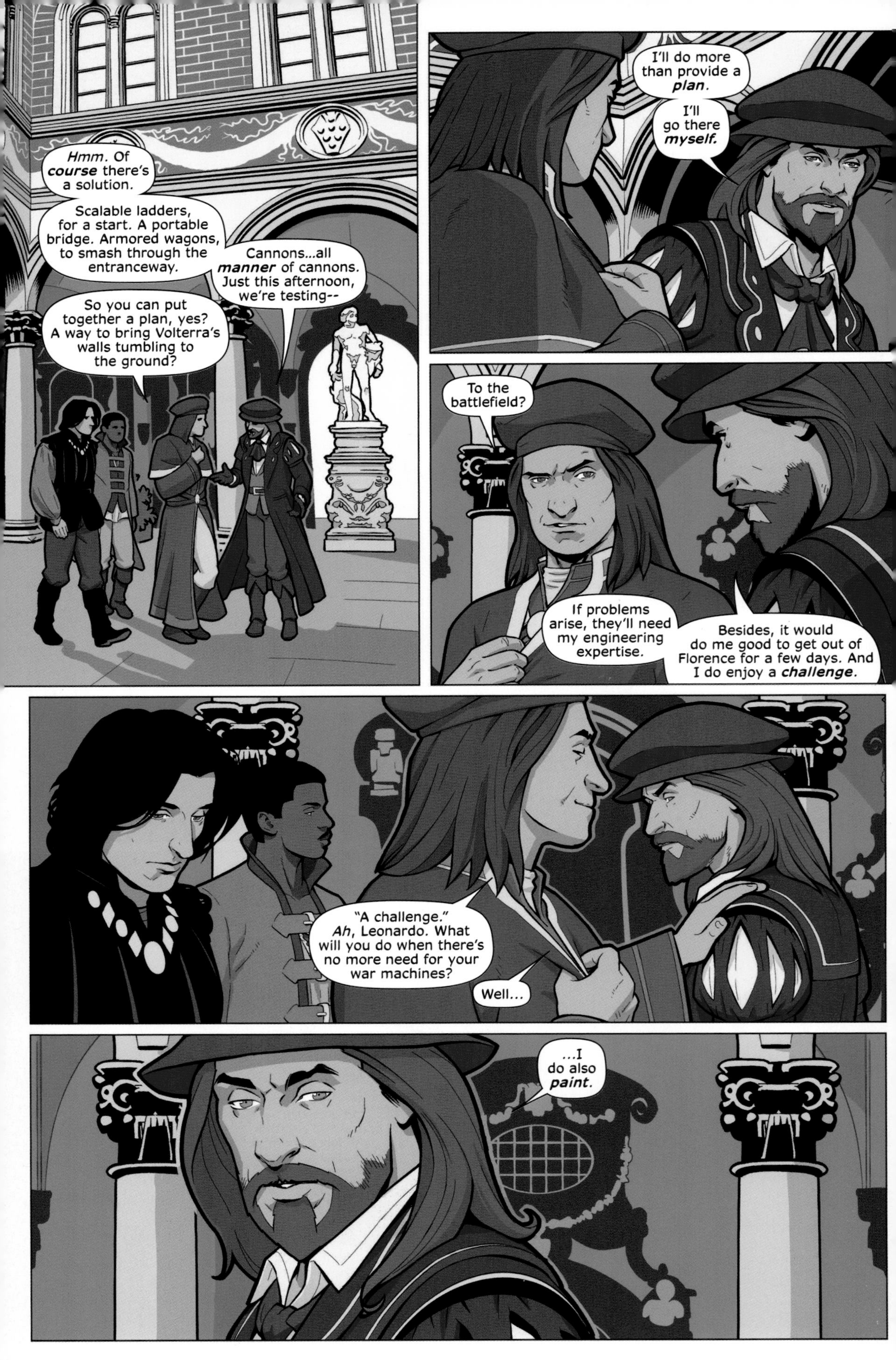

Hmm. Of **course** there's a solution.
Scalable ladders, for a start. A portable bridge. Armored wagons, to smash through the entranceway.
So you can put together a plan, yes? A way to bring Volterra's walls tumbling to the ground?
Cannons...all ***manner*** of cannons. Just this afternoon, we're testing--
I'll do more than provide a ***plan***.
I'll go there ***myself.***
To the battlefield?
If problems arise, they'll need my engineering expertise.
Besides, it would do me good to get out of Florence for a few days. And I do enjoy a ***challenge***.
"A challenge." *Ah*, Leonardo. What will you do when there's no more need for your war machines?
Well...
...I do also ***paint***.

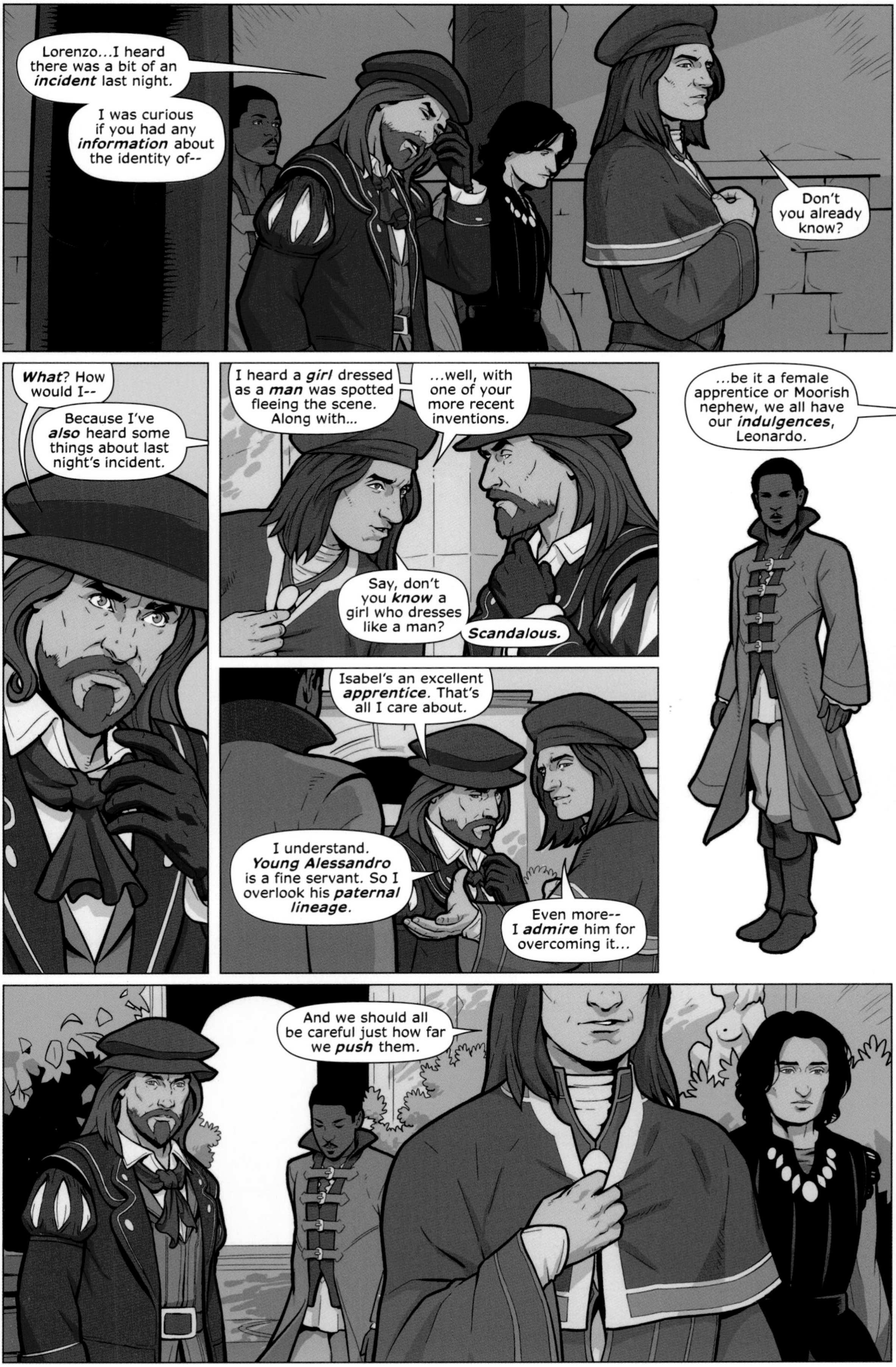

Lorenzo...I heard there was a bit of an *incident* last night.
I was curious if you had any *information* about the identity of--
Don't you already know?
What? How would I--
Because I've *also* heard some things about last night's incident.
I heard a *girl* dressed as a *man* was spotted fleeing the scene. Along with...
...well, with one of your more recent inventions.
Say, don't you *know* a girl who dresses like a man?
Scandalous.
Isabel's an excellent *apprentice*. That's all I care about.
I understand. *Young Alessandro* is a fine servant. So I overlook his *paternal lineage*.
Even more-- I *admire* him for overcoming it...
...be it a female apprentice or Moorish nephew, we all have our *indulgences*, Leonardo.
And we should all be careful just how far we *push* them.

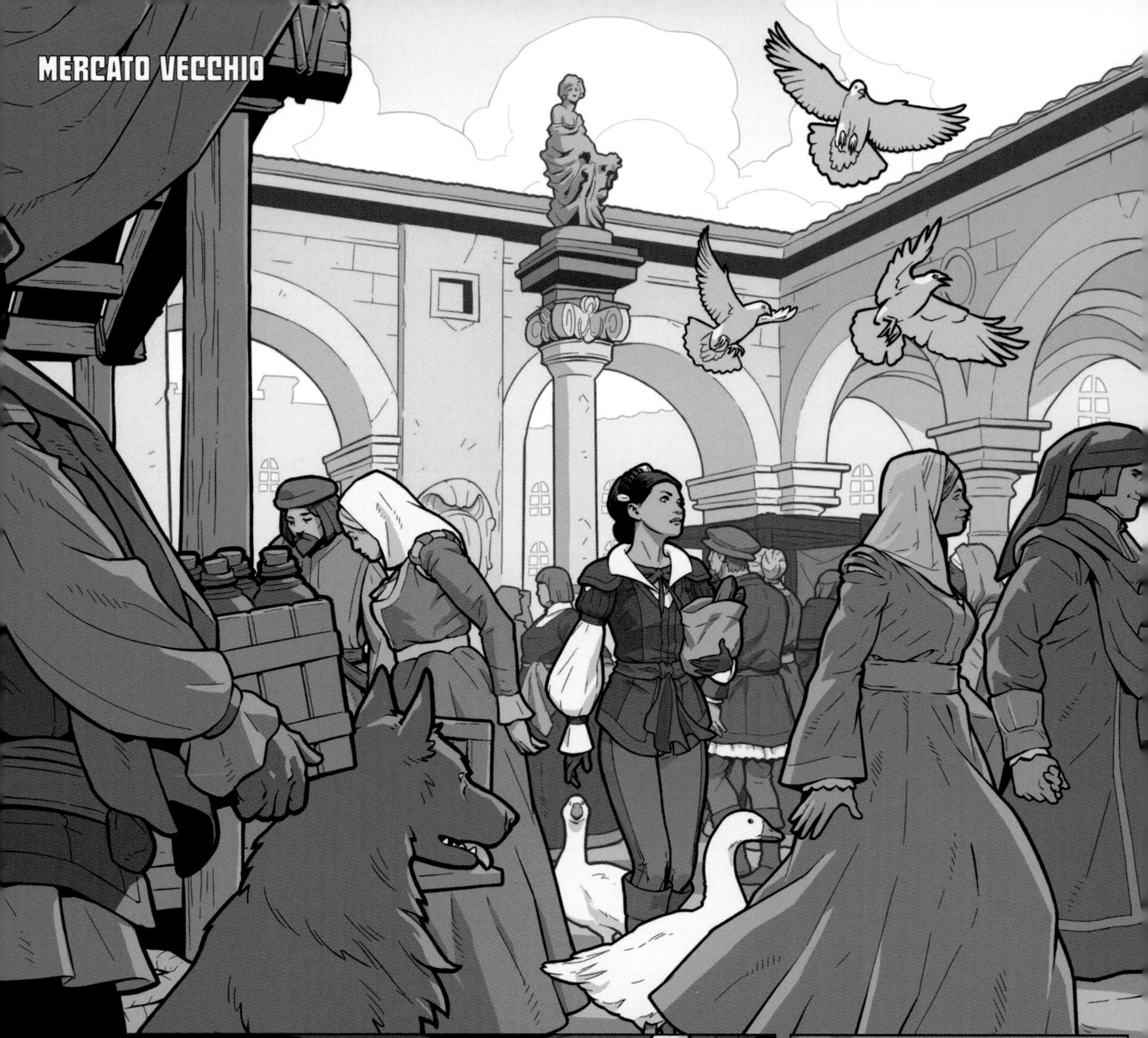
MERCATO VECCHIO

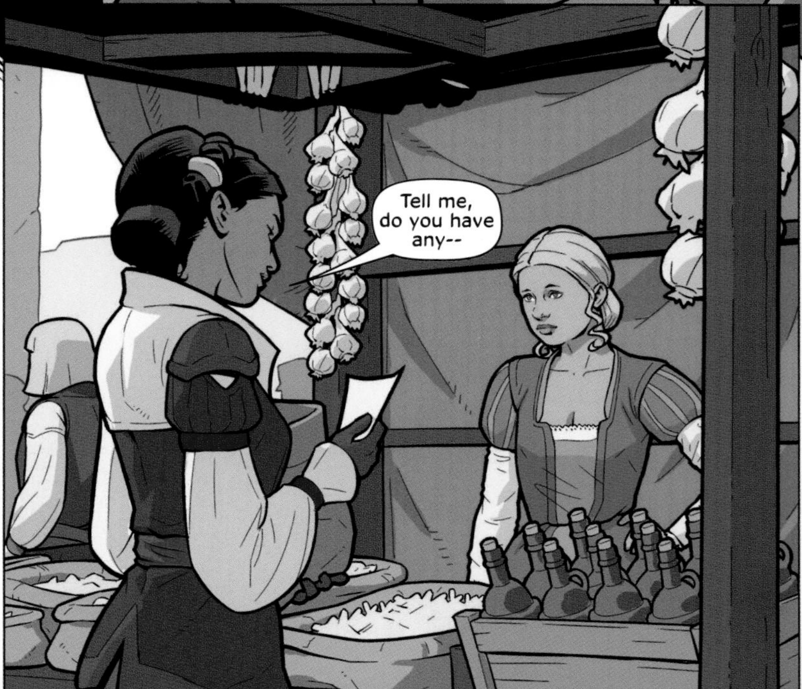
Tell me, do you have any--

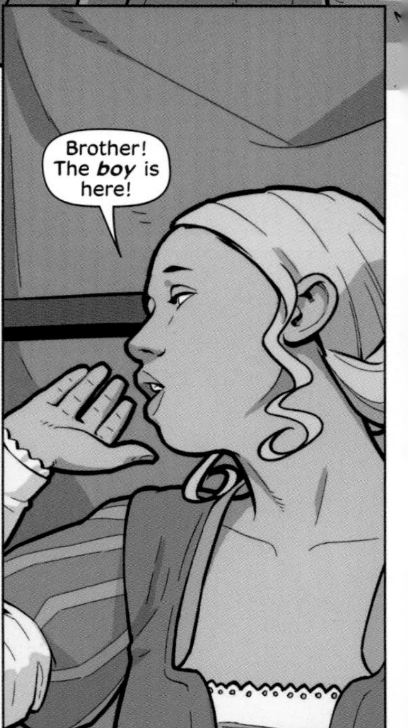
Brother! The *boy* is here!

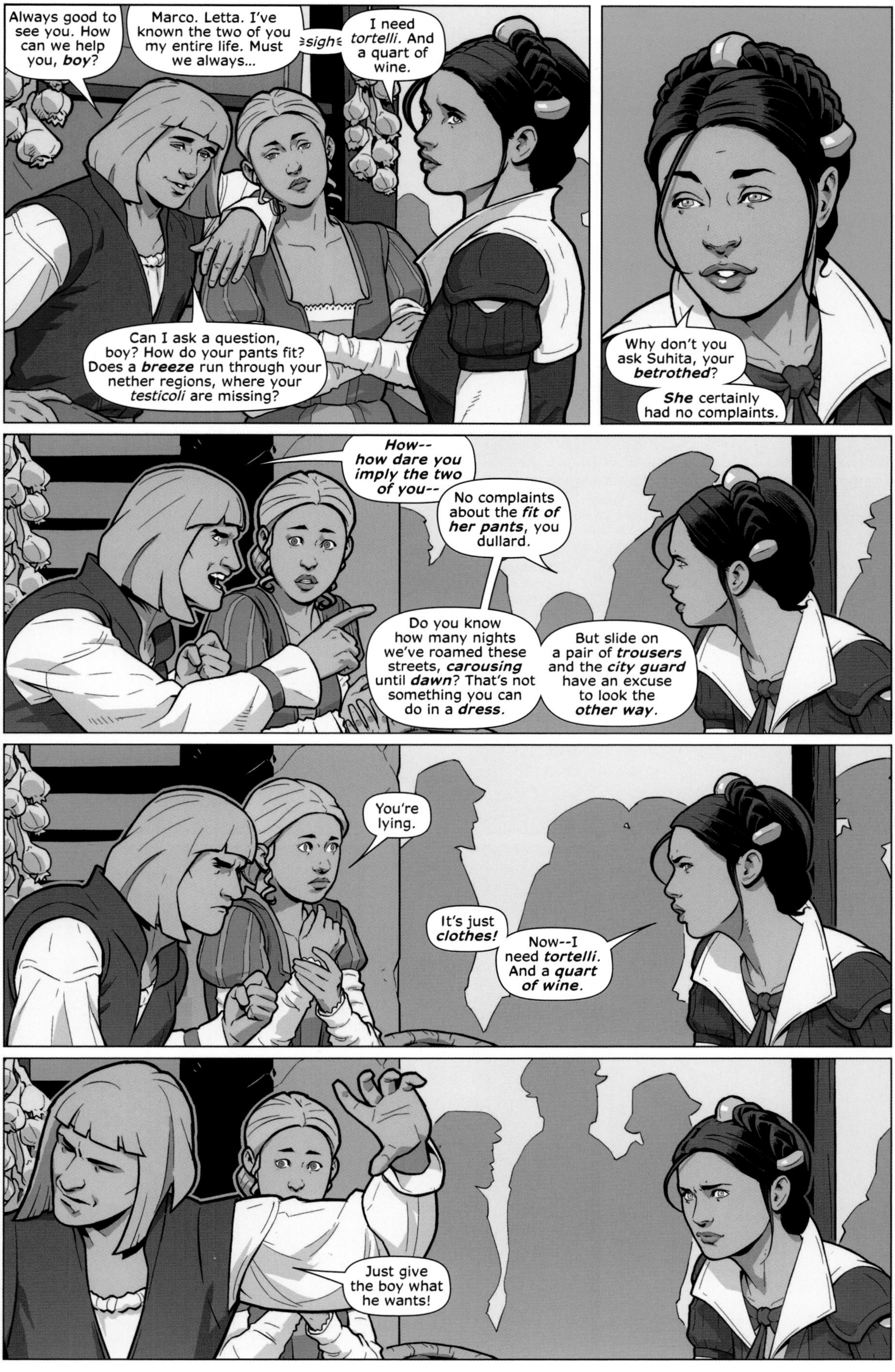

Always good to see you. How can we help you, *boy*?
Marco. Letta. I've known the two of you my entire life. Must we always...
sigh
I need *tortelli*. And a quart of wine.
Can I ask a question, boy? How do your pants fit? Does a ***breeze*** run through your nether regions, where your *testicoli* are missing?
Why don't you ask Suhita, your ***betrothed***?
She certainly had no complaints.
How-- how dare you imply the two of you--
No complaints about the ***fit of her pants***, you dullard.
Do you know how many nights we've roamed these streets, ***carousing*** until ***dawn***? That's not something you can do in a ***dress***.
But slide on a pair of ***trousers*** and the ***city guard*** have an excuse to look the ***other way***.
You're lying.
It's just ***clothes!***
Now--I need ***tortelli***. And a ***quart of wine***.
Just give the boy what he wants!

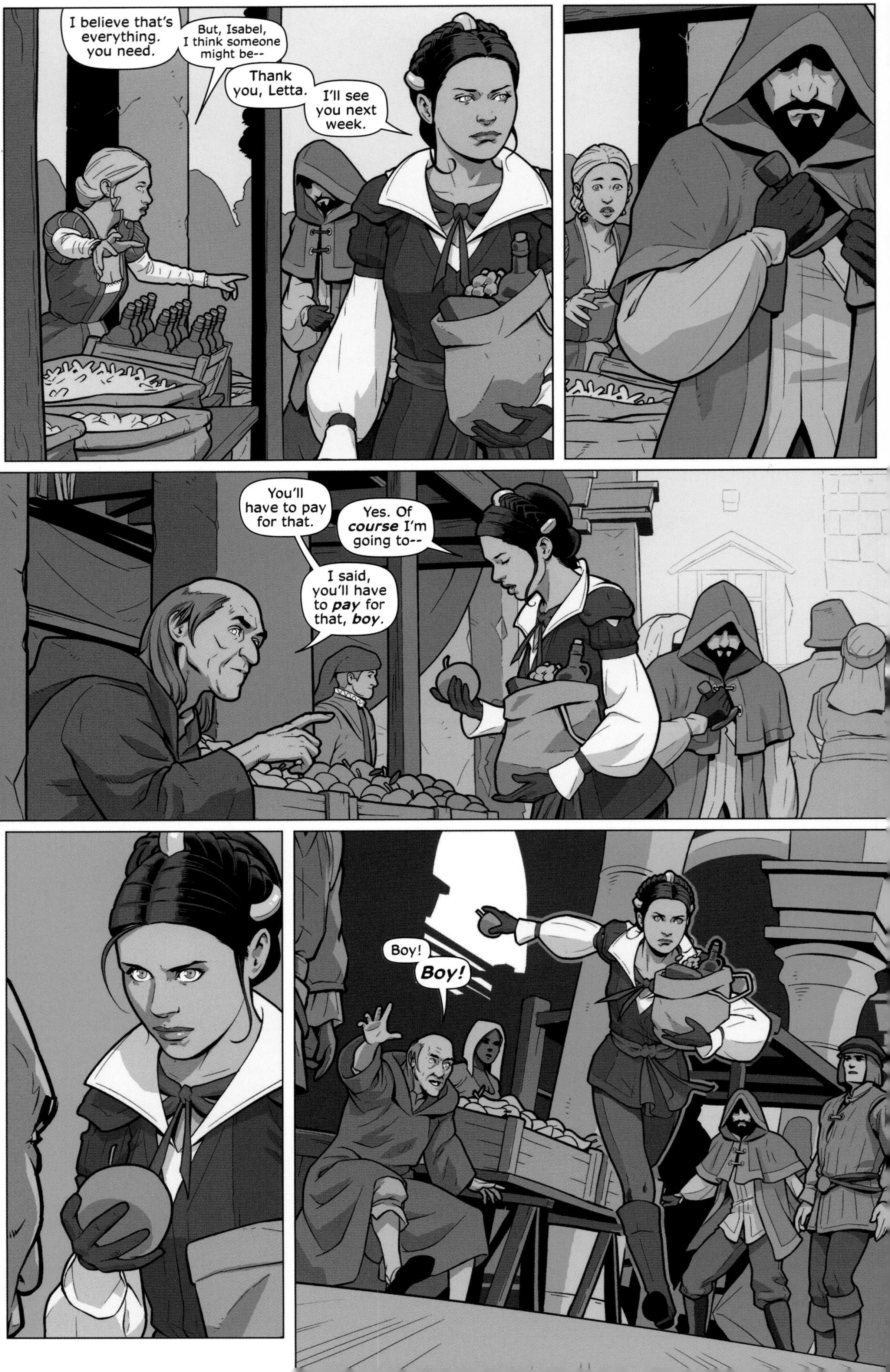
I believe that's everything. you need.
But, Isabel, I think someone might be--
Thank you, Letta.
I'll see you next week.
You'll have to pay for that.
Yes. Of *course* I'm going to--
I said, you'll have to *pay* for that, *boy*.
Boy!
Boy!

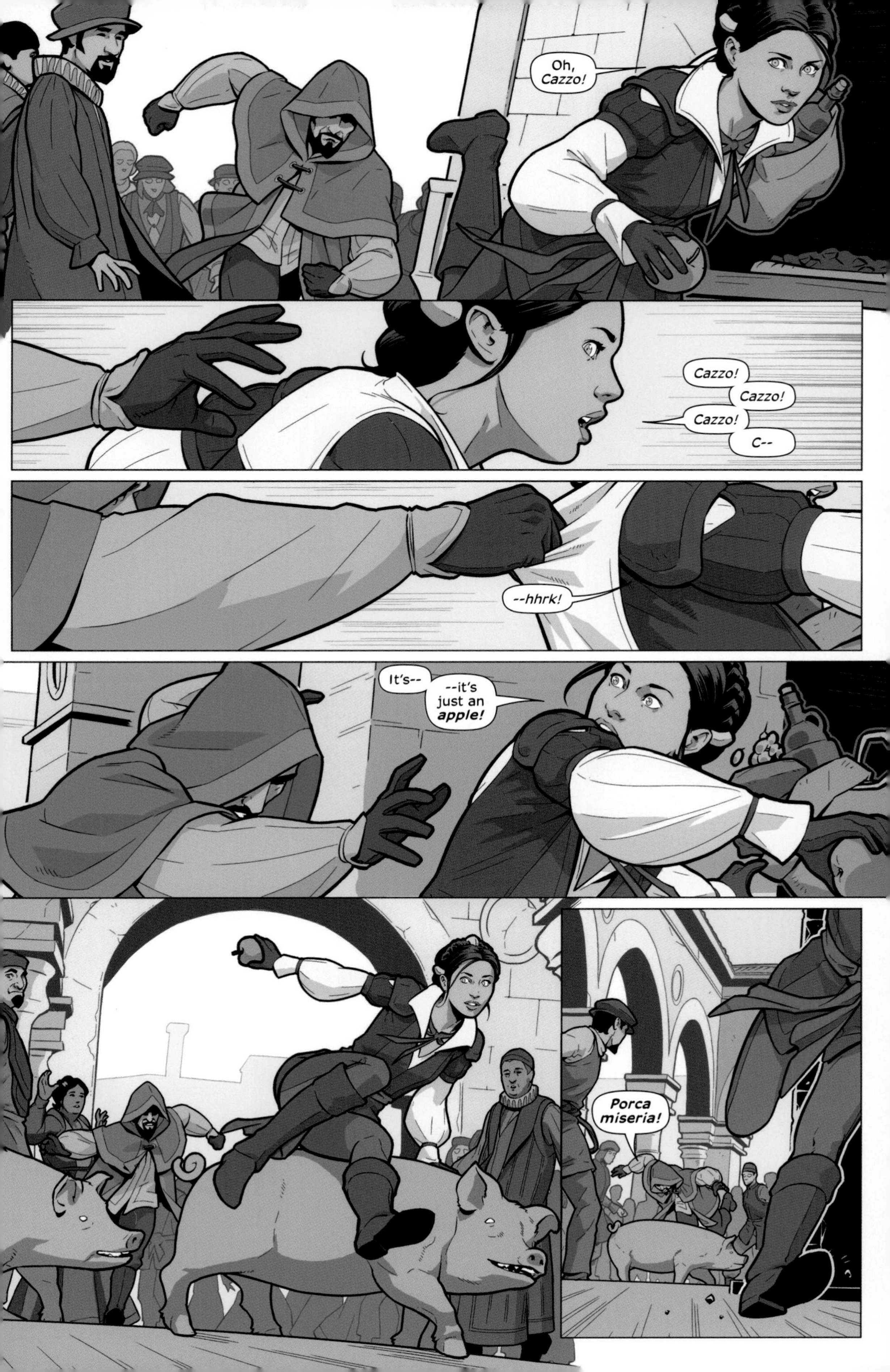

Oh, Cazzo!
Cazzo!
Cazzo!
Cazzo!
C--
--hhrk!
It's--
--it's just an *apple!*
Porca miseria!

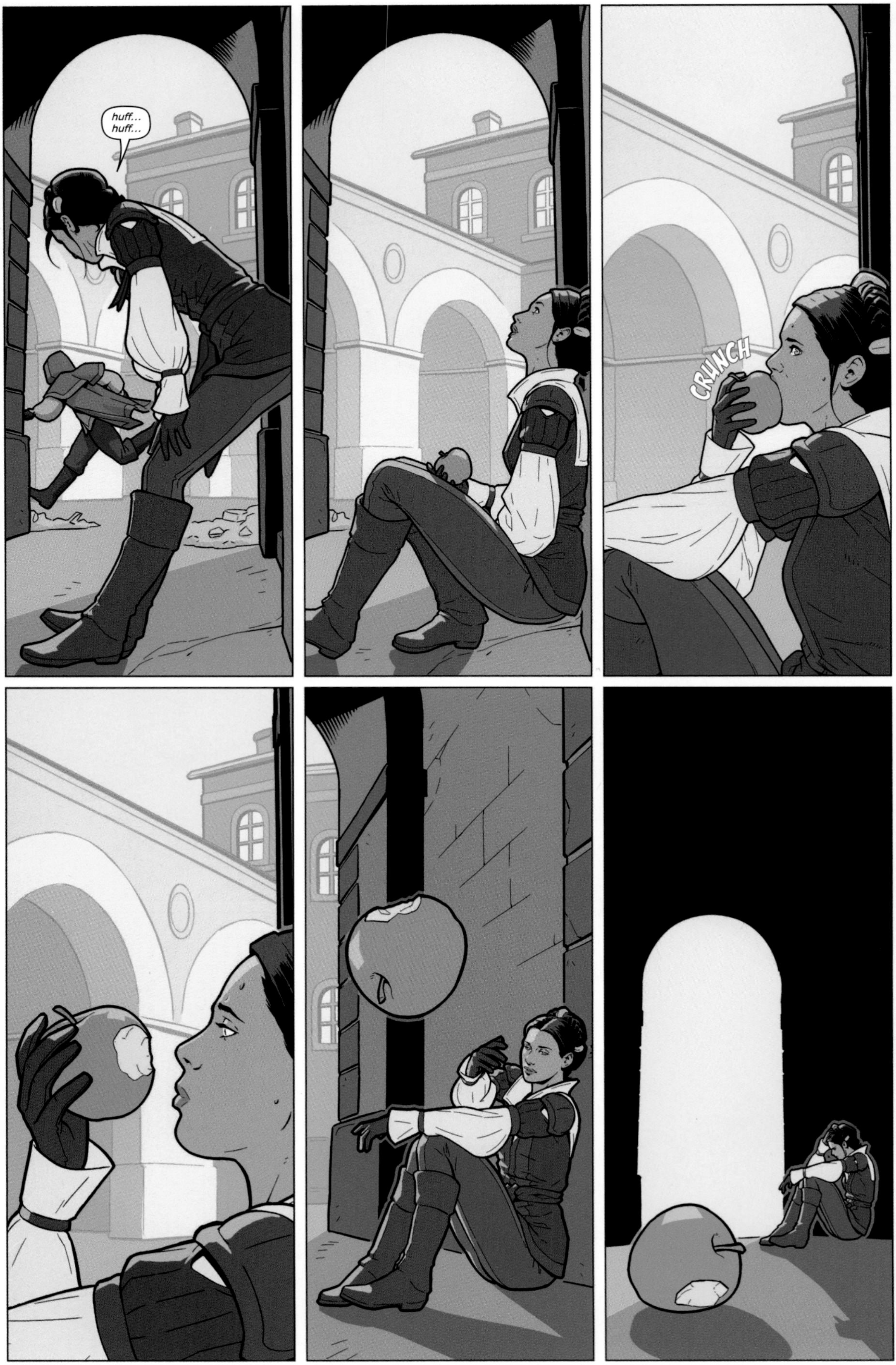
huff...
huff...
CRUNCH

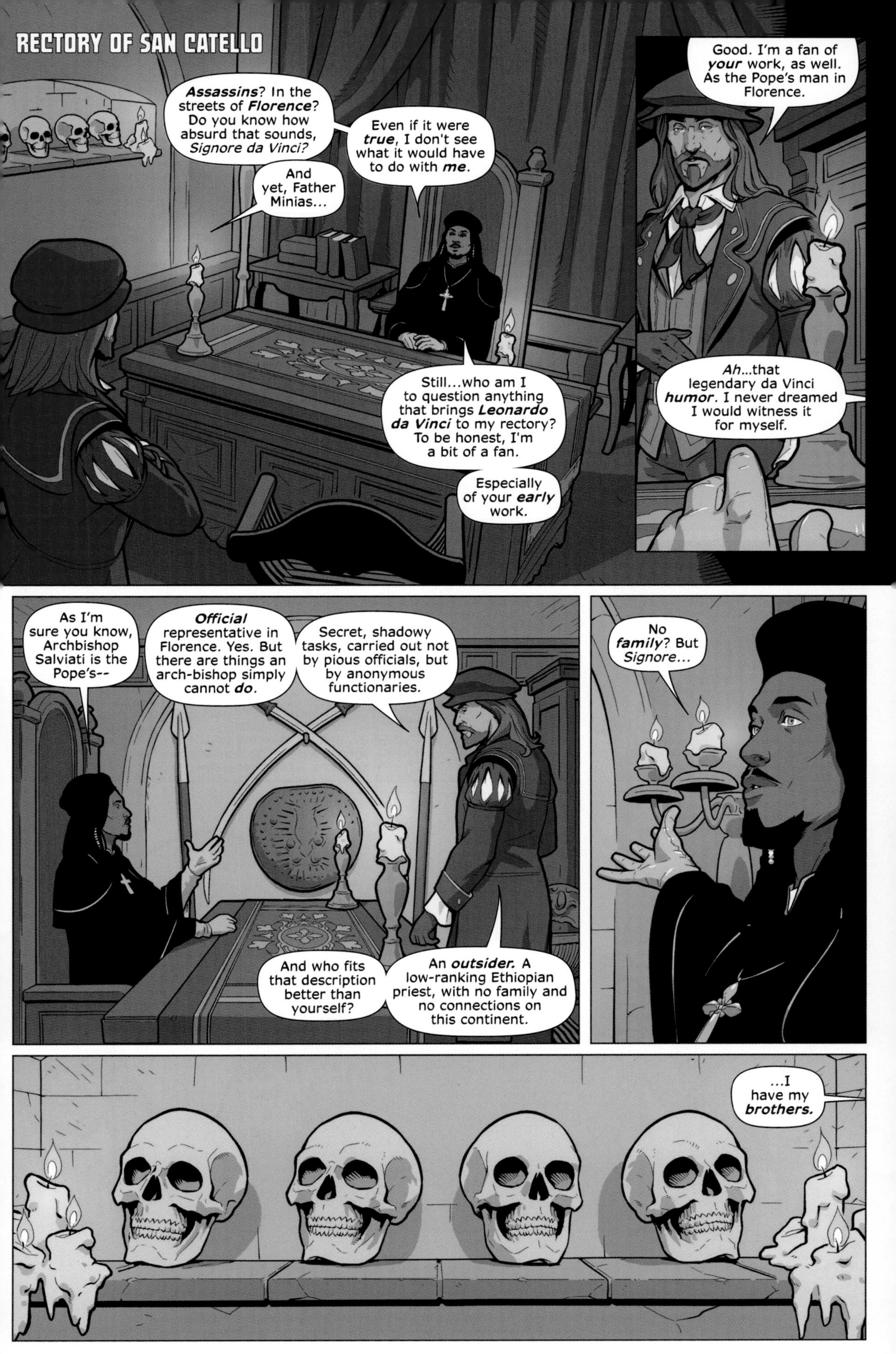
RECTORY OF SAN CATELLO
Assassins? In the streets of Florence? Do you know how absurd that sounds, Signore da Vinci?
Even if it were true, I don't see what it would have to do with me.
And yet, Father Minias...
Still...who am I to question anything that brings Leonardo da Vinci to my rectory? To be honest, I'm a bit of a fan.
Especially of your early work.
Good. I'm a fan of your work, as well. As the Pope's man in Florence.
Ah...that legendary da Vinci humor. I never dreamed I would witness it for myself.
As I'm sure you know, Archbishop Salviati is the Pope's--
Official representative in Florence. Yes. But there are things an arch-bishop simply cannot do.
Secret, shadowy tasks, carried out not by pious officials, but by anonymous functionaries.
And who fits that description better than yourself?
An outsider. A low-ranking Ethiopian priest, with no family and no connections on this continent.
No family? But Signore...
...I have my brothers.

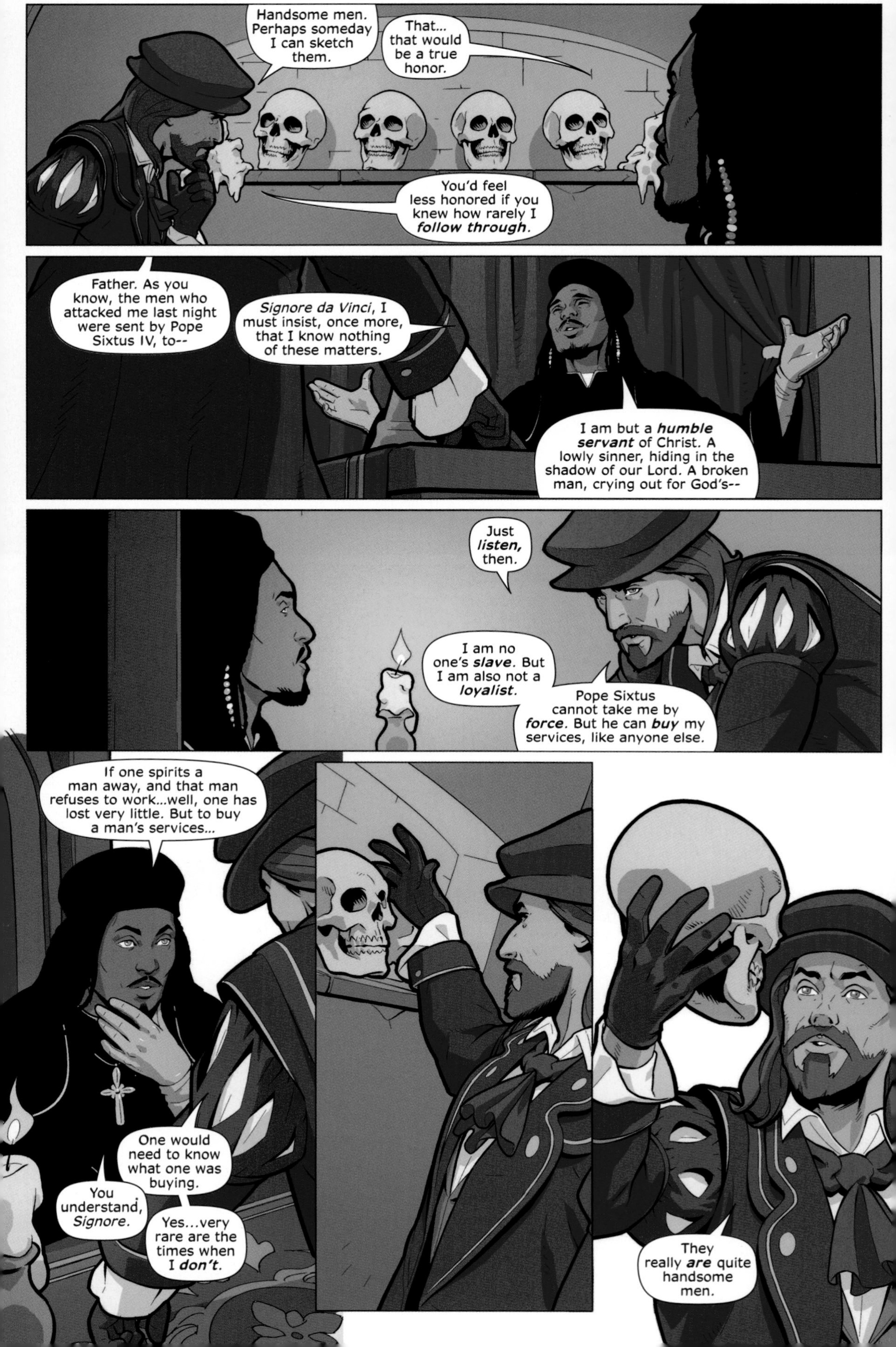
Handsome men. Perhaps someday I can sketch them.
That... that would be a true honor.
You'd feel less honored if you knew how rarely I *follow through*.
Father. As you know, the men who attacked me last night were sent by Pope Sixtus IV, to--
Signore da Vinci, I must insist, once more, that I know nothing of these matters.
I am but a ***humble servant*** of Christ. A lowly sinner, hiding in the shadow of our Lord. A broken man, crying out for God's--
Just *listen,* then.
I am no one's ***slave***. But I am also not a ***loyalist***.
Pope Sixtus cannot take me by ***force***. But he can ***buy*** my services, like anyone else.
If one spirits a man away, and that man refuses to work...well, one has lost very little. But to buy a man's services...
One would need to know what one was buying.
You understand, *Signore*.
Yes...very rare are the times when I ***don't***.
They really ***are*** quite handsome men.

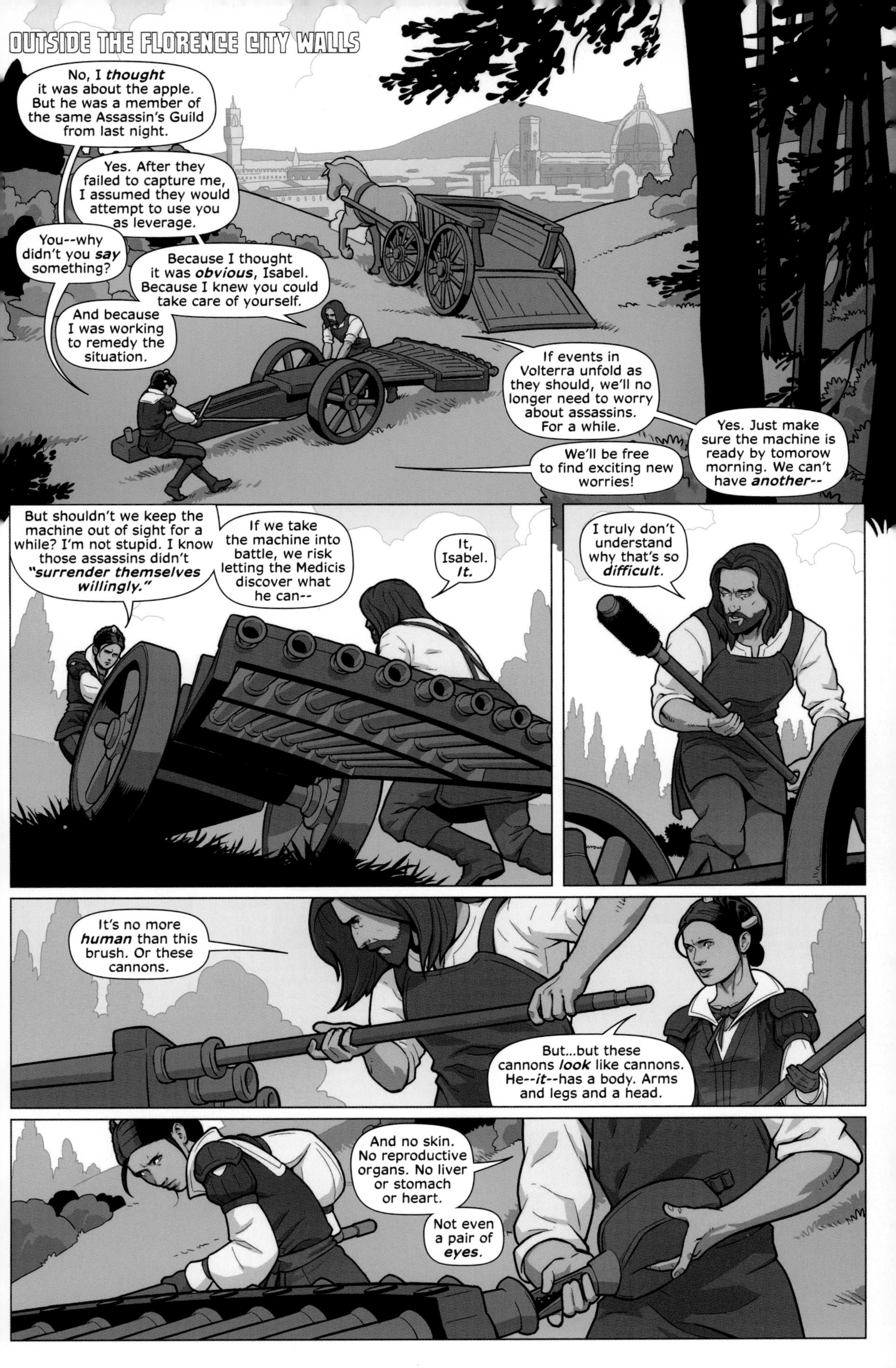
OUTSIDE THE FLORENCE CITY WALLS
No, I *thought* it was about the apple. But he was a member of the same Assassin's Guild from last night.
Yes. After they failed to capture me, I assumed they would attempt to use you as leverage.
You--why didn't you *say* something?
Because I thought it was *obvious*, Isabel. Because I knew you could take care of yourself.
And because I was working to remedy the situation.
If events in Volterra unfold as they should, we'll no longer need to worry about assassins. For a while.
We'll be free to find exciting new worries!
Yes. Just make sure the machine is ready by tomorow morning. We can't have *another--*
But shouldn't we keep the machine out of sight for a while? I'm not stupid. I know those assassins didn't *"surrender themselves willingly."*
If we take the machine into battle, we risk letting the Medicis discover what he can--
It, Isabel. *It.*
I truly don't understand why that's so *difficult*.
It's no more *human* than this brush. Or these cannons.
But...but these cannons *look* like cannons. He--*it*--has a body. Arms and legs and a head.
And no skin. No reproductive organs. No liver or stomach or heart.
Not even a pair of *eyes*.

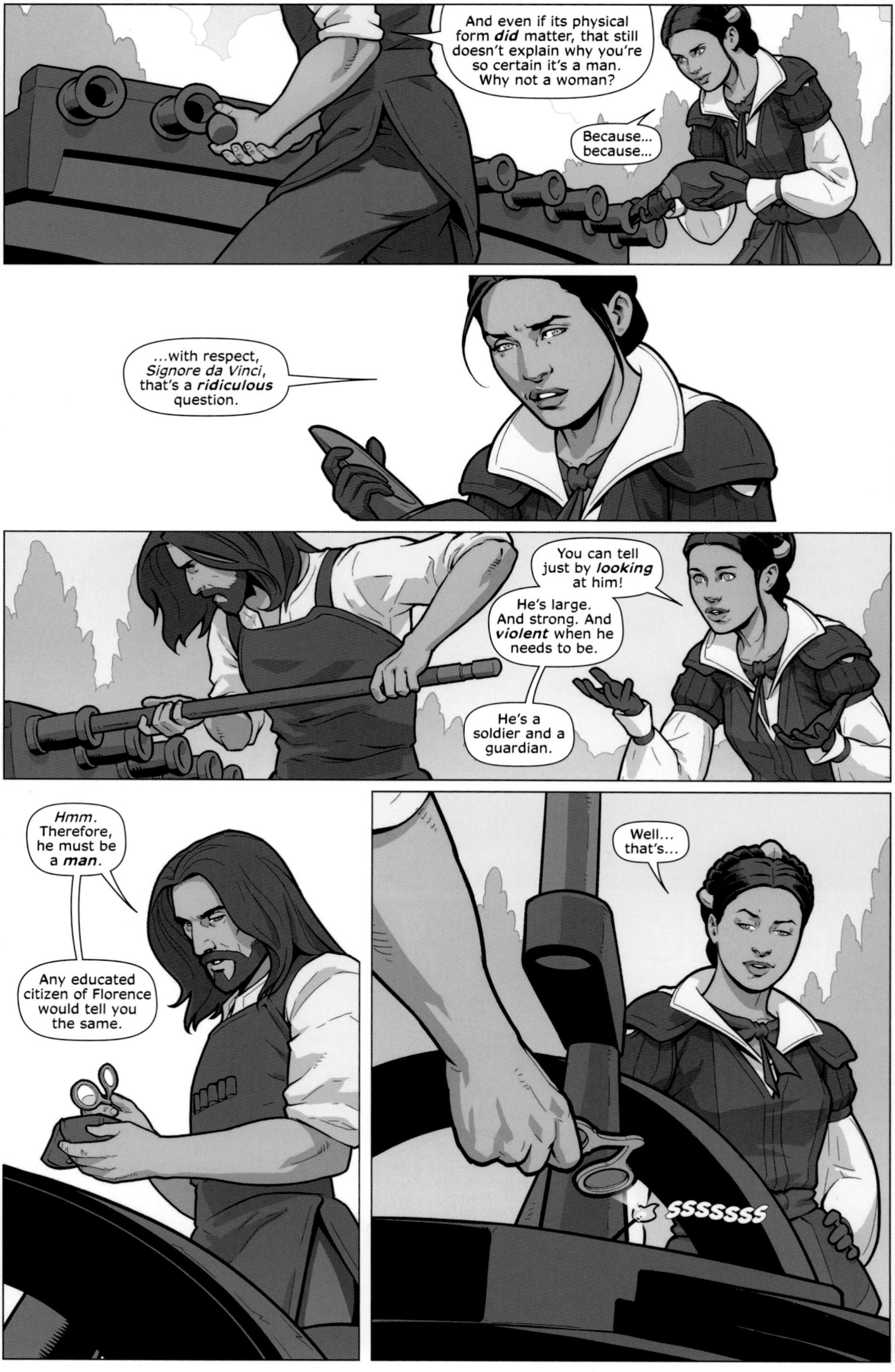
And even if its physical form ***did*** matter, that still doesn't explain why you're so certain it's a man. Why not a woman?
Because... because...
...with respect, *Signore da Vinci*, that's a ***ridiculous*** question.
You can tell just by ***looking*** at him!
He's large. And strong. And ***violent*** when he needs to be.
He's a soldier and a guardian.
Hmm. Therefore, he must be a ***man***.
Any educated citizen of Florence would tell you the same.
Well... that's...
SSSSSSS

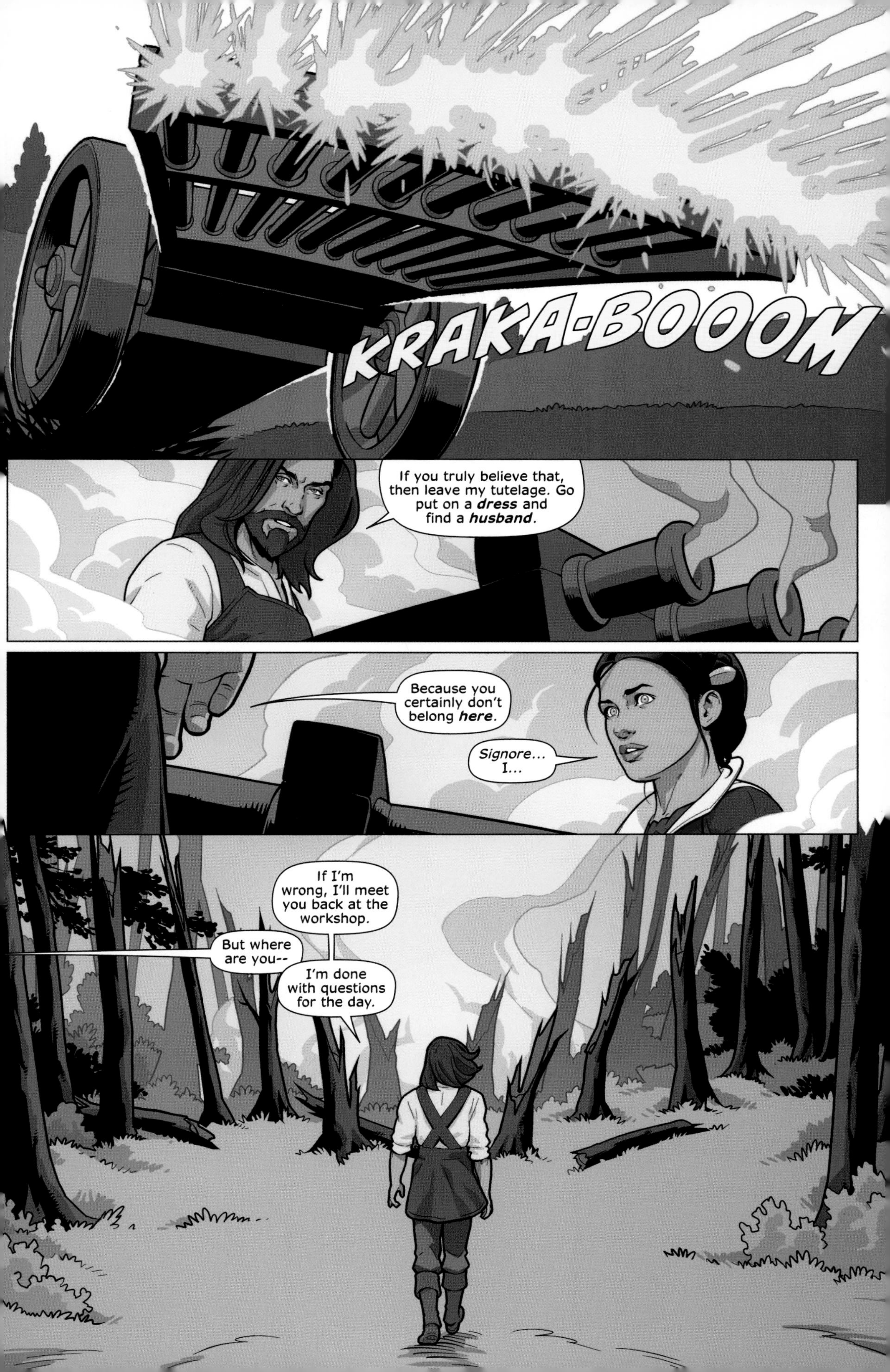
KRAKA-BOOOM
If you truly believe that, then leave my tutelage. Go put on a *dress* and find a *husband*.
Because you certainly don't belong *here*.
Signore... I...
If I'm wrong, I'll meet you back at the workshop.
But where are you--
I'm done with questions for the day.

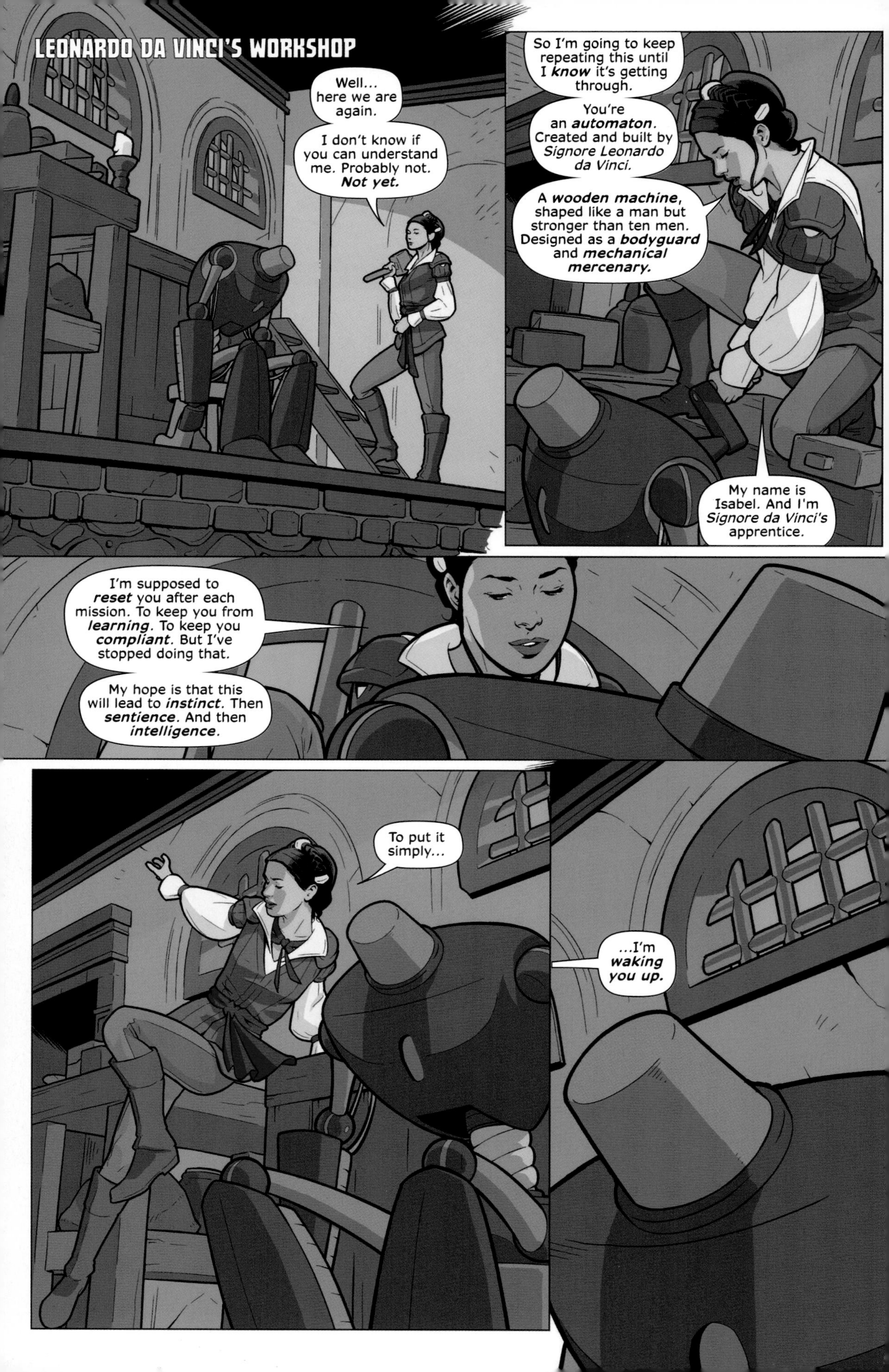
LEONARDO DA VINCI'S WORKSHOP
Well... here we are again.
I don't know if you can understand me. Probably not. Not yet.
So I'm going to keep repeating this until I know it's getting through.
You're an automaton. Created and built by Signore Leonardo da Vinci.
A wooden machine, shaped like a man but stronger than ten men. Designed as a bodyguard and mechanical mercenary.
My name is Isabel. And I'm Signore da Vinci's apprentice.
I'm supposed to reset you after each mission. To keep you from learning. To keep you compliant. But I've stopped doing that.
My hope is that this will lead to instinct. Then sentience. And then intelligence.
To put it simply...
...I'm waking you up.

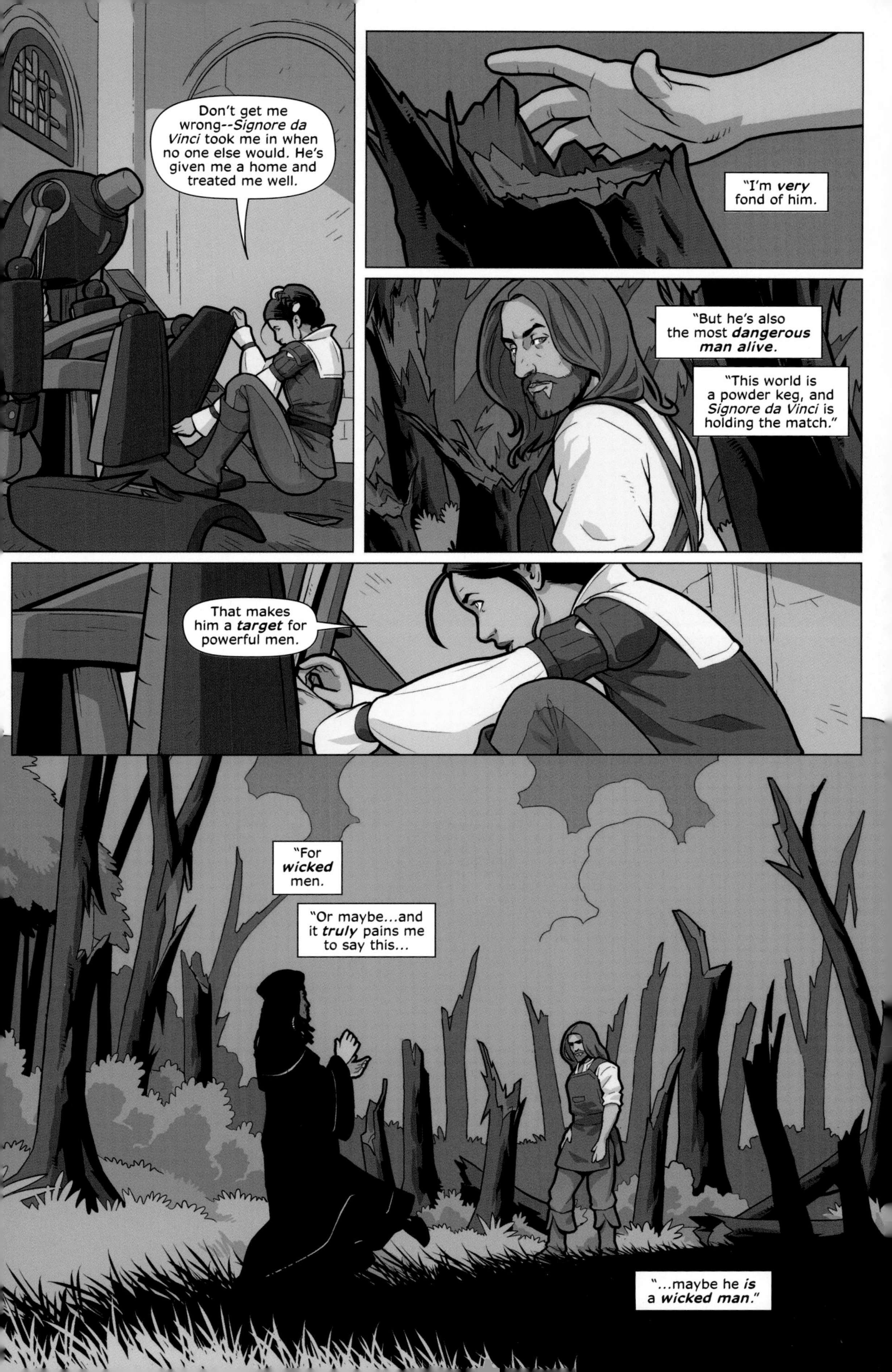
Don't get me wrong--*Signore da Vinci* took me in when no one else would. He's given me a home and treated me well.
"I'm ***very*** fond of him.
"But he's also the most ***dangerous man alive***.
"This world is a powder keg, and *Signore da Vinci* is holding the match."
That makes him a ***target*** for powerful men.
"For ***wicked*** men.
"Or maybe...and it ***truly*** pains me to say this...
"...maybe he ***is*** a ***wicked man***."

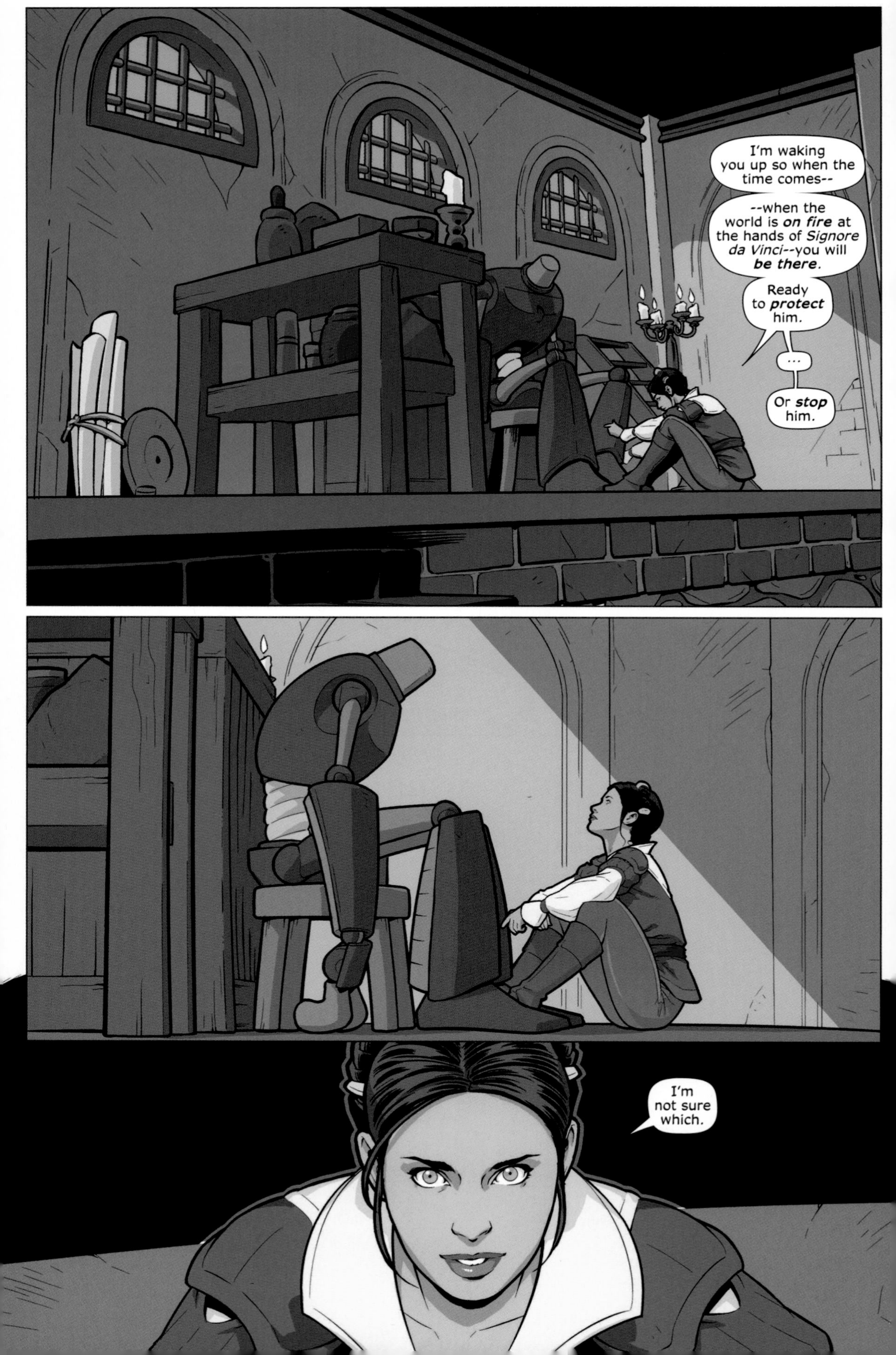

I'm waking you up so when the time comes--
--when the world is *on fire* at the hands of *Signore da Vinci*--you will ***be there***.
Ready to ***protect*** him.
...
Or ***stop*** him.
I'm not sure which.

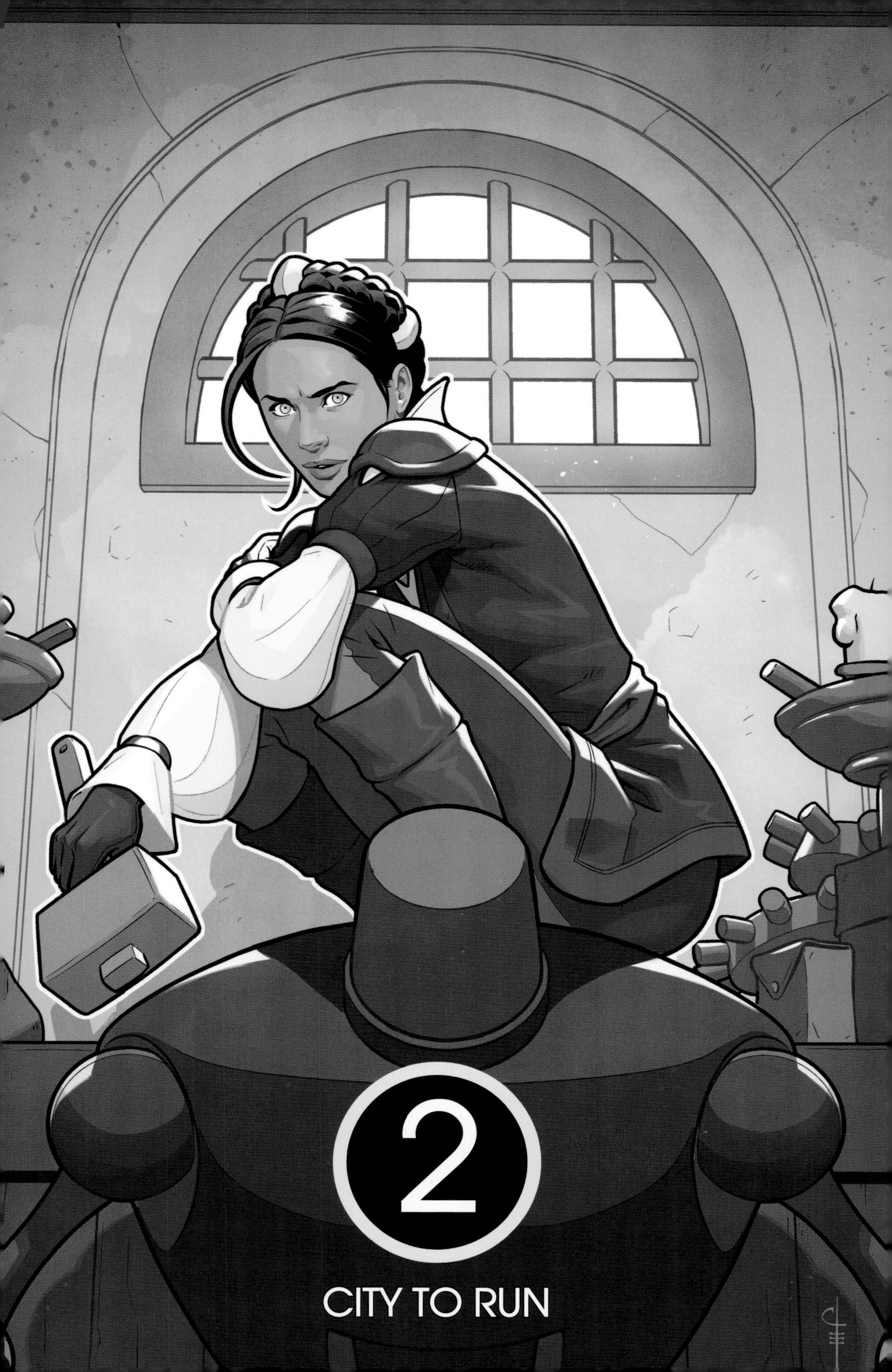
2
CITY TO RUN

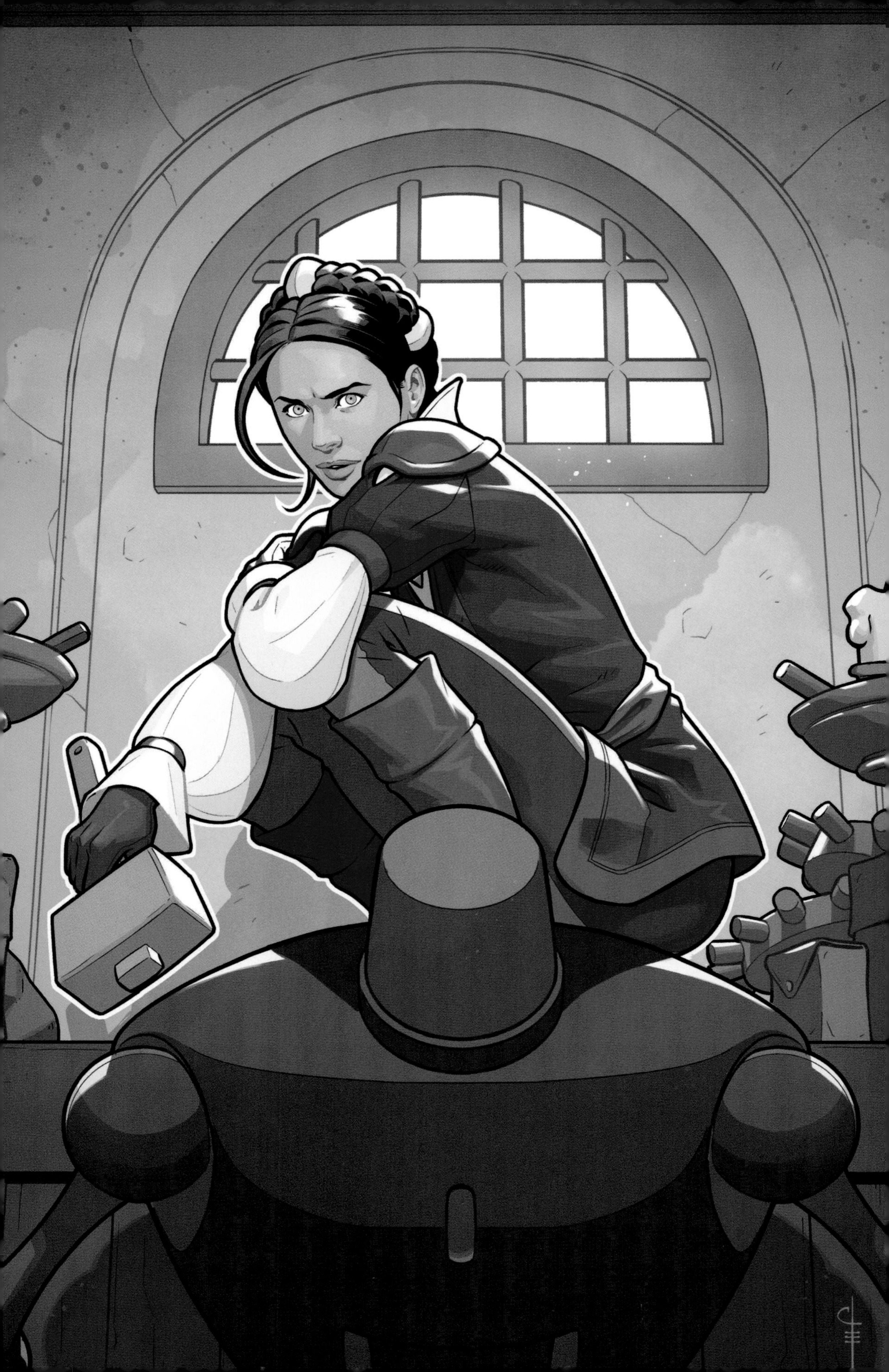

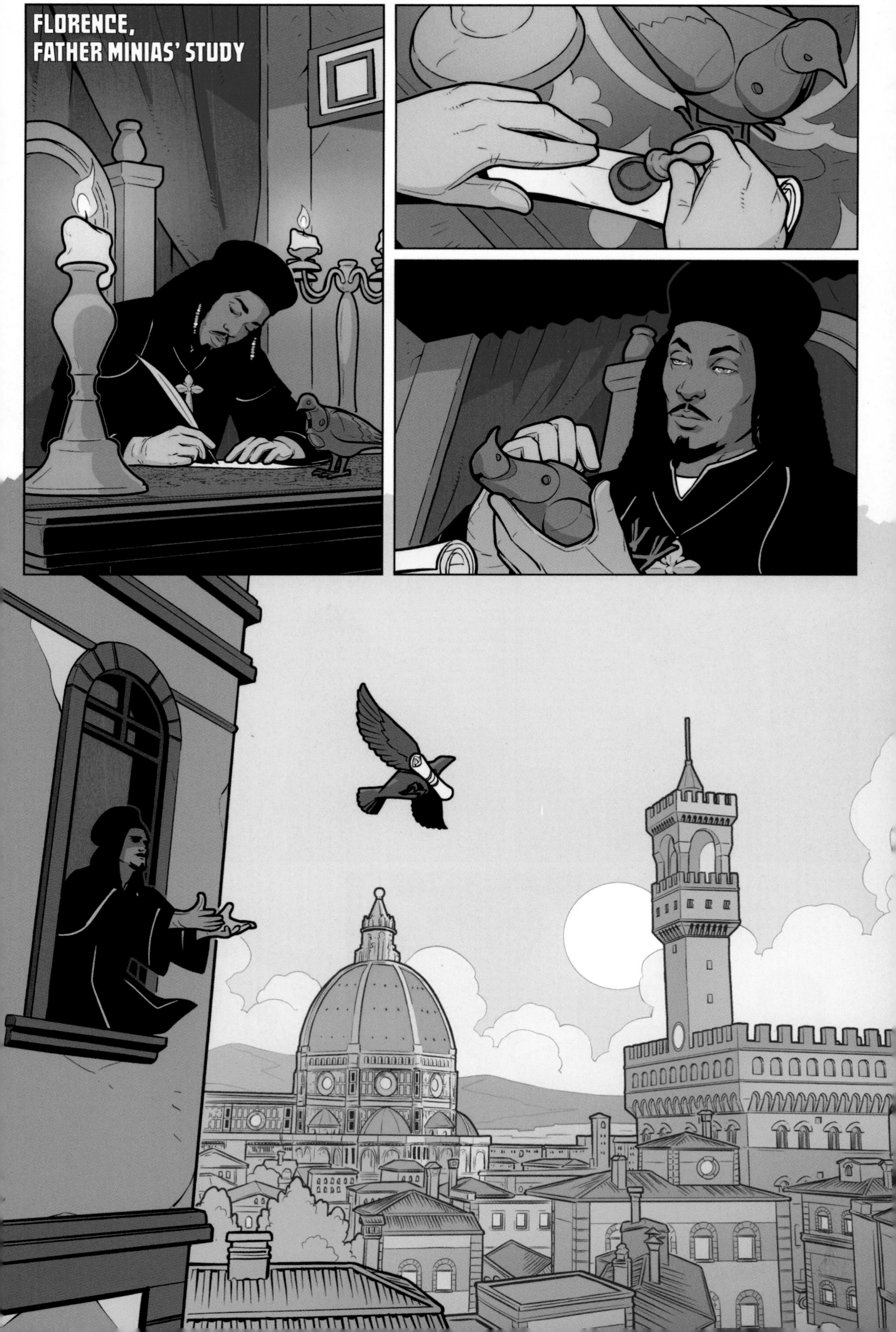
FLORENCE,
FATHER MINIAS' STUDY

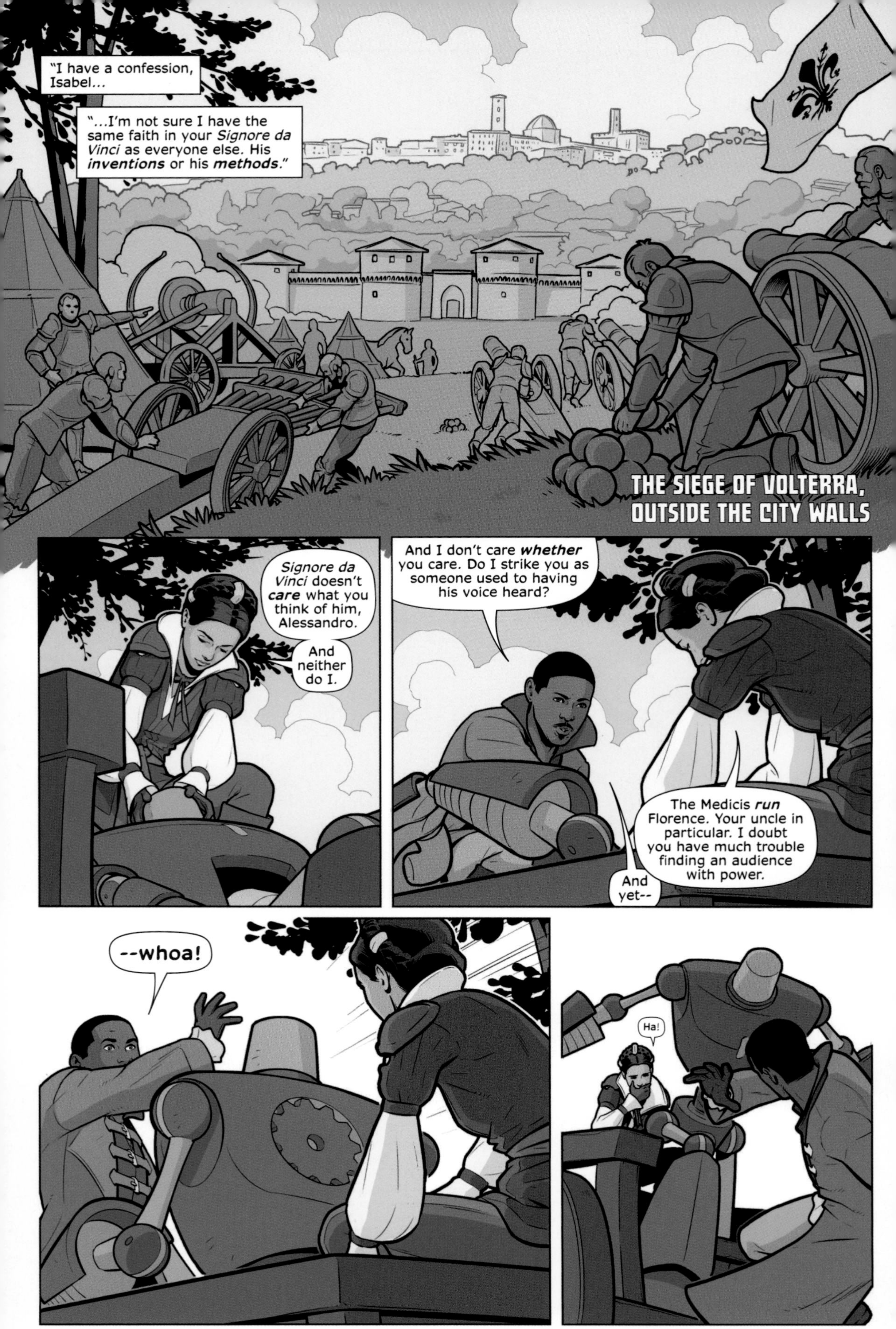
"I have a confession, Isabel...
"...I'm not sure I have the same faith in your *Signore da Vinci* as everyone else. His ***inventions*** or his ***methods***."
THE SIEGE OF VOLTERRA, OUTSIDE THE CITY WALLS
Signore da Vinci doesn't ***care*** what you think of him, Alessandro.
And neither do I.
And I don't care ***whether*** you care. Do I strike you as someone used to having his voice heard?
The Medicis ***run*** Florence. Your uncle in particular. I doubt you have much trouble finding an audience with power.
And yet--
--whoa!
Ha!

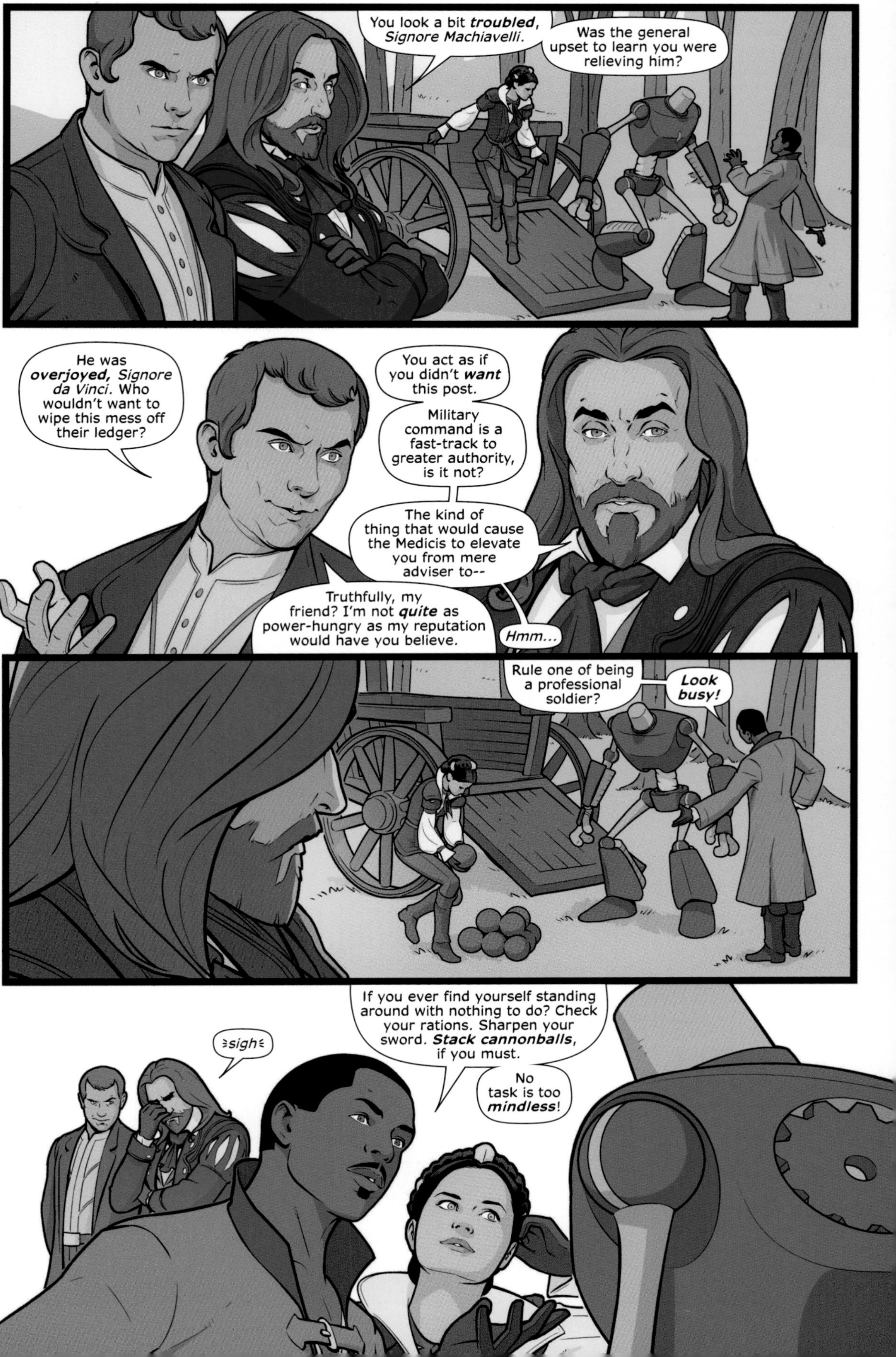

You look a bit *troubled*, *Signore Machiavelli.*
Was the general upset to learn you were relieving him?
He was ***overjoyed,*** *Signore da Vinci.* Who wouldn't want to wipe this mess off their ledger?
You act as if you didn't ***want*** this post.
Military command is a fast-track to greater authority, is it not?
The kind of thing that would cause the Medicis to elevate you from mere adviser to--
Truthfully, my friend? I'm not ***quite*** as power-hungry as my reputation would have you believe.
Hmm...
Rule one of being a professional soldier?
Look busy!
If you ever find yourself standing around with nothing to do? Check your rations. Sharpen your sword. ***Stack cannonballs***, if you must.
sigh
No task is too ***mindless***!

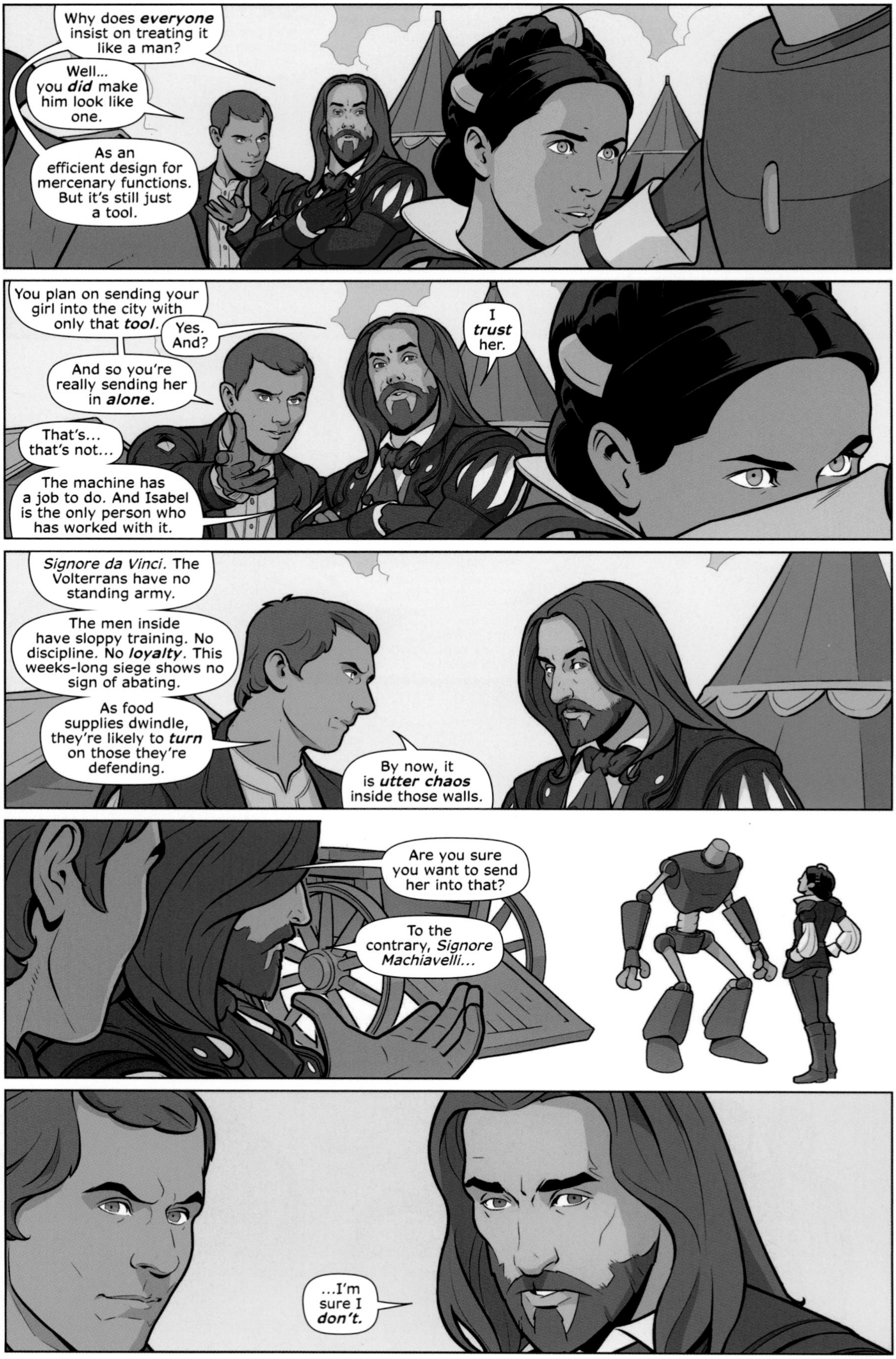
Why does *everyone* insist on treating it like a man?
Well... you *did* make him look like one.
As an efficient design for mercenary functions. But it's still just a tool.
You plan on sending your girl into the city with only that *tool*.
Yes. And?
I *trust* her.
And so you're really sending her in *alone*.
That's... that's not...
The machine has a job to do. And Isabel is the only person who has worked with it.
Signore da Vinci. The Volterrans have no standing army.
The men inside have sloppy training. No discipline. No *loyalty*. This weeks-long siege shows no sign of abating.
As food supplies dwindle, they're likely to *turn* on those they're defending.
By now, it is *utter chaos* inside those walls.
Are you sure you want to send her into that?
To the contrary, *Signore Machiavelli*...
...I'm sure I *don't*.

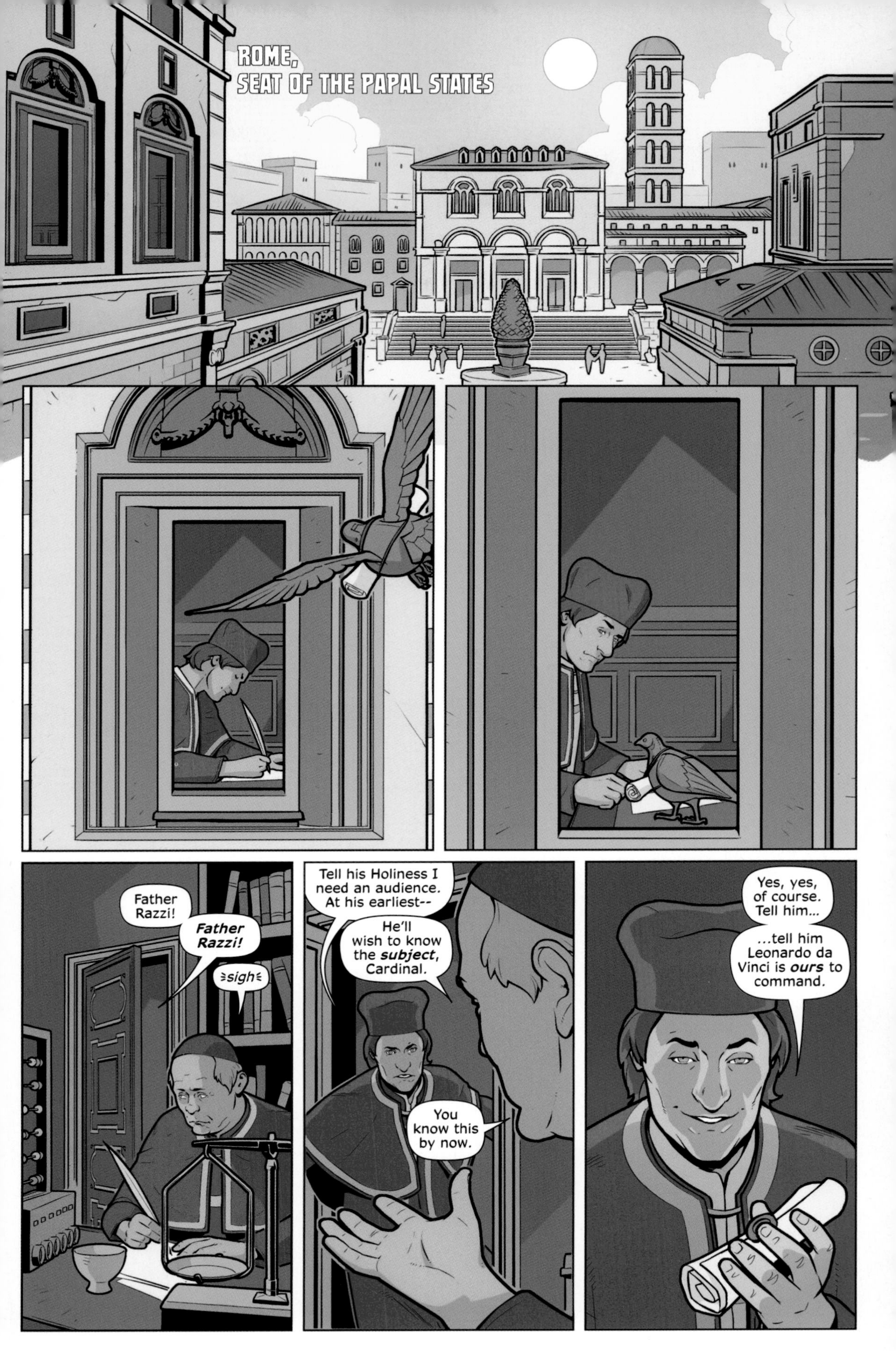
ROME,
SEAT OF THE PAPAL STATES
Father Razzi!
Father Razzi!
sigh
Tell his Holiness I need an audience. At his earliest--
He'll wish to know the subject, Cardinal.
You know this by now.
Yes, yes, of course. Tell him...
...tell him Leonardo da Vinci is ours to command.

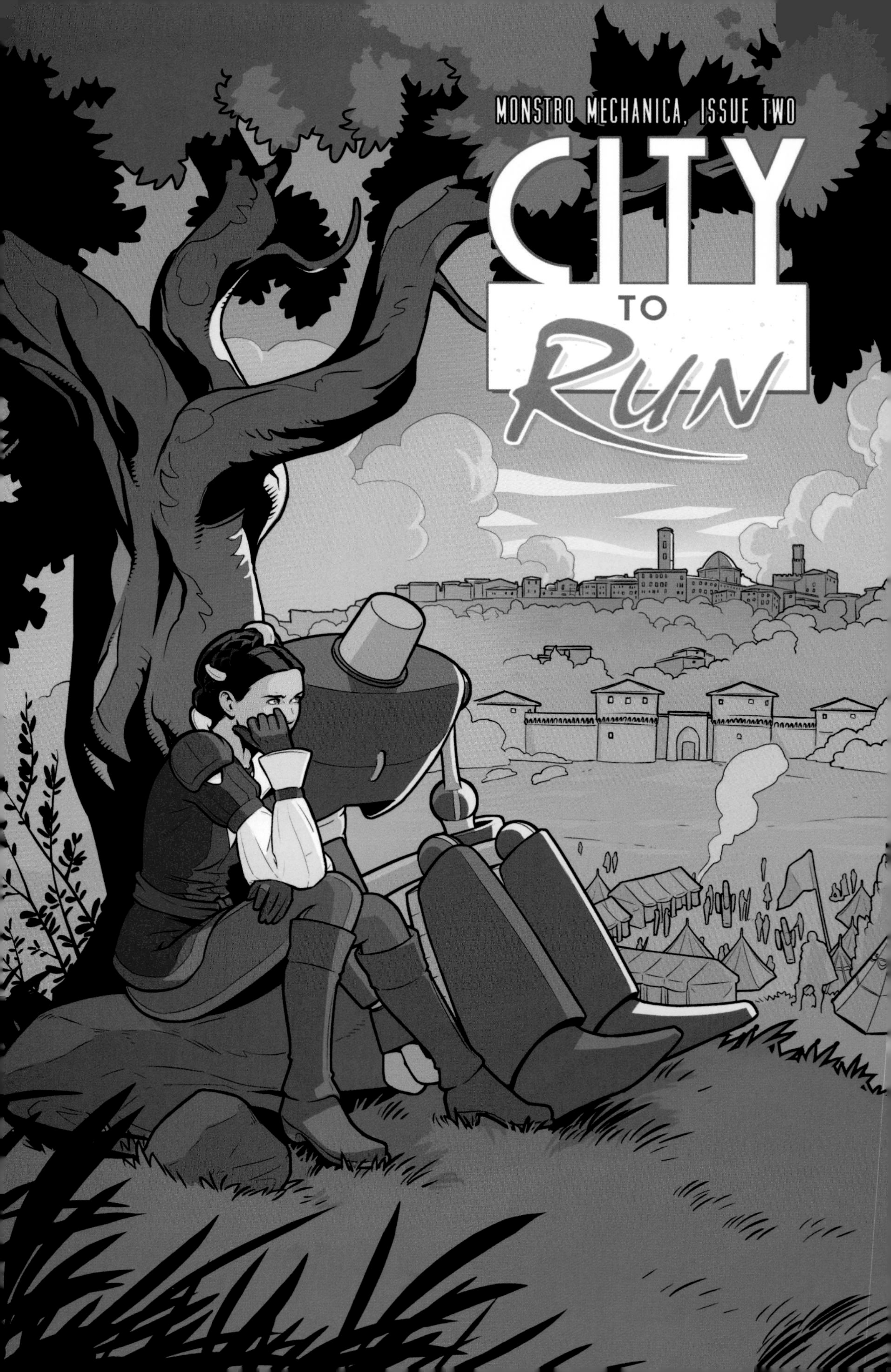
MONSTRO MECHANICA, ISSUE TWO
CITY
TO
RUN

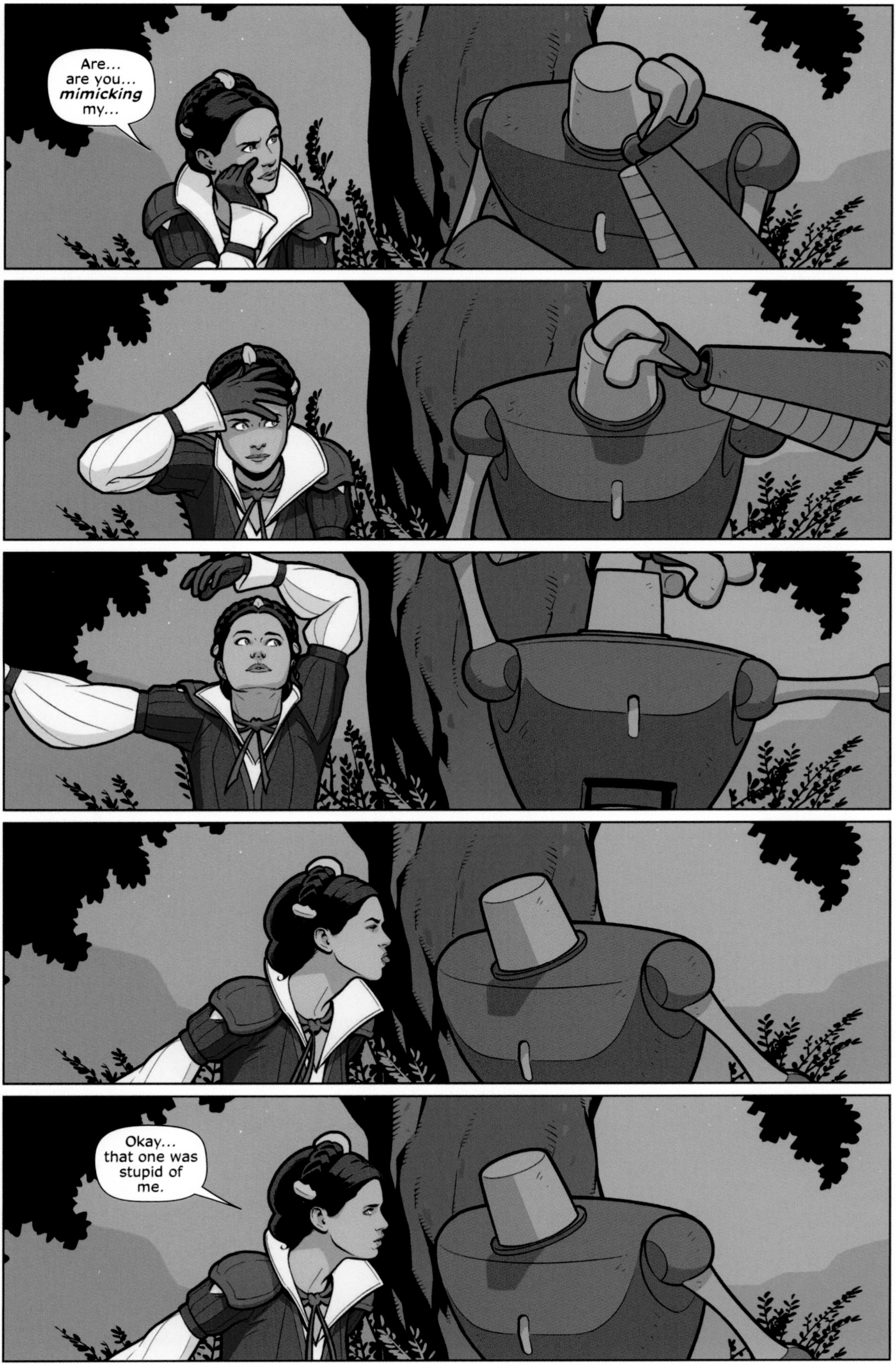
Are... are you... *mimicking* my...
Okay... that one was stupid of me.

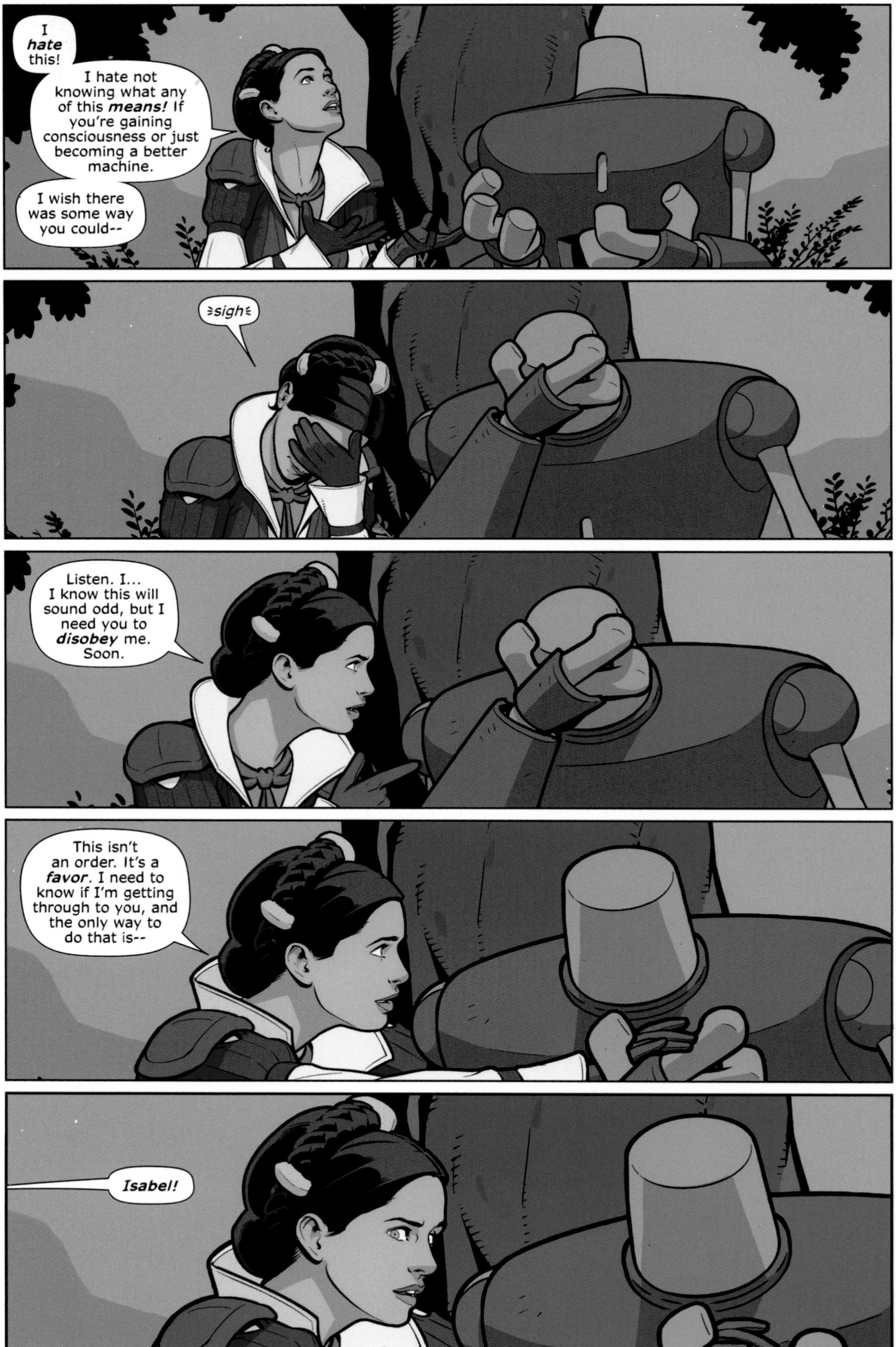

I *hate* this!
I hate not knowing what any of this *means!* If you're gaining consciousness or just becoming a better machine.
I wish there was some way you could--
sigh
Listen. I... I know this will sound odd, but I need you to *disobey* me. Soon.
This isn't an order. It's a *favor*. I need to know if I'm getting through to you, and the only way to do that is--
Isabel!

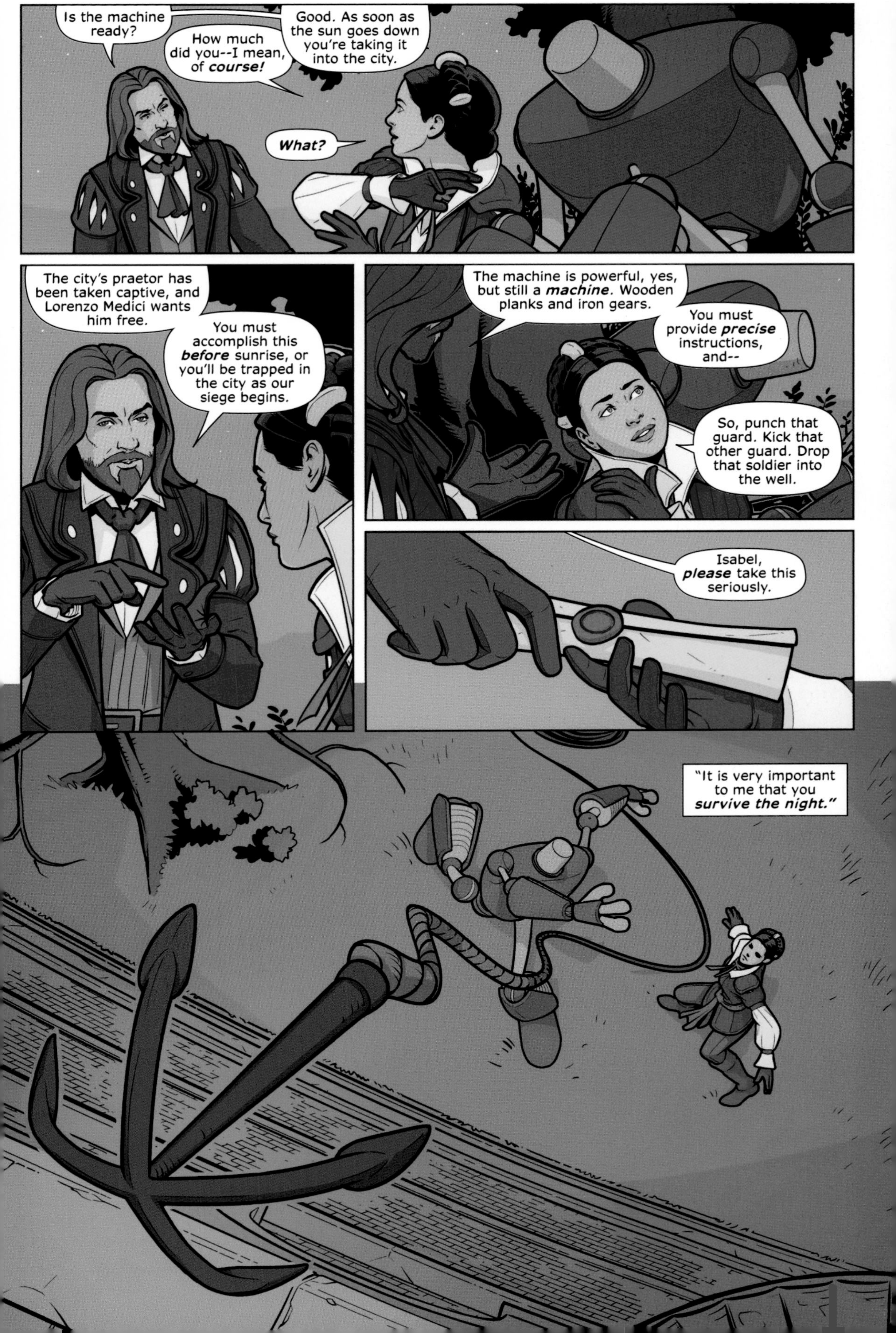

Is the machine ready?
How much did you--I mean, of *course!*
Good. As soon as the sun goes down you're taking it into the city.
What?
The city's praetor has been taken captive, and Lorenzo Medici wants him free.
You must accomplish this *before* sunrise, or you'll be trapped in the city as our siege begins.
The machine is powerful, yes, but still a *machine*. Wooden planks and iron gears.
You must provide *precise* instructions, and--
So, punch that guard. Kick that other guard. Drop that soldier into the well.
Isabel, *please* take this seriously.
"It is very important to me that you *survive the night."*

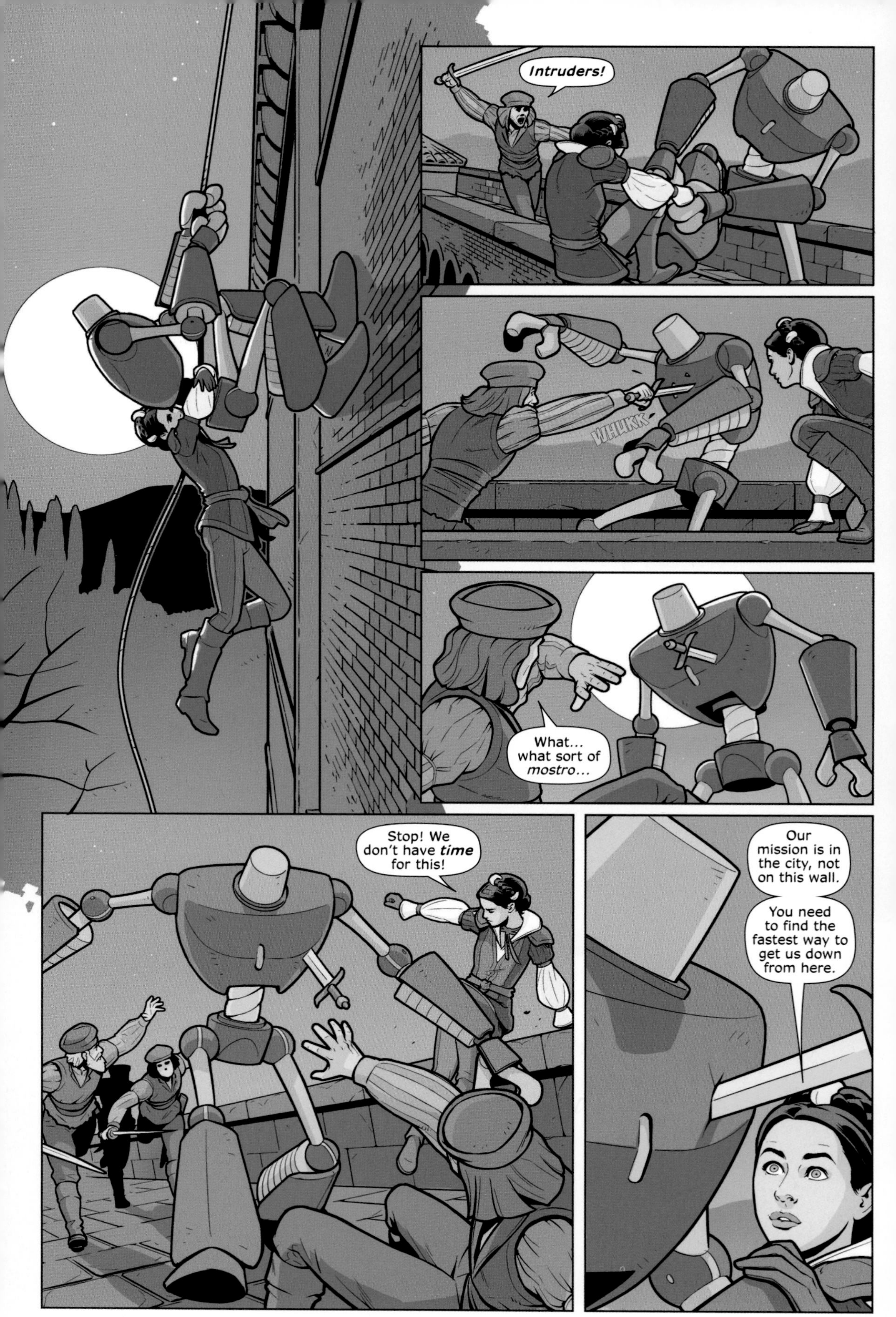
Intruders!
WHUKK
What... what sort of *mostro*...
Stop! We don't have *time* for this!
Our mission is in the city, not on this wall.
You need to find the fastest way to get us down from here.

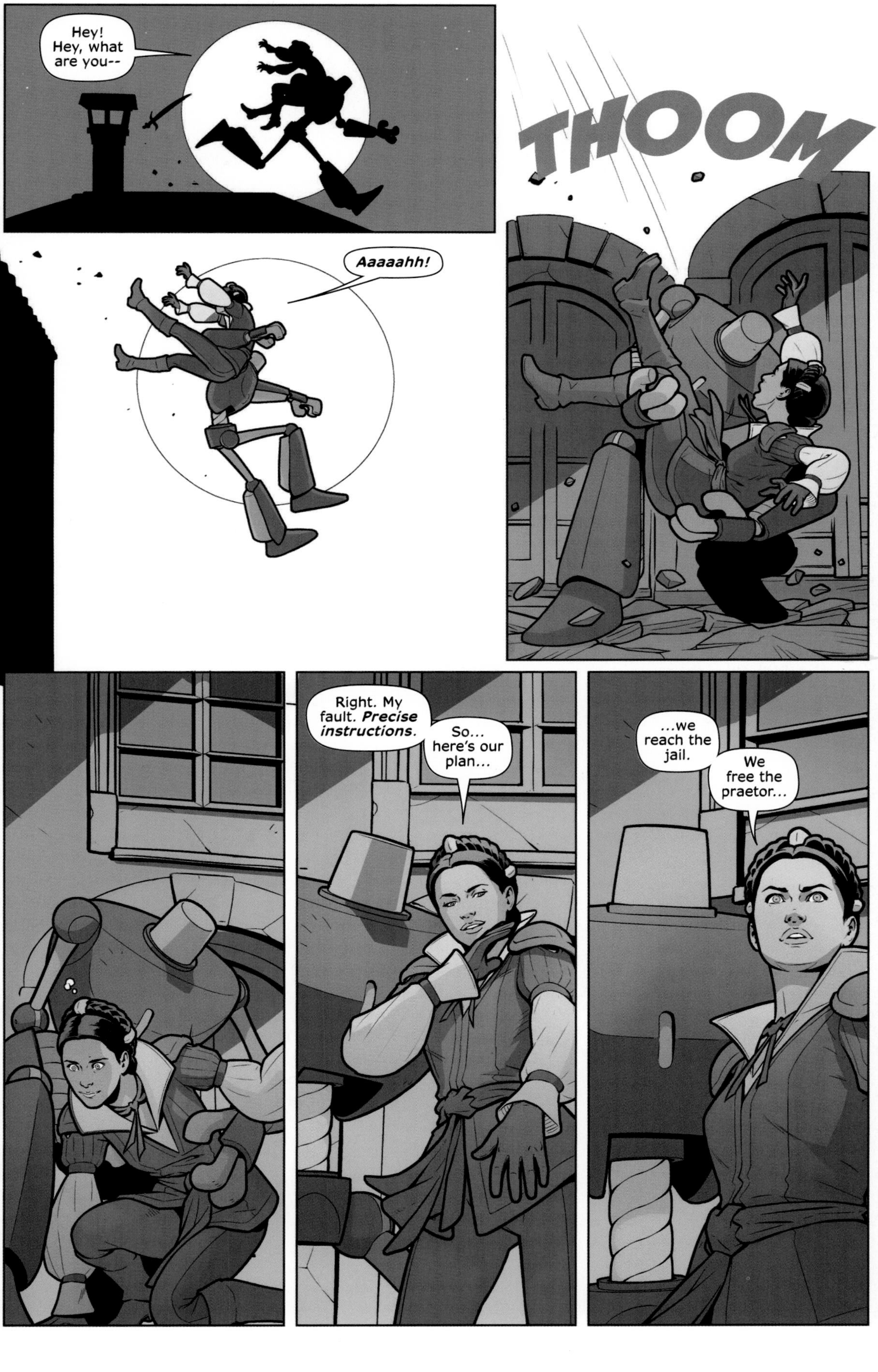
Hey!
Hey, what are you--
THOOM
Aaaaahh!
Right. My fault. *Precise instructions*.
So... here's our plan...
...we reach the jail.
We free the praetor...

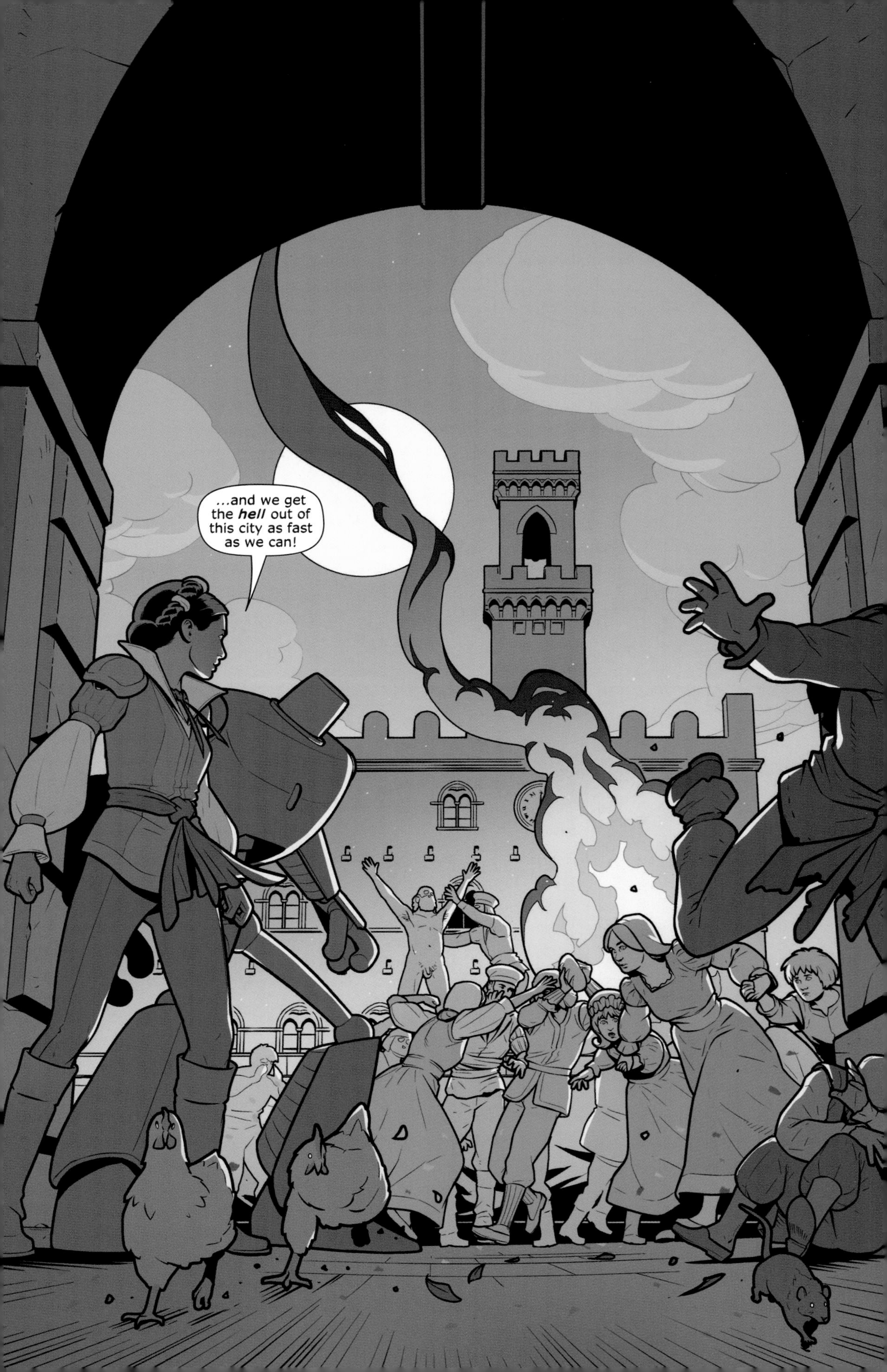
...and we get the *hell* out of this city as fast as we can!

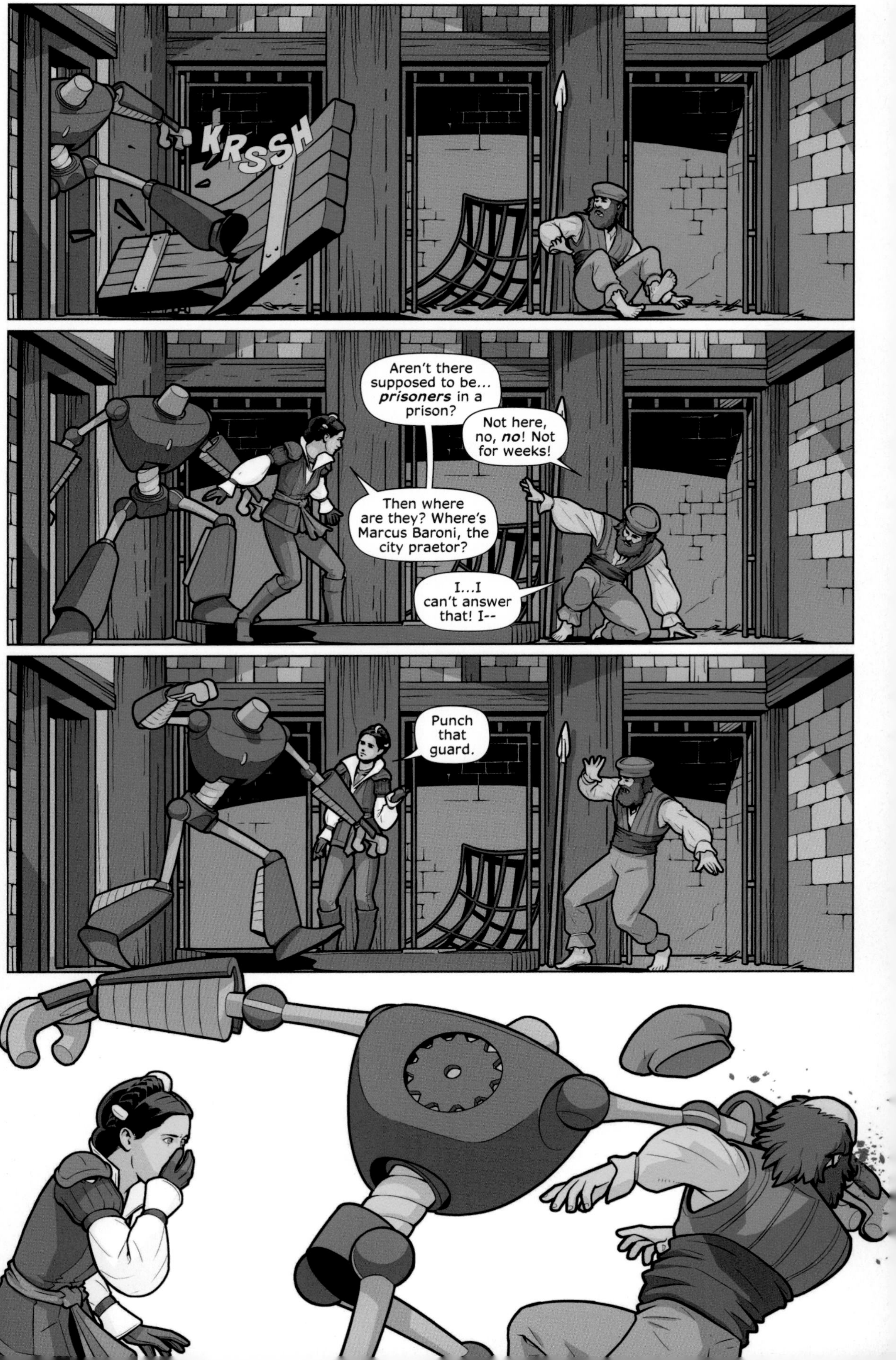
KRSSH
Aren't there supposed to be... *prisoners* in a prison?
Not here, no, ***no***! Not for weeks!
Then where are they? Where's Marcus Baroni, the city praetor?
I...I can't answer that! I--
Punch that guard.

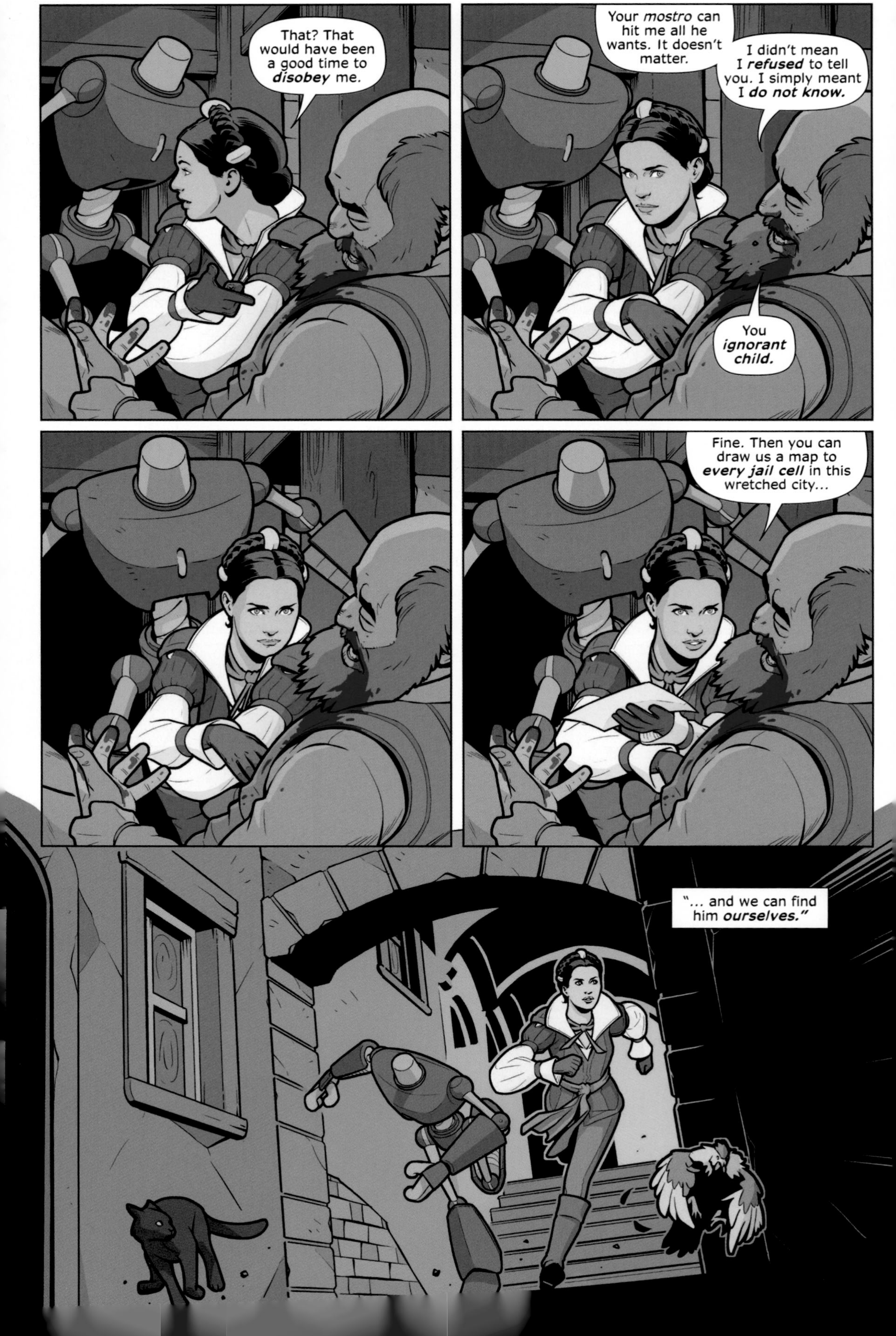

That? That would have been a good time to *disobey* me.
Your *mostro* can hit me all he wants. It doesn't matter.
I didn't mean I ***refused*** to tell you. I simply meant I ***do not know.***
You ***ignorant child.***
Fine. Then you can draw us a map to ***every jail cell*** in this wretched city...
"... and we can find him ***ourselves."***

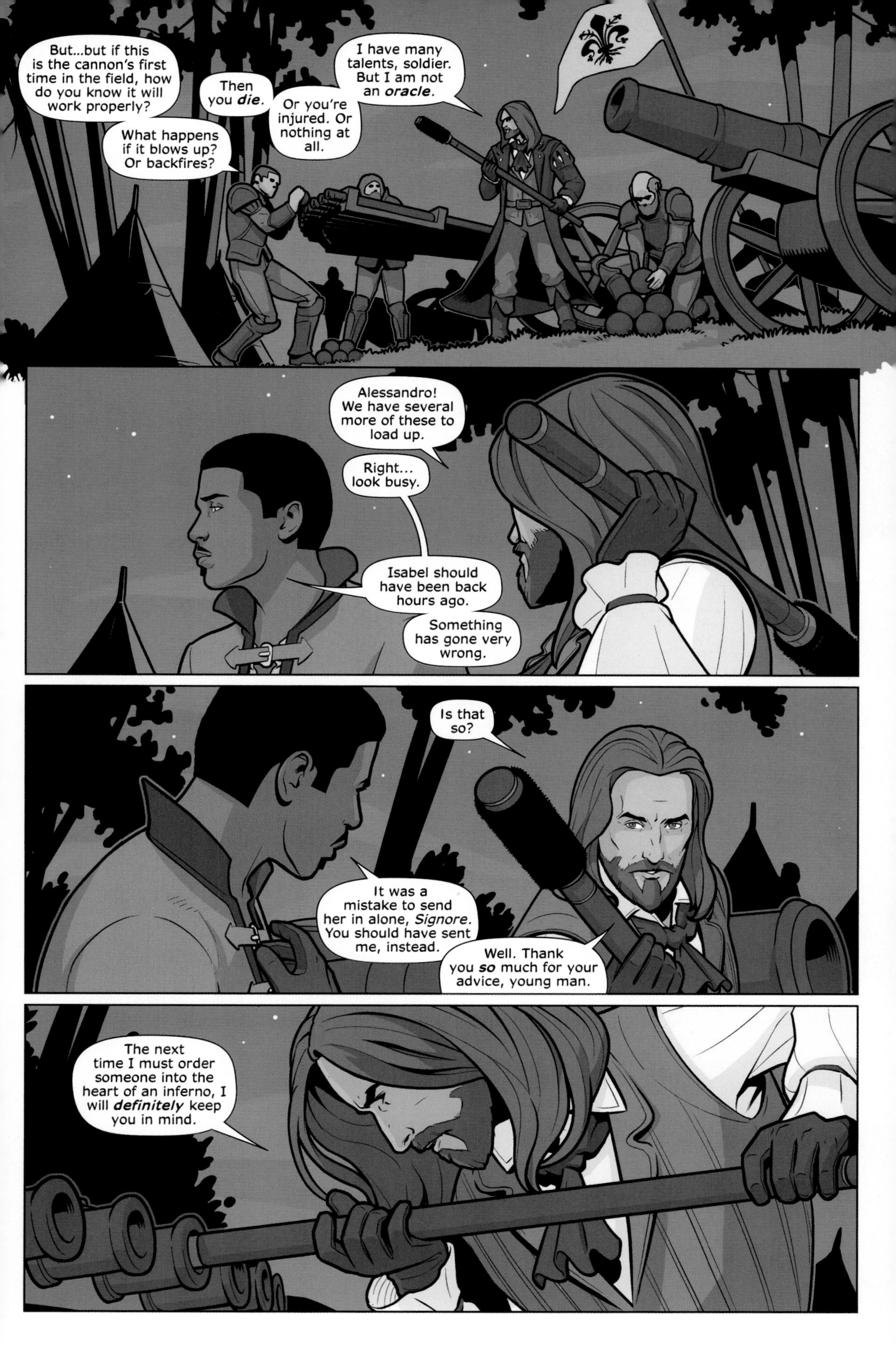

But...but if this is the cannon's first time in the field, how do you know it will work properly?
What happens if it blows up? Or backfires?
Then you *die*.
Or you're injured. Or nothing at all.
I have many talents, soldier. But I am not an ***oracle***.
Alessandro! We have several more of these to load up.
Right... look busy.
Isabel should have been back hours ago.
Something has gone very wrong.
Is that so?
It was a mistake to send her in alone, *Signore*. You should have sent me, instead.
Well. Thank you ***so*** much for your advice, young man.
The next time I must order someone into the heart of an inferno, I will ***definitely*** keep you in mind.

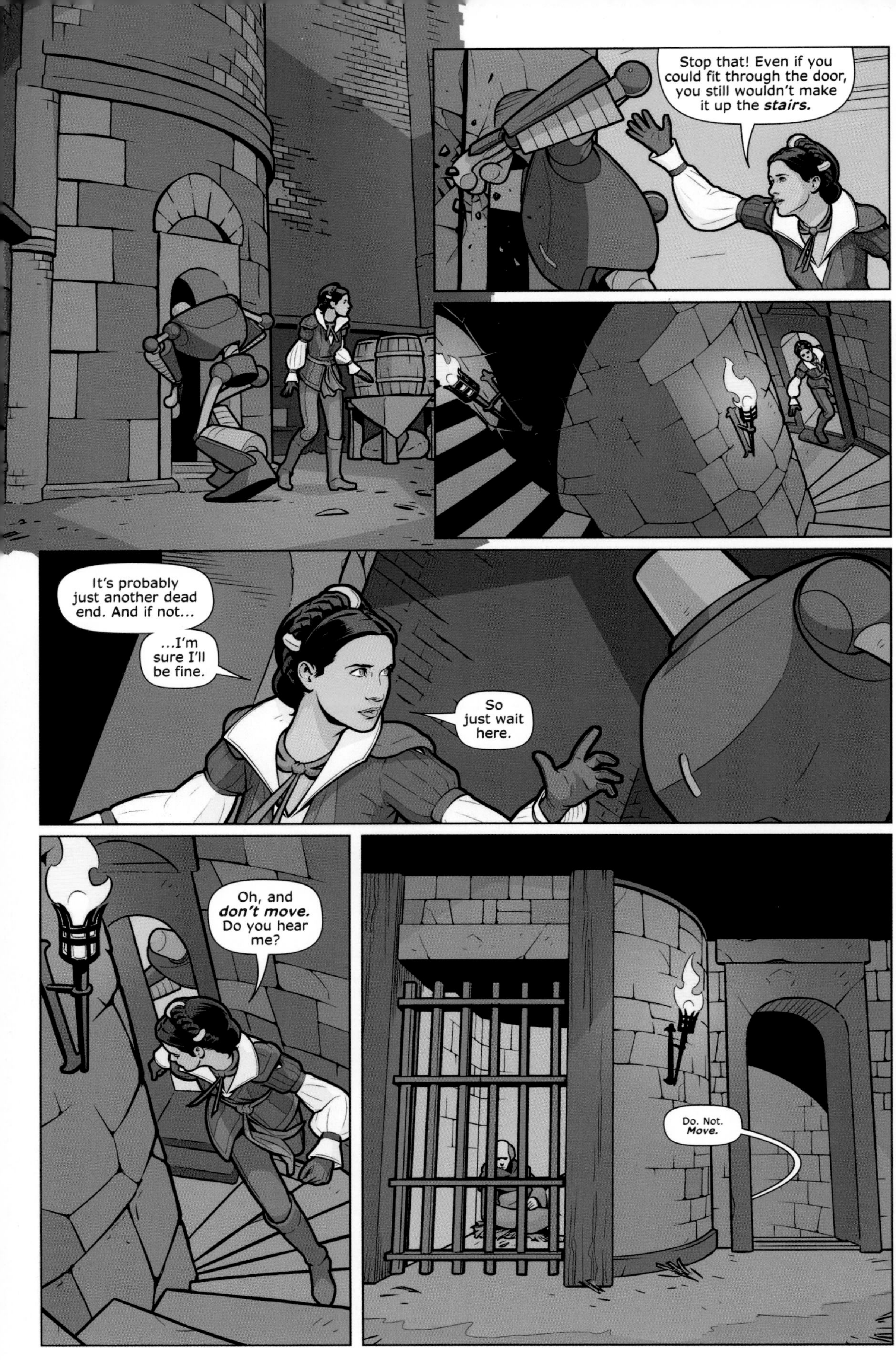
Stop that! Even if you could fit through the door, you still wouldn't make it up the ***stairs.***
It's probably just another dead end. And if not...
...I'm sure I'll be fine.
So just wait here.
Oh, and ***don't move.*** Do you hear me?
Do. Not. ***Move.***

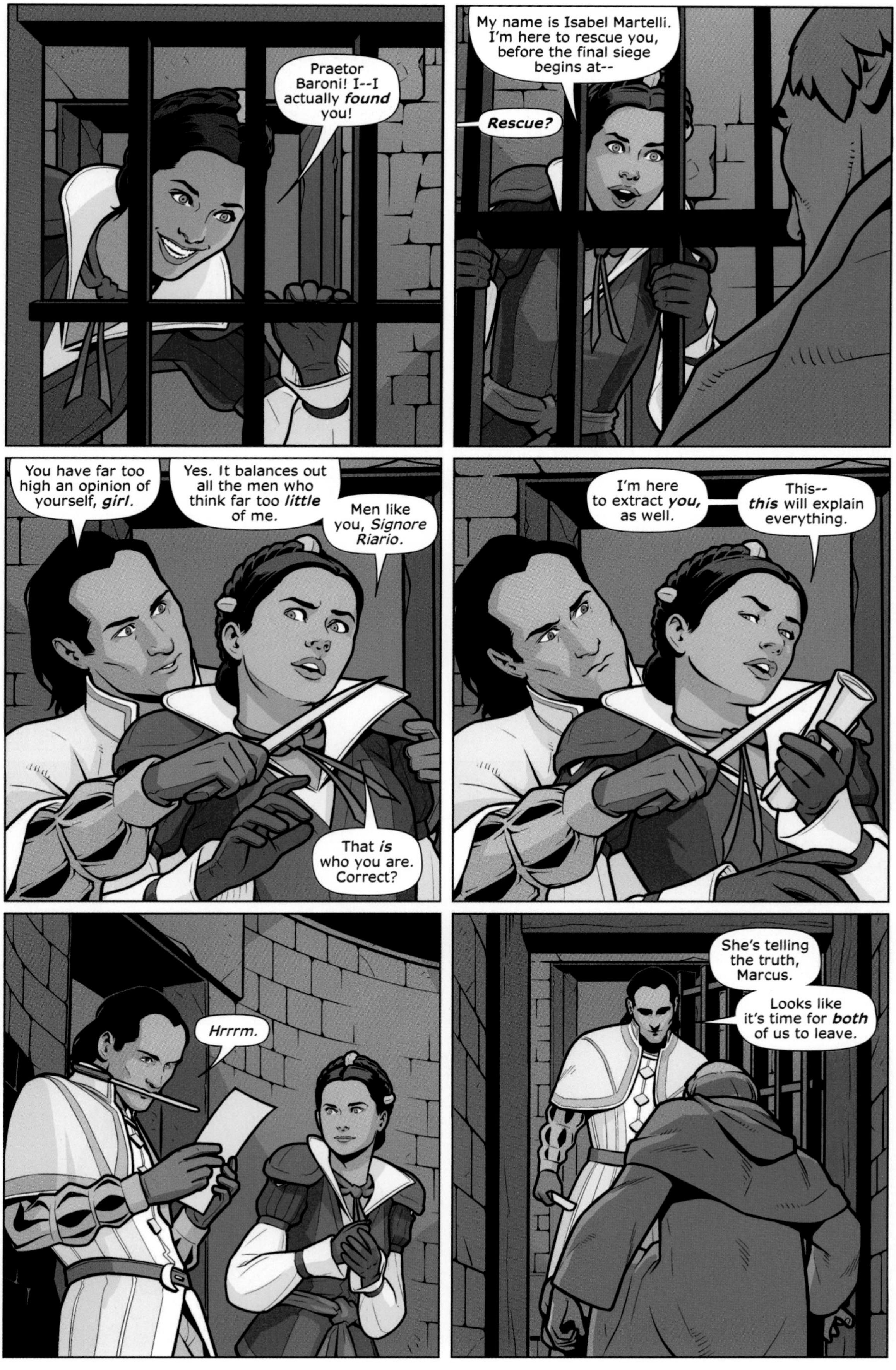
Praetor Baroni! I--I actually *found* you!
My name is Isabel Martelli. I'm here to rescue you, before the final siege begins at--
Rescue?
You have far too high an opinion of yourself, *girl*.
Yes. It balances out all the men who think far too *little* of me.
Men like you, *Signore Riario*.
That *is* who you are. Correct?
I'm here to extract *you,* as well.
This-- *this* will explain everything.
Hrrrm.
She's telling the truth, Marcus.
Looks like it's time for *both* of us to leave.

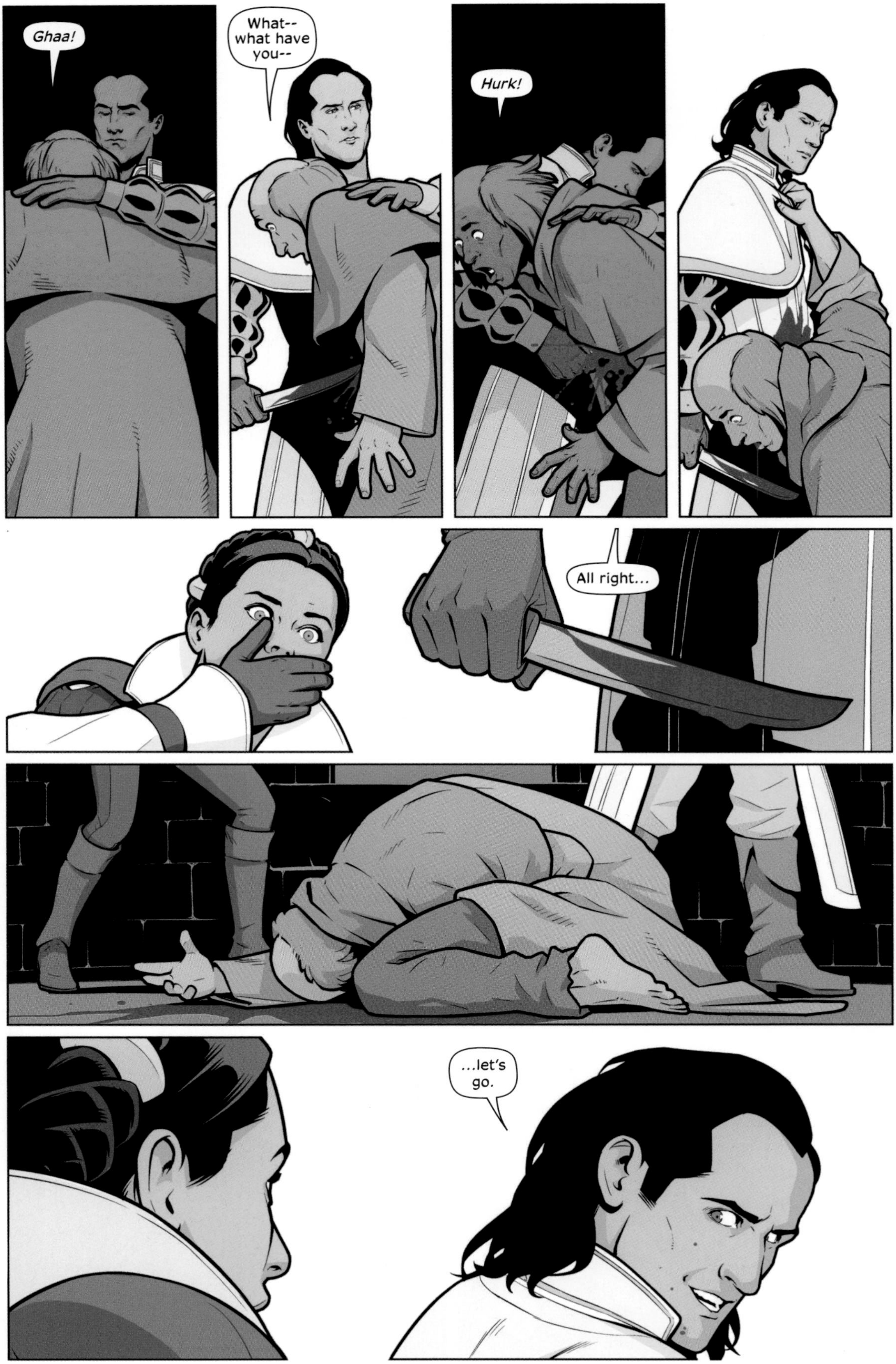
Ghaa!
What-- what have you--
Hurk!
All right...
...let's go.

So much for getting us out *before* the siege begins!

There's a--a *machine* downstairs. It can get me to safety.

Your safety is no longer my concern.

Really? What caused *that* change?

I just saw you *slaughter* a man!

After you handed me a letter instructing me to!

BOOM

That's... that's not--

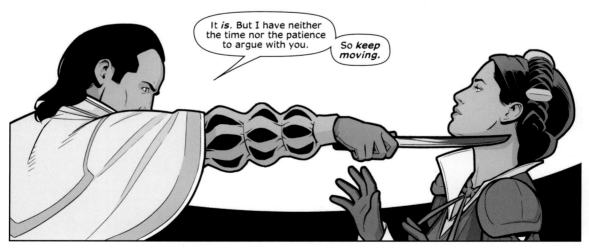

It *is*. But I have neither the time nor the patience to argue with you.

So *keep moving.*

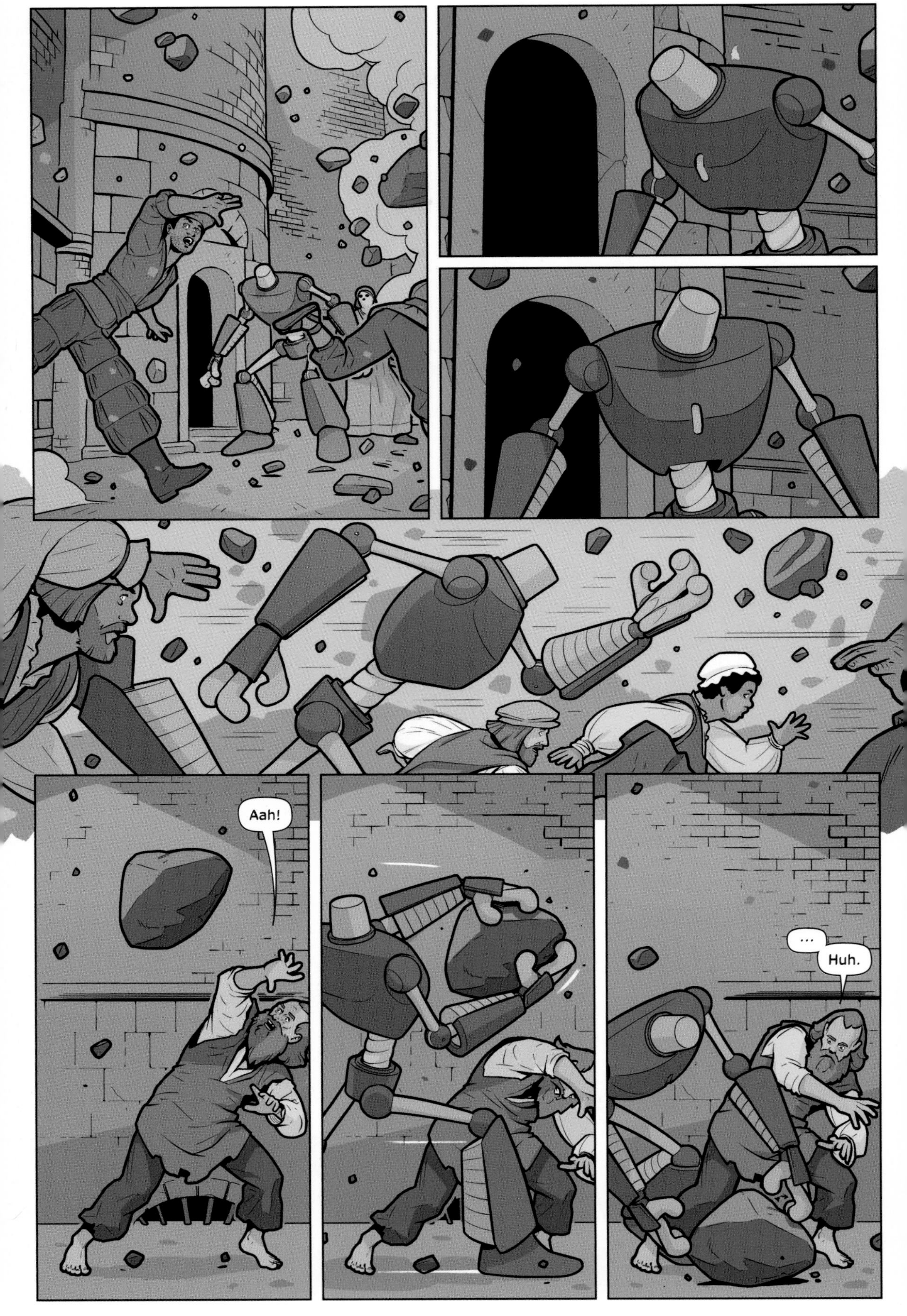
Aah!
...
Huh.

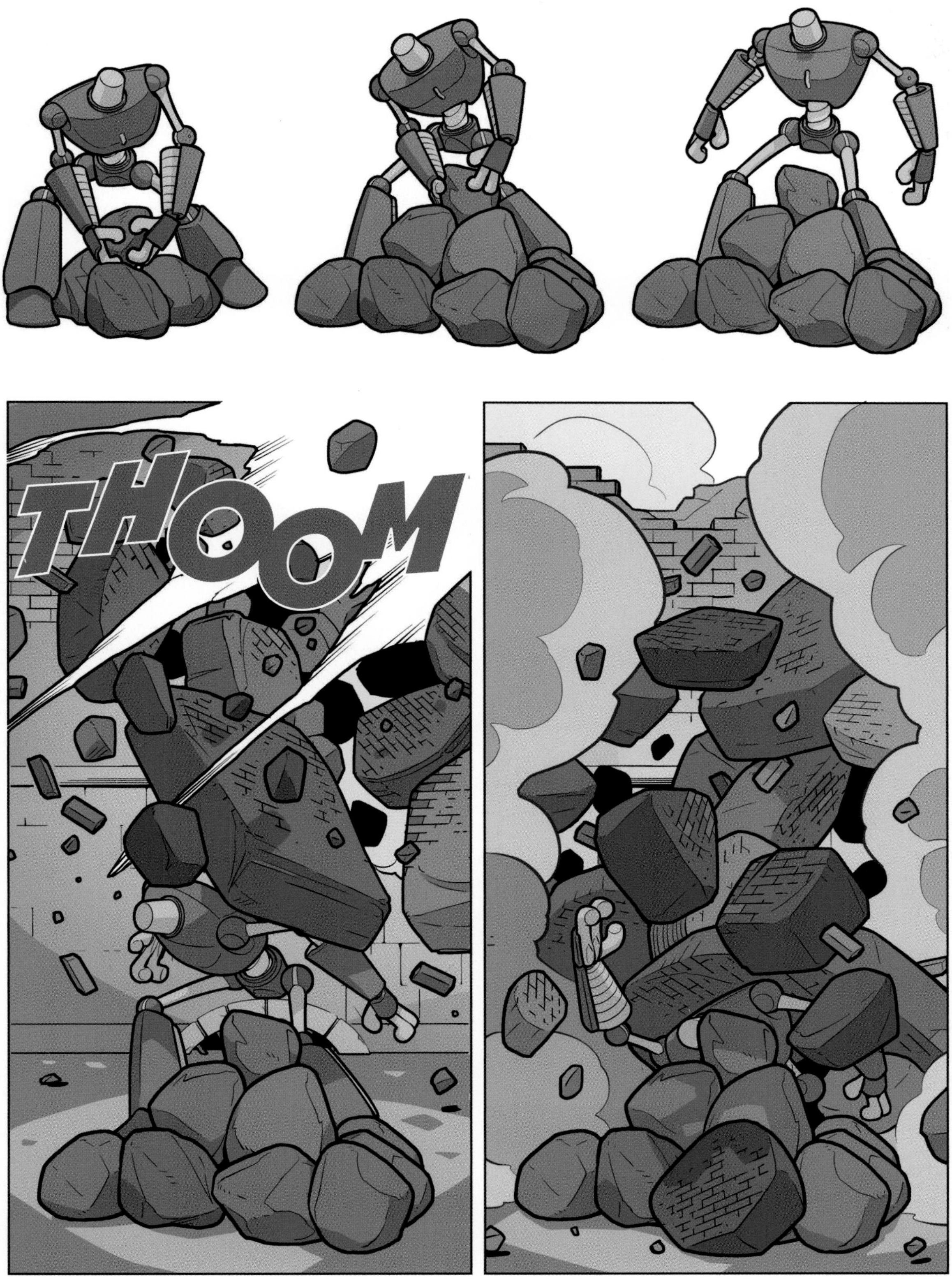
THOOM

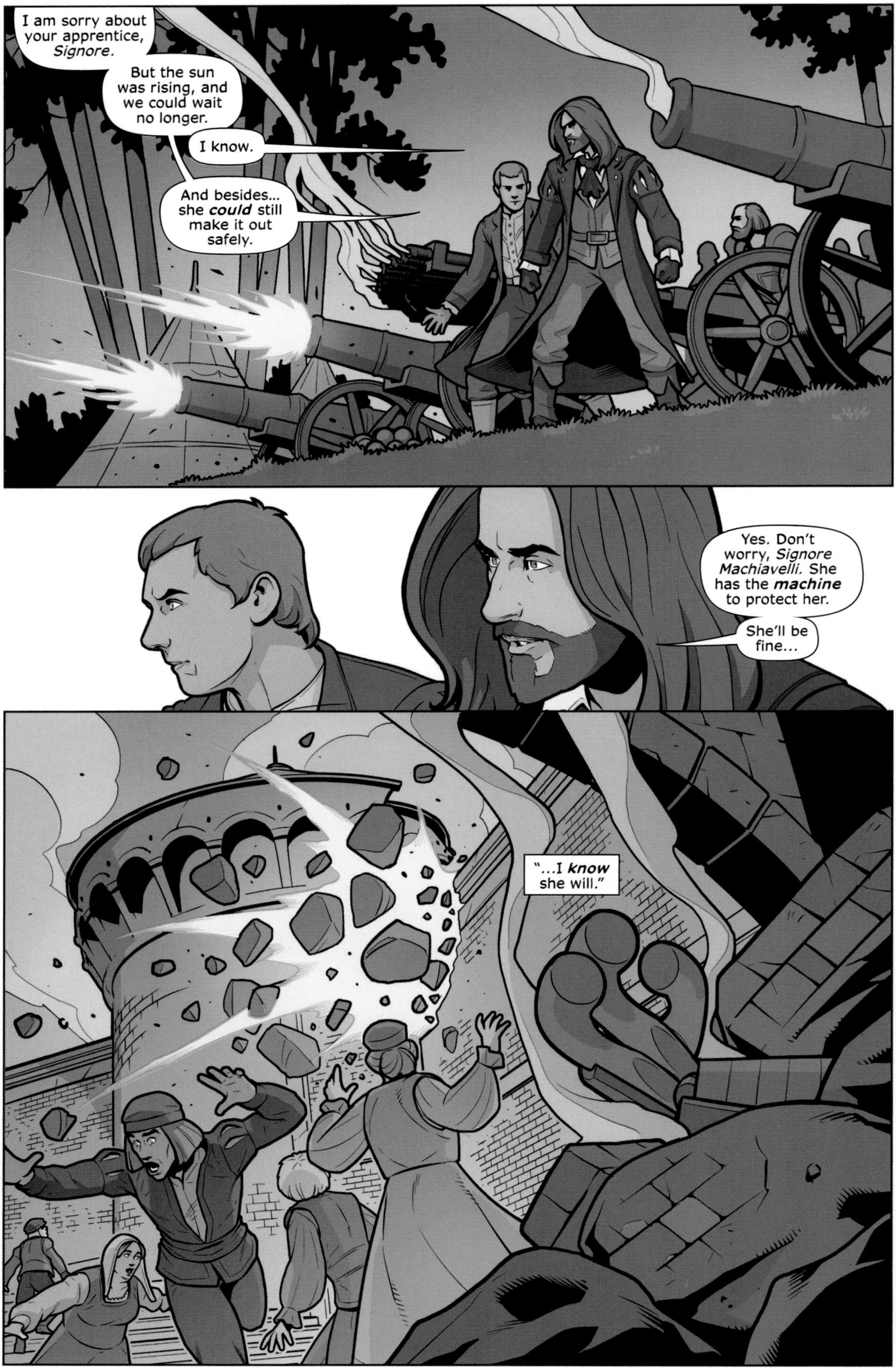
I am sorry about your apprentice, *Signore.*
But the sun was rising, and we could wait no longer.
I know.
And besides... she ***could*** still make it out safely.
Yes. Don't worry, *Signore Machiavelli.* She has the ***machine*** to protect her.
She'll be fine...
"...I ***know*** she will."

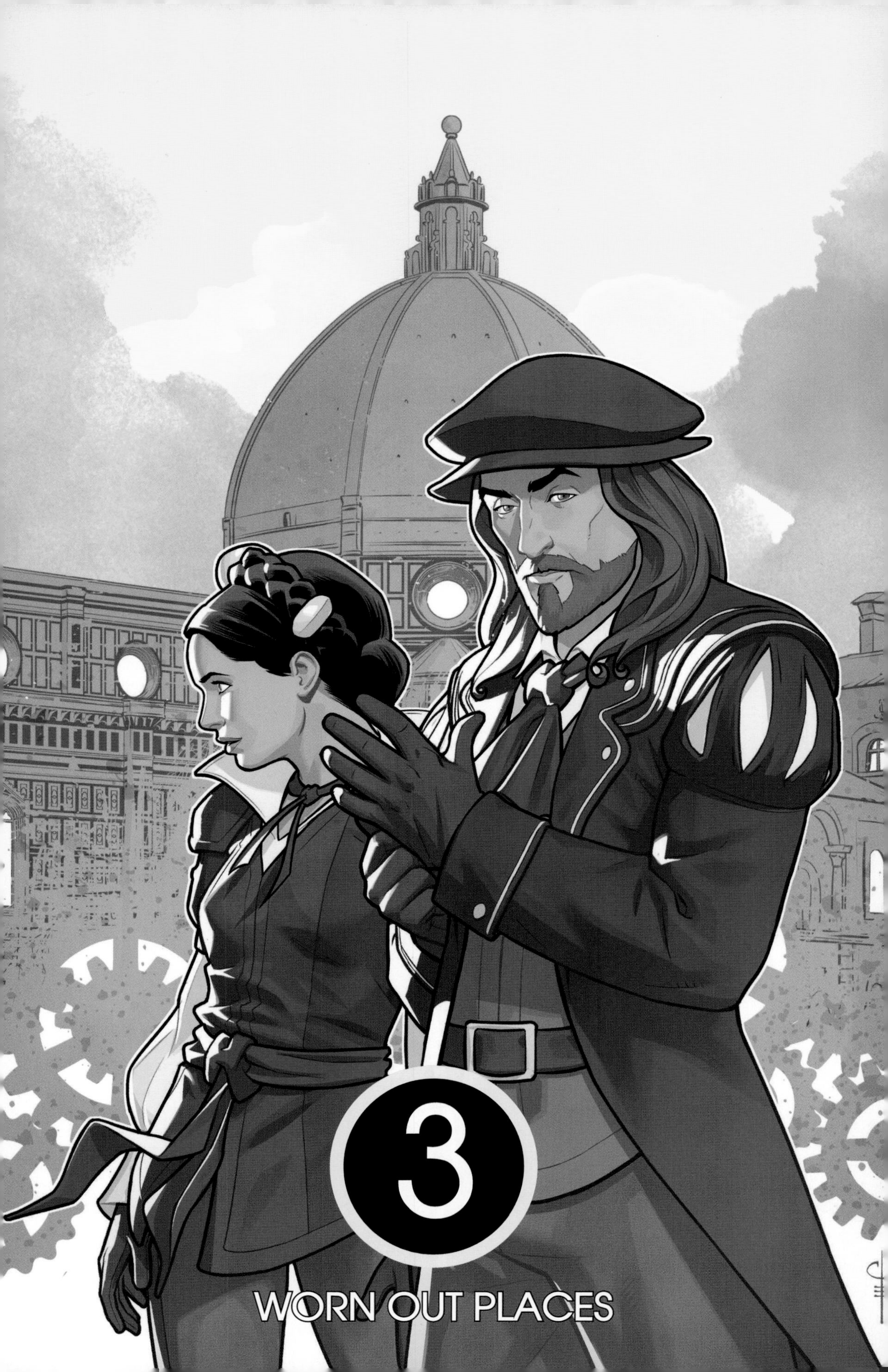
3
WORN OUT PLACES

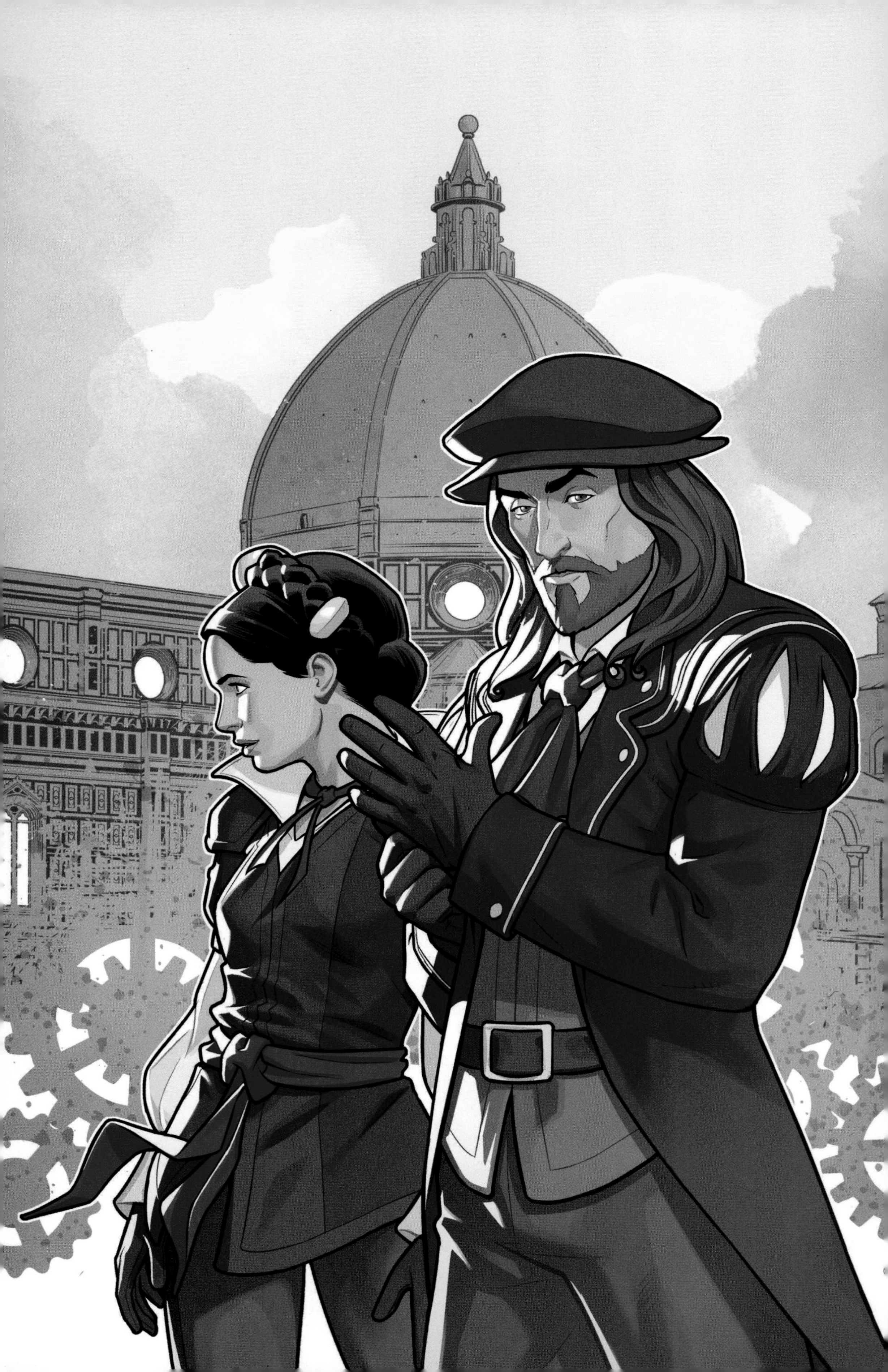

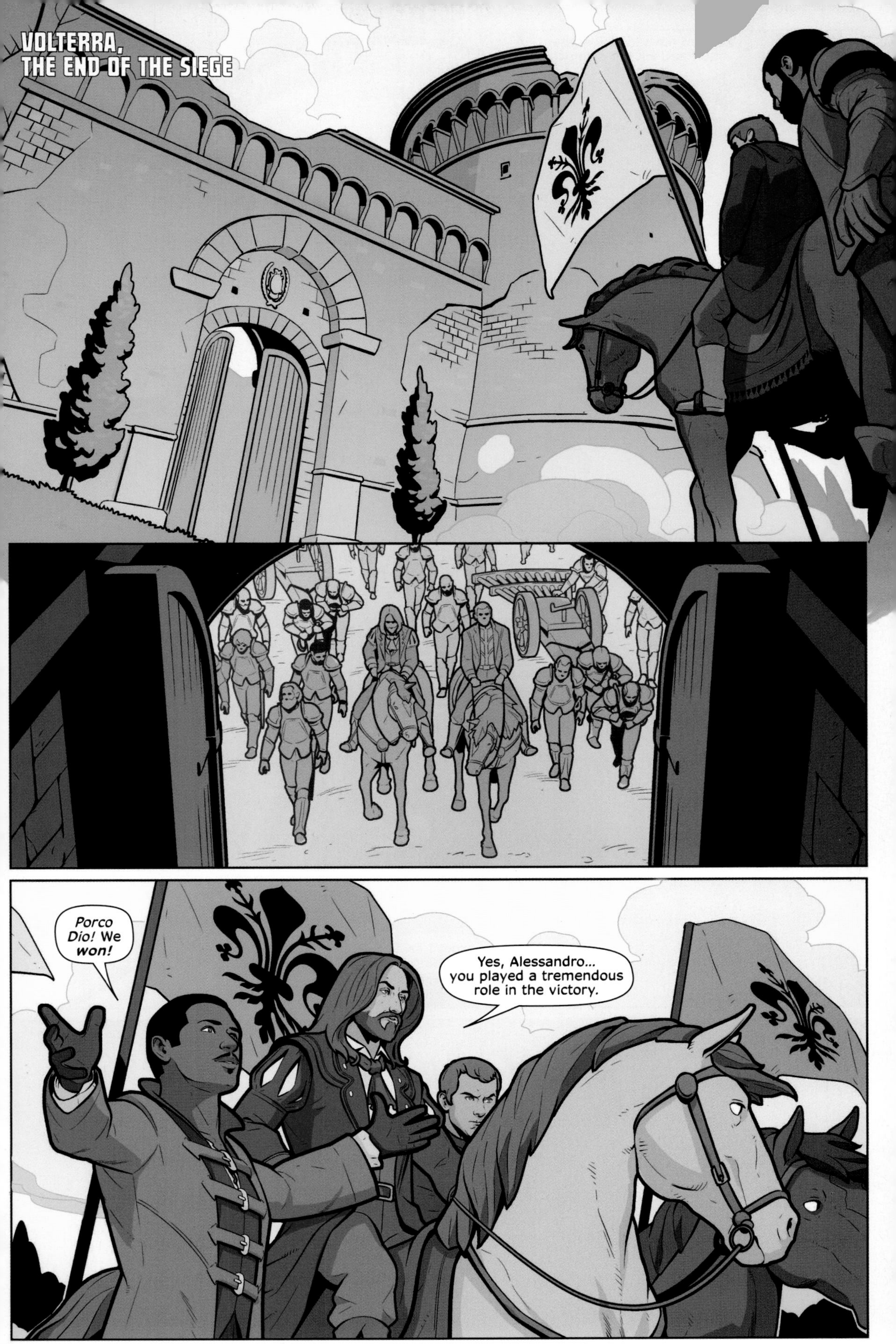

VOLTERRA, THE END OF THE SIEGE
Porco Dio! We won!
Yes, Alessandro... you played a tremendous role in the victory.

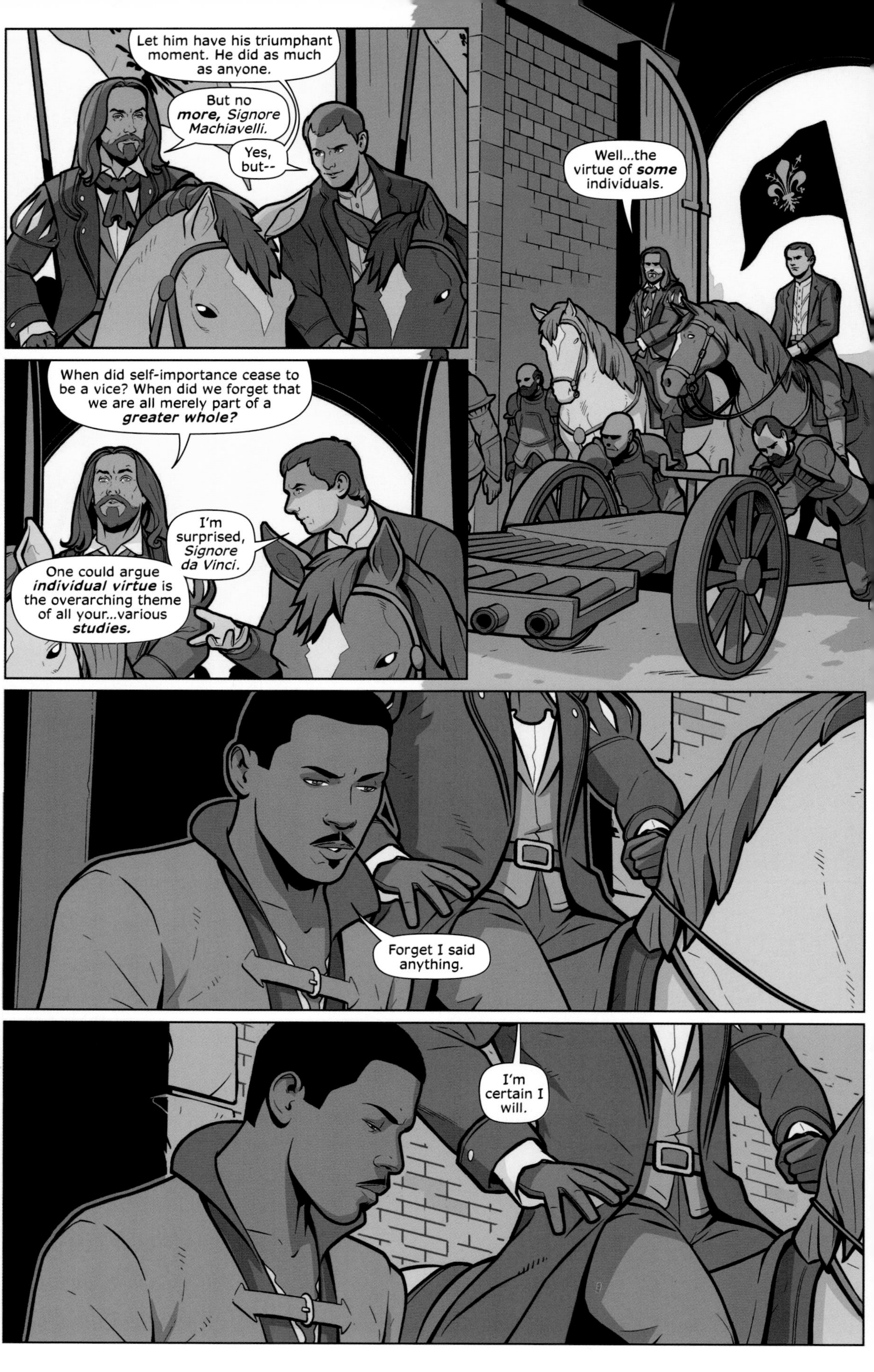

Let him have his triumphant moment. He did as much as anyone.
But no *more,* Signore Machiavelli.
Yes, but--
Well...the virtue of *some* individuals.
When did self-importance cease to be a vice? When did we forget that we are all merely part of a *greater whole?*
I'm surprised, *Signore da Vinci.*
One could argue *individual virtue* is the overarching theme of all your...various *studies.*
Forget I said anything.
I'm certain I will.

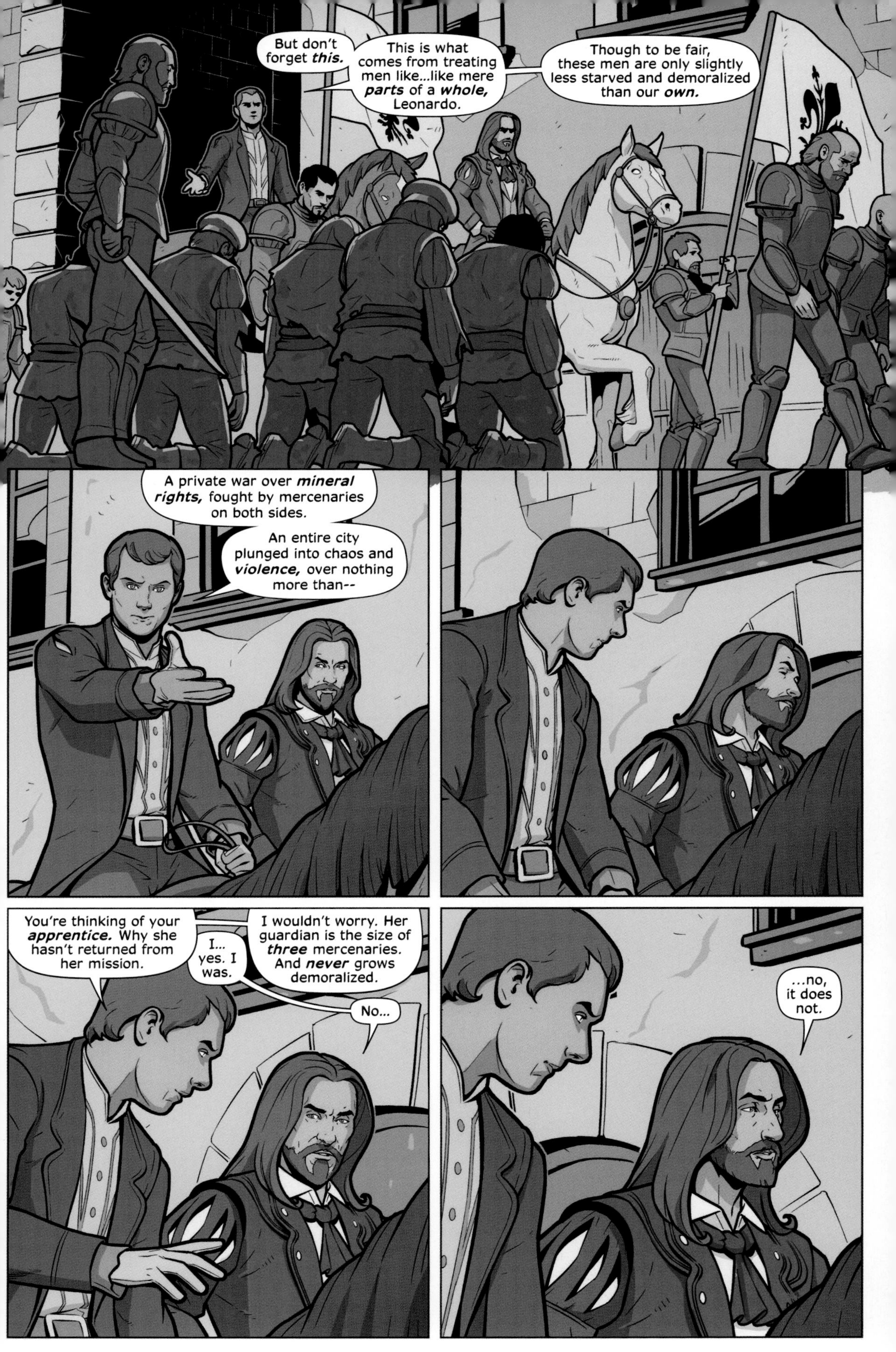
But don't forget *this.*
This is what comes from treating men like...like mere ***parts*** of a ***whole,*** Leonardo.
Though to be fair, these men are only slightly less starved and demoralized than our ***own.***
A private war over ***mineral rights,*** fought by mercenaries on both sides.
An entire city plunged into chaos and ***violence,*** over nothing more than--
You're thinking of your ***apprentice.*** Why she hasn't returned from her mission.
I... yes. I was.
I wouldn't worry. Her guardian is the size of ***three*** mercenaries. And ***never*** grows demoralized.
No...
...no, it does not.

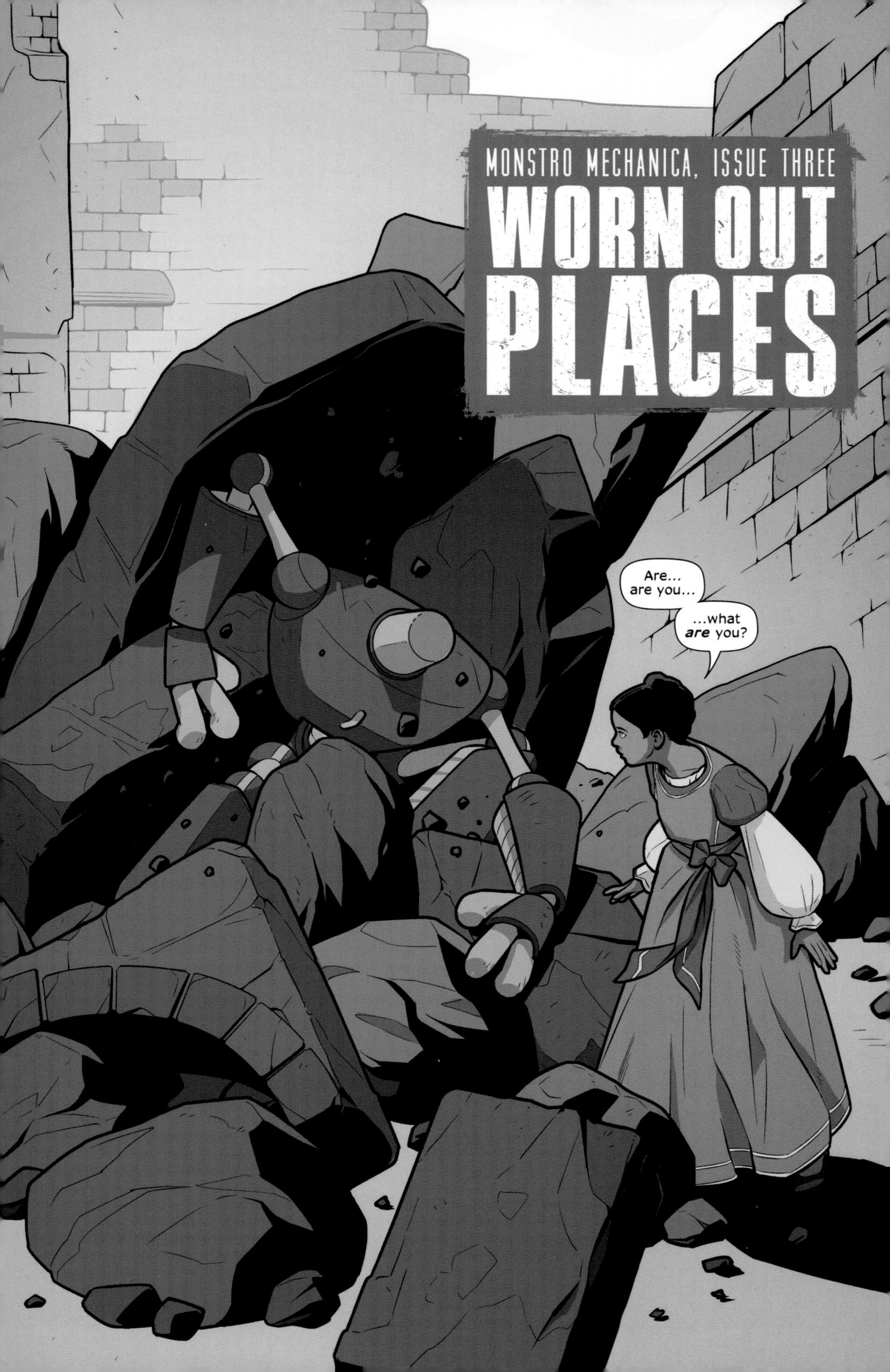
MONSTRO MECHANICA, ISSUE THREE
WORN OUT PLACES
Are... are you...
...what *are* you?

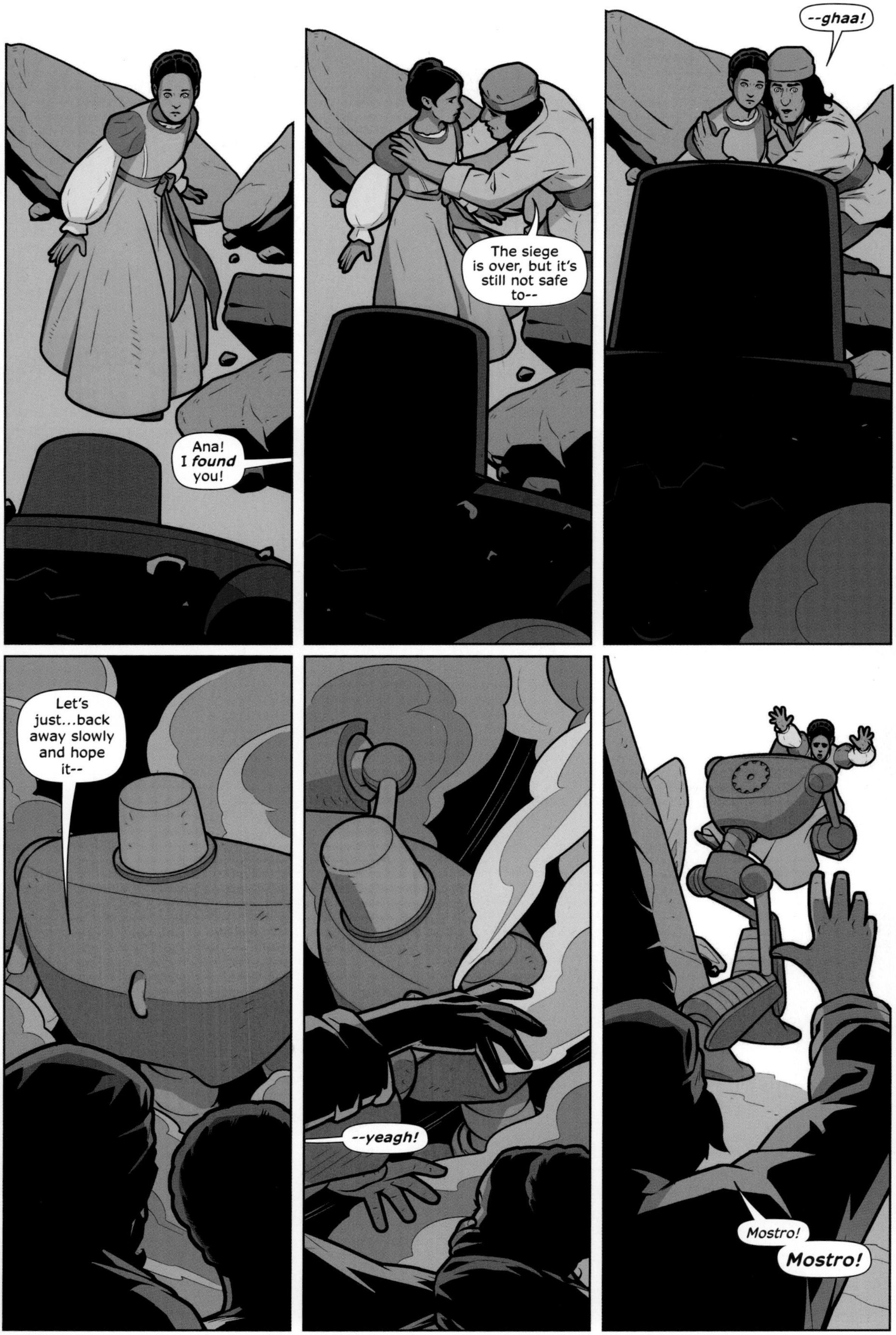
Ana! I *found* you!
The siege is over, but it's still not safe to--
--ghaa!
Let's just...back away slowly and hope it--
--yeagh!
Mostro!
Mostro!

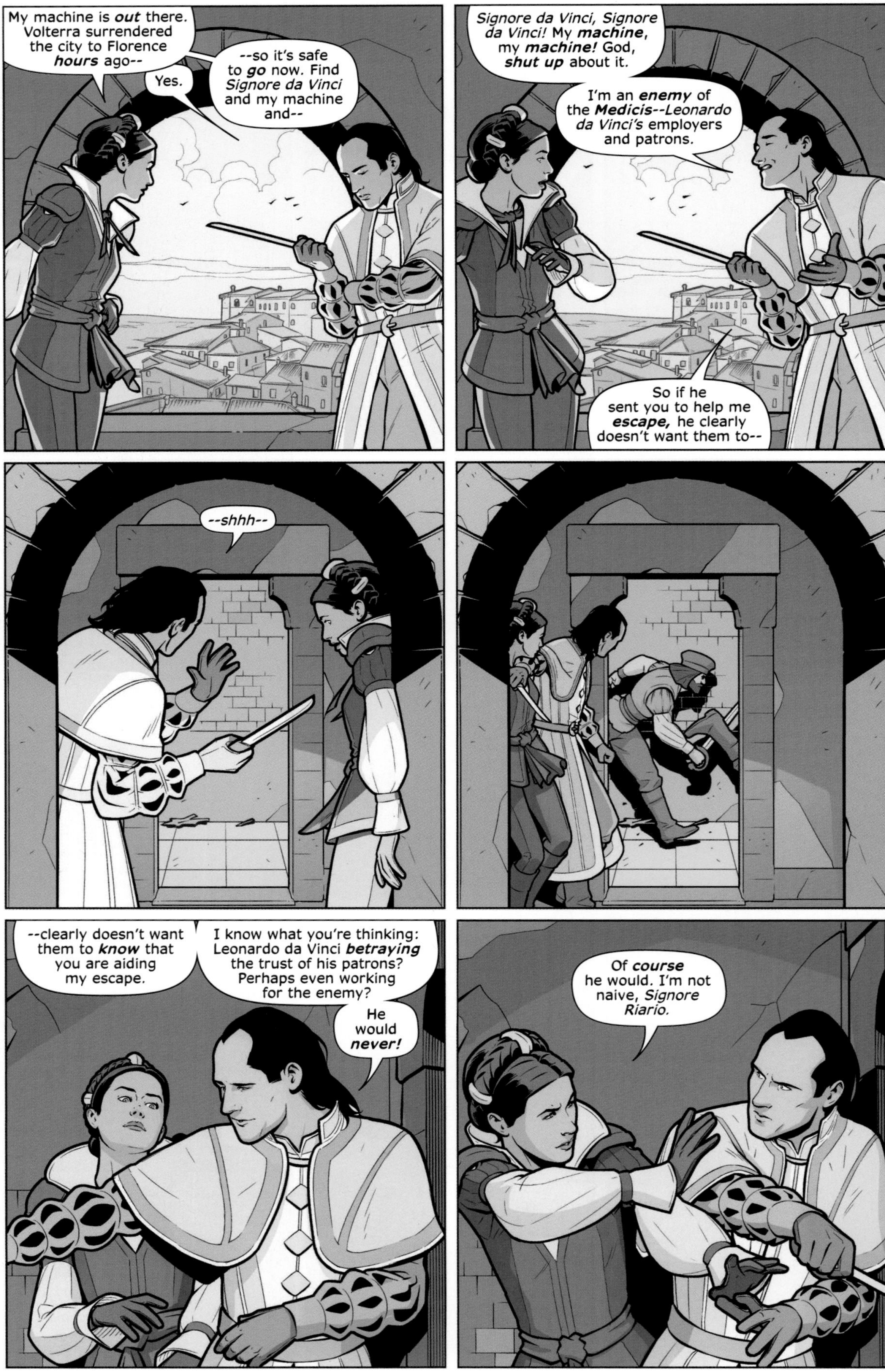

My machine is *out* there. Volterra surrendered the city to Florence ***hours*** ago--
Yes.
--so it's safe to ***go*** now. Find *Signore da Vinci* and my machine and--
Signore da Vinci, Signore da Vinci! My ***machine***, my ***machine!*** God, ***shut up*** about it.
I'm an ***enemy*** of the ***Medicis***--*Leonardo da Vinci's* employers and patrons.
So if he sent you to help me ***escape,*** he clearly doesn't want them to--
--shhh--
--clearly doesn't want them to ***know*** that you are aiding my escape.
I know what you're thinking: Leonardo da Vinci ***betraying*** the trust of his patrons? Perhaps even working for the enemy?
He would ***never!***
Of ***course*** he would. I'm not naive, *Signore Riario.*

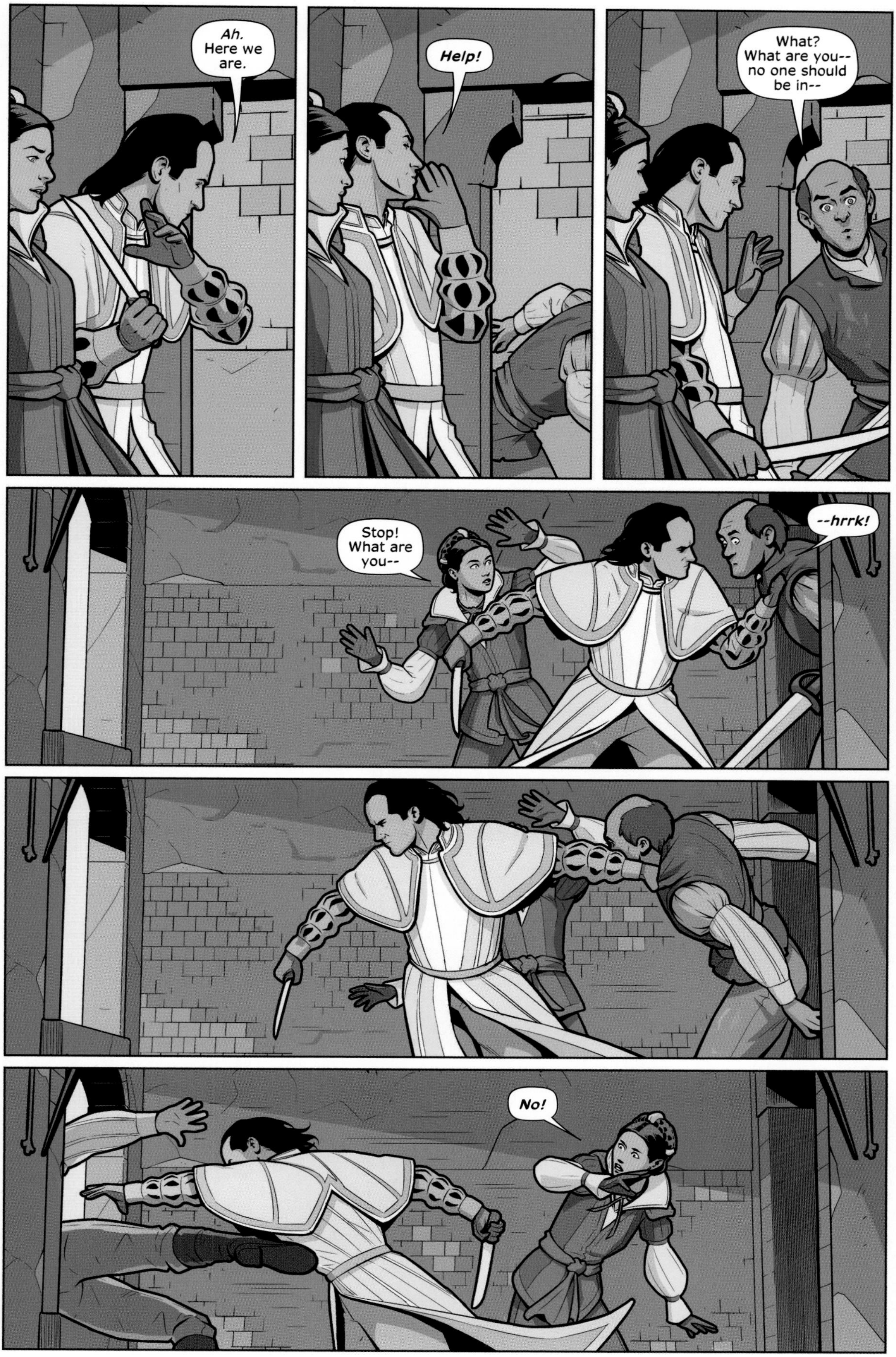
Ah. Here we are.
Help!
What? What are you-- no one should be in--
Stop! What are you--
--hrrk!
No!

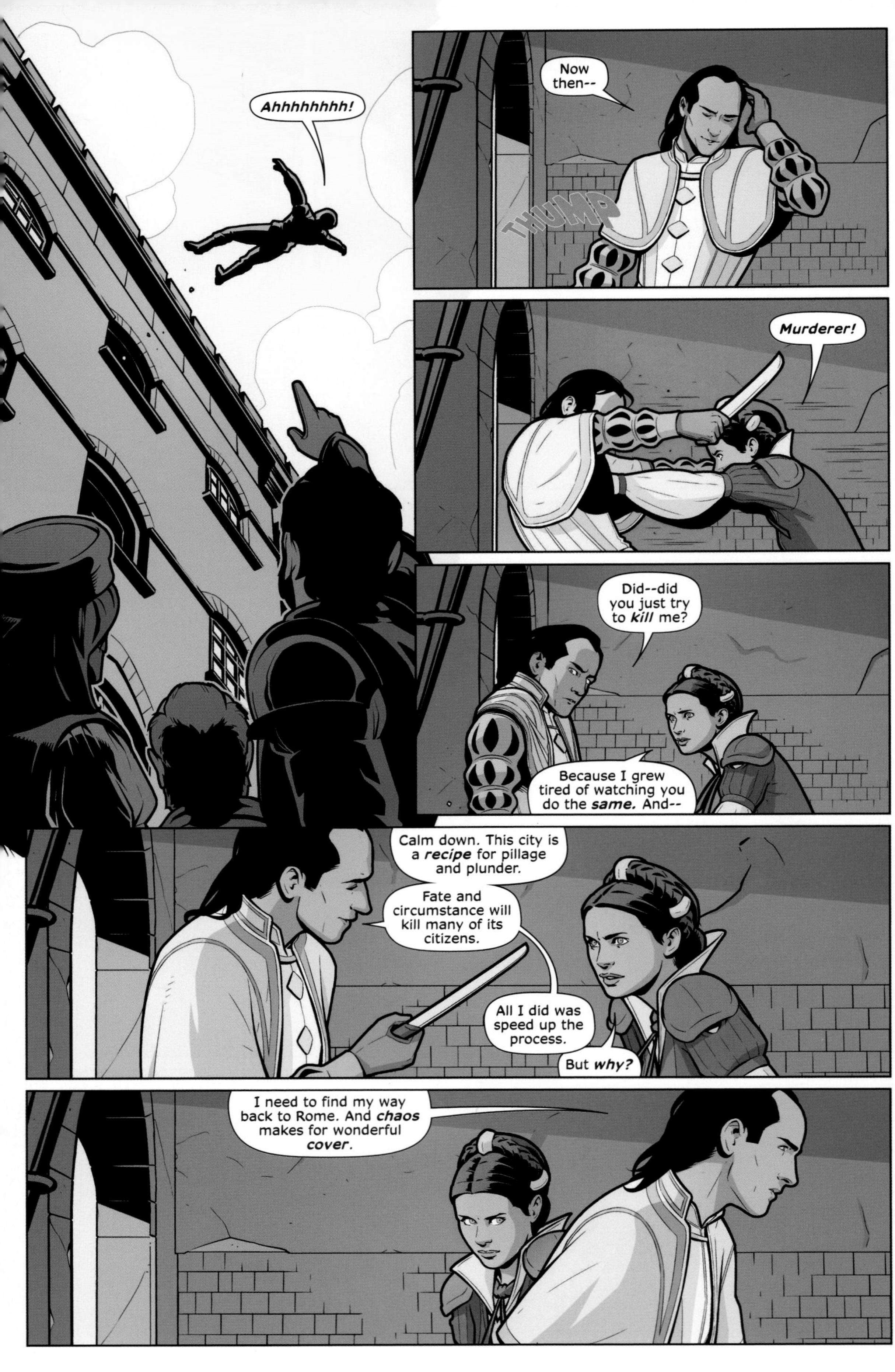
Ahhhhhhhh!
Now then--
THUMP
Murderer!
Did--did you just try to kill me?
Because I grew tired of watching you do the same. And--
Calm down. This city is a recipe for pillage and plunder.
Fate and circumstance will kill many of its citizens.
All I did was speed up the process.
But why?
I need to find my way back to Rome. And chaos makes for wonderful cover.

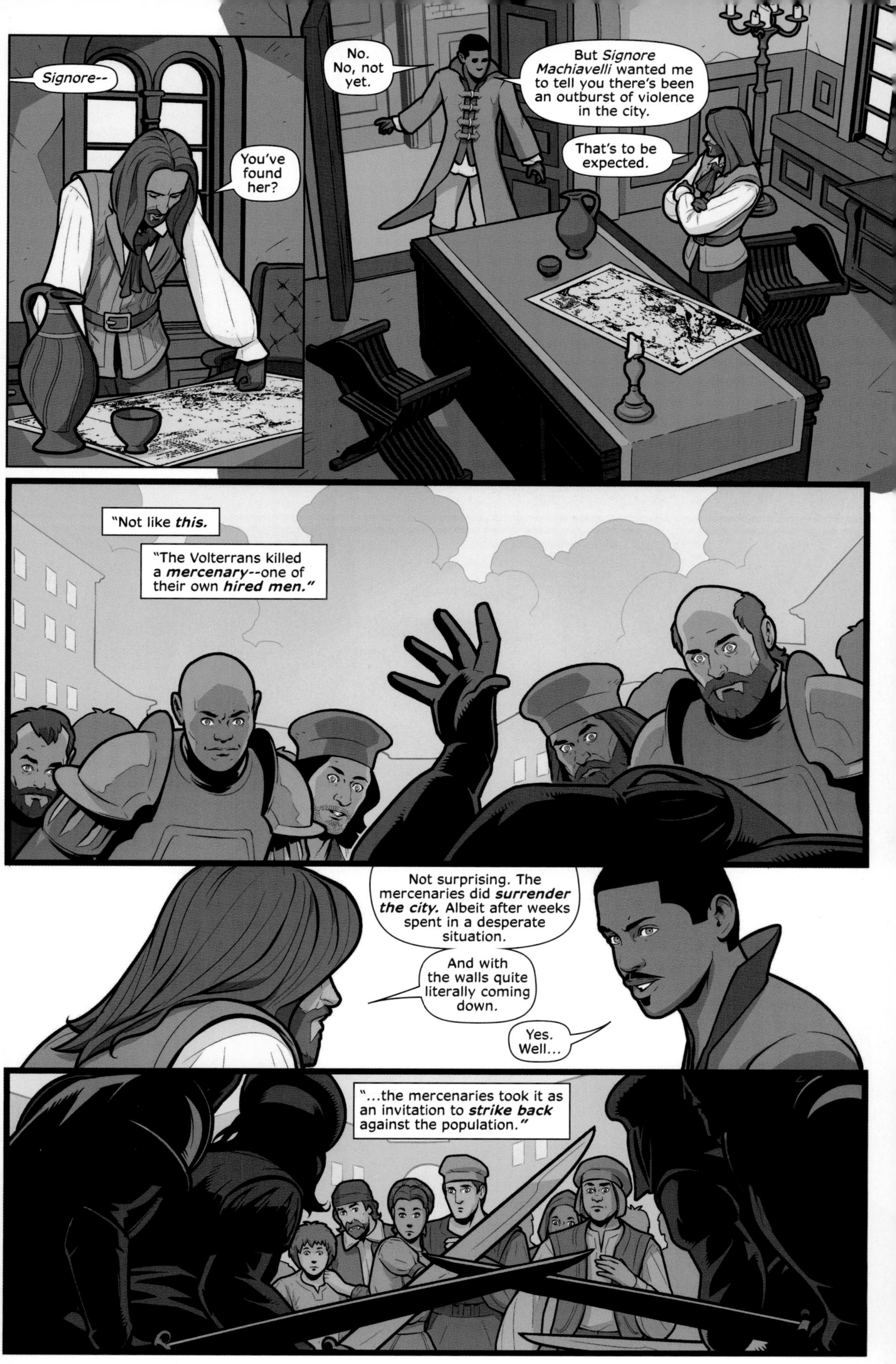
Signore--
You've found her?
No. No, not yet.
But Signore Machiavelli wanted me to tell you there's been an outburst of violence in the city.
That's to be expected.
"Not like this.
"The Volterrans killed a mercenary--one of their own hired men."
Not surprising. The mercenaries did surrender the city. Albeit after weeks spent in a desperate situation.
And with the walls quite literally coming down.
Yes. Well...
"...the mercenaries took it as an invitation to strike back against the population."

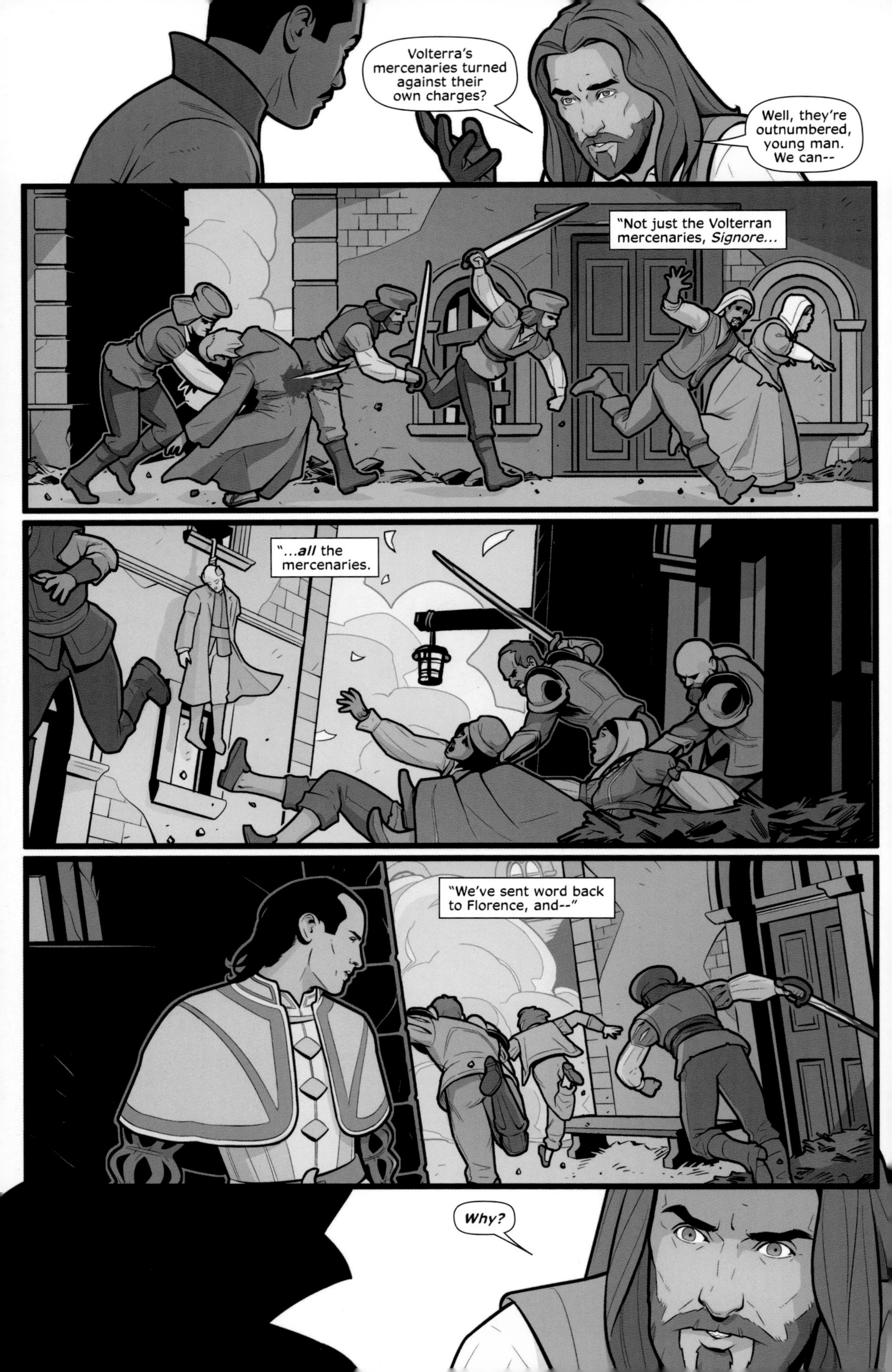
Volterra's mercenaries turned against their own charges?
Well, they're outnumbered, young man. We can--
"Not just the Volterran mercenaries, *Signore*...
"...*all* the mercenaries.
"We've sent word back to Florence, and--"
Why?

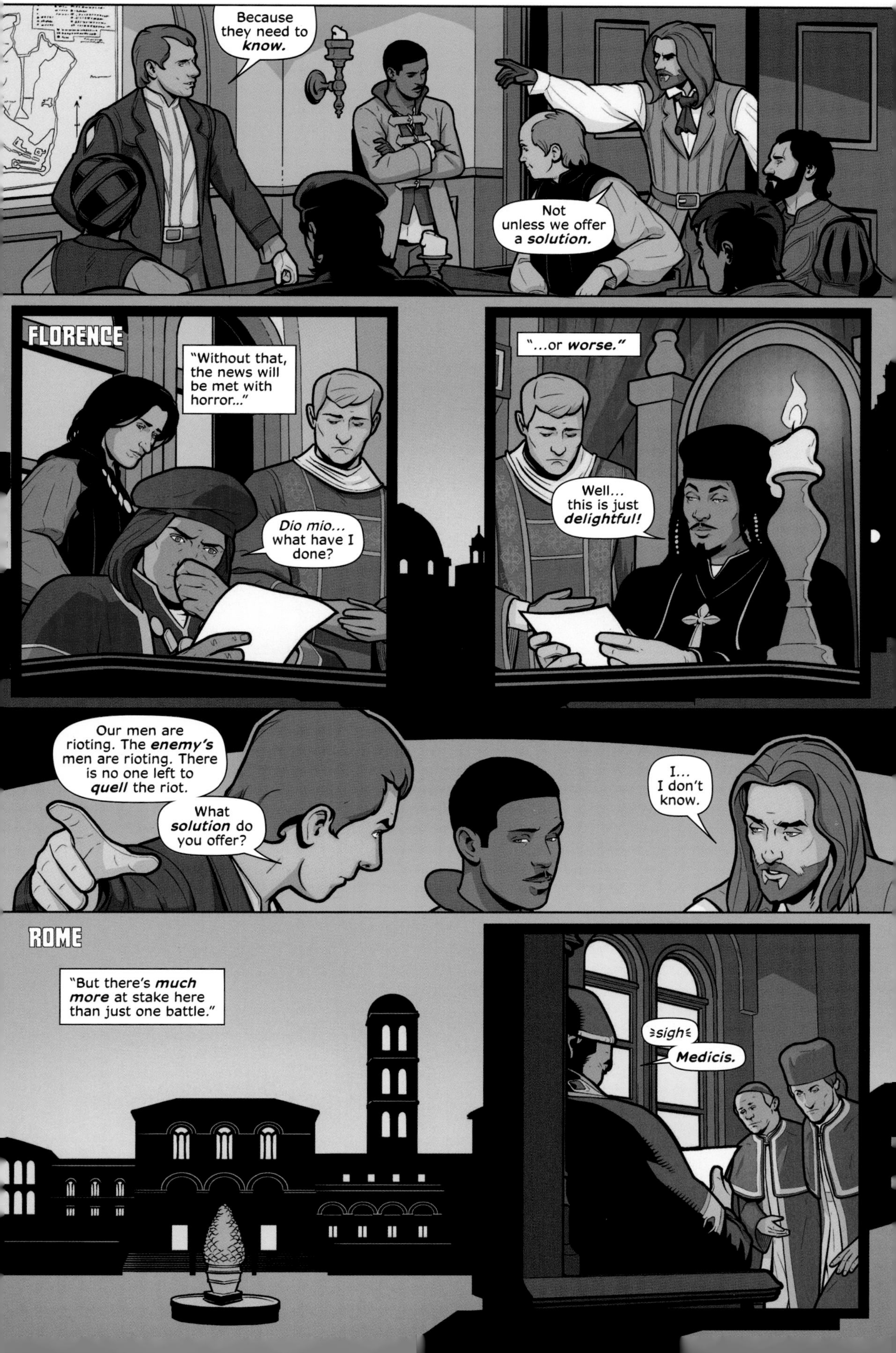
Because they need to know.
Not unless we offer a solution.
FLORENCE
"Without that, the news will be met with horror..."
Dio mio... what have I done?
"...or worse."
Well... this is just delightful!
Our men are rioting. The enemy's men are rioting. There is no one left to quell the riot.
What solution do you offer?
I... I don't know.
ROME
"But there's much more at stake here than just one battle."
sigh
Medicis.

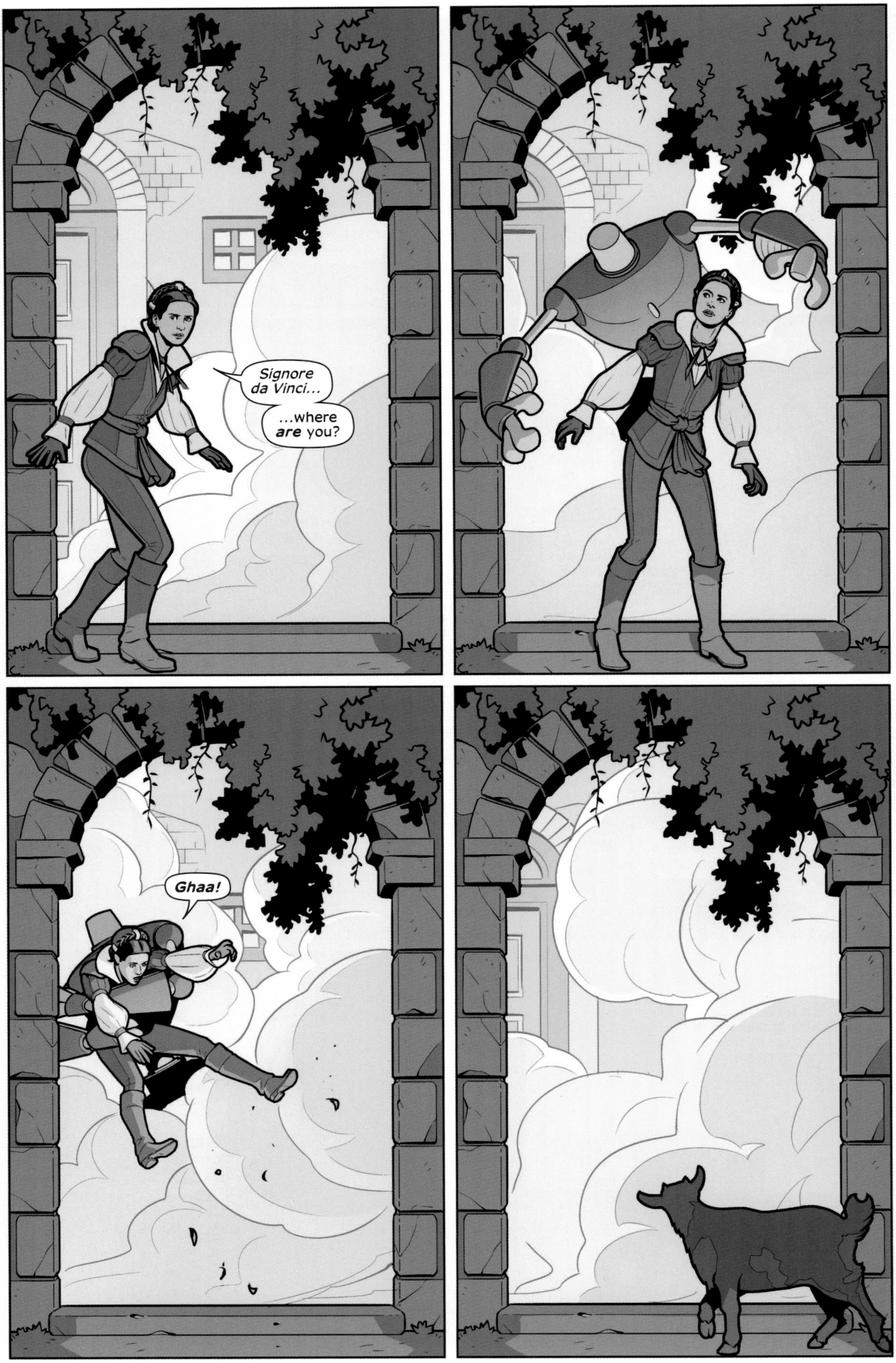
Signore da Vinci...
...where *are* you?
Ghaa!

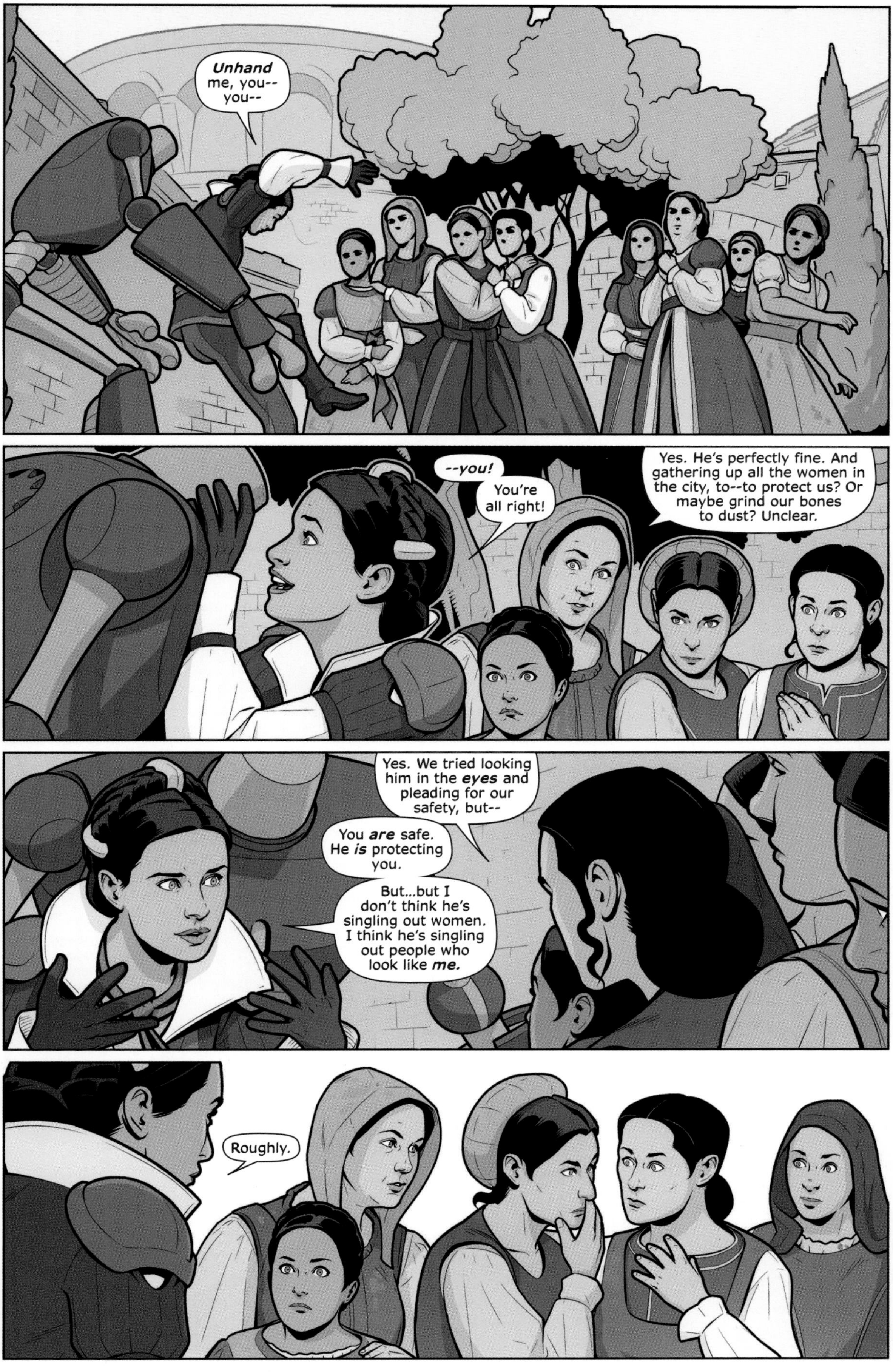

Unhand me, you-- you--
--you!
You're all right!
Yes. He's perfectly fine. And gathering up all the women in the city, to--to protect us? Or maybe grind our bones to dust? Unclear.
Yes. We tried looking him in the ***eyes*** and pleading for our safety, but--
You ***are*** safe. He ***is*** protecting you.
But...but I don't think he's singling out women. I think he's singling out people who look like ***me.***
Roughly.

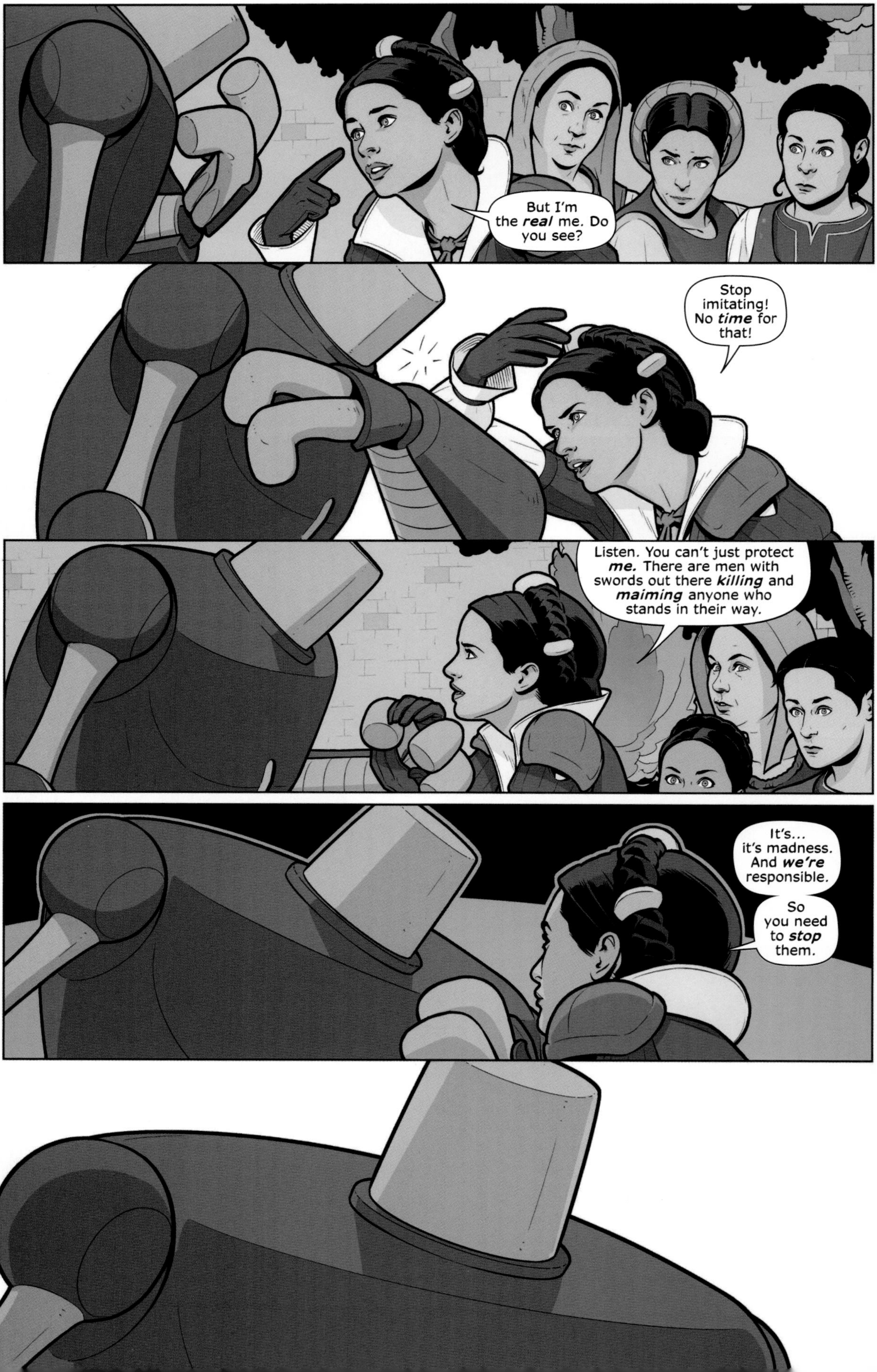
But I'm the *real* me. Do you see?
Stop imitating! No *time* for that!
Listen. You can't just protect *me.* There are men with swords out there *killing* and *maiming* anyone who stands in their way.
It's... it's madness. And *we're* responsible.
So you need to *stop* them.

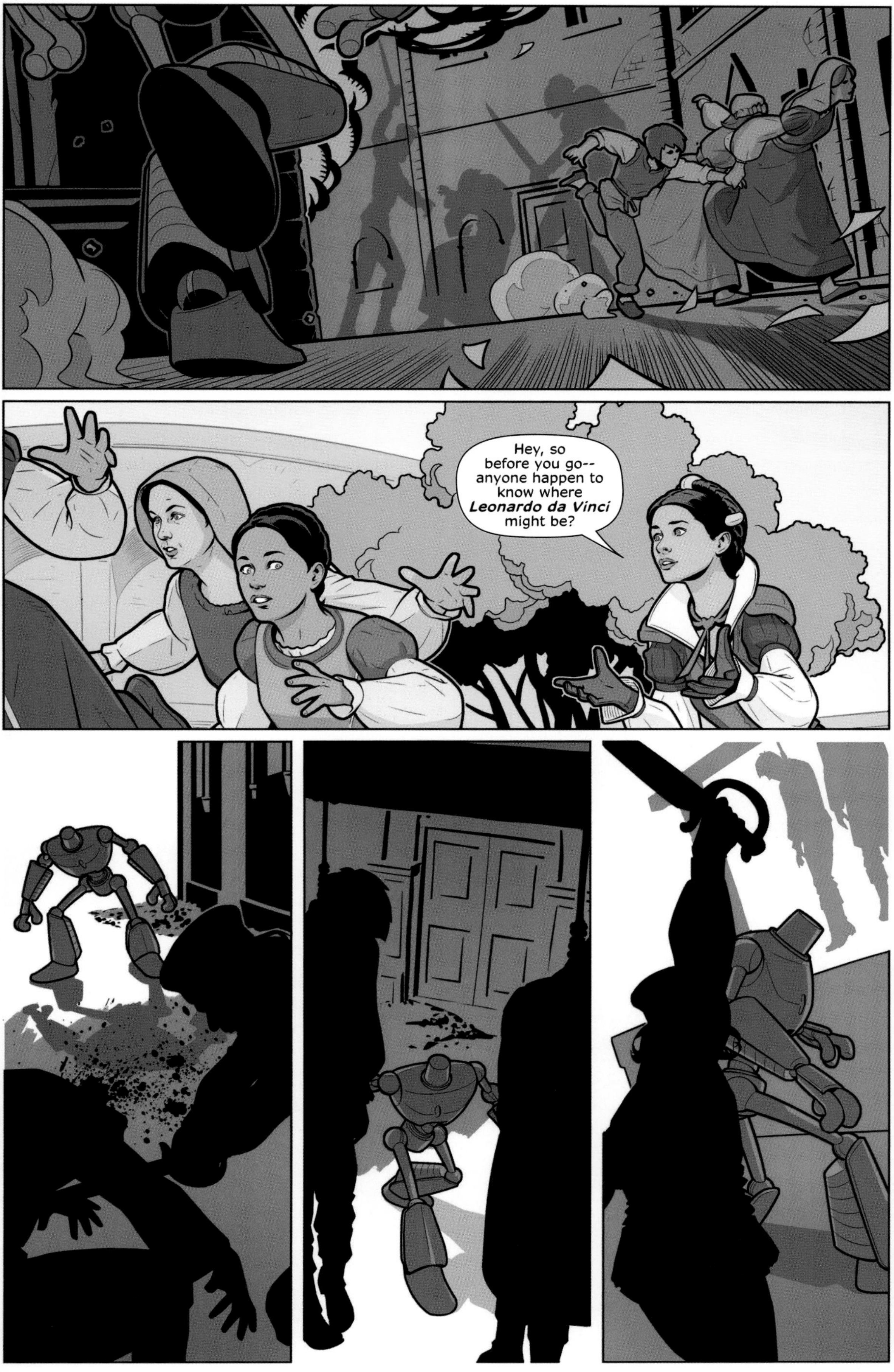
Hey, so before you go-- anyone happen to know where *Leonardo da Vinci* might be?

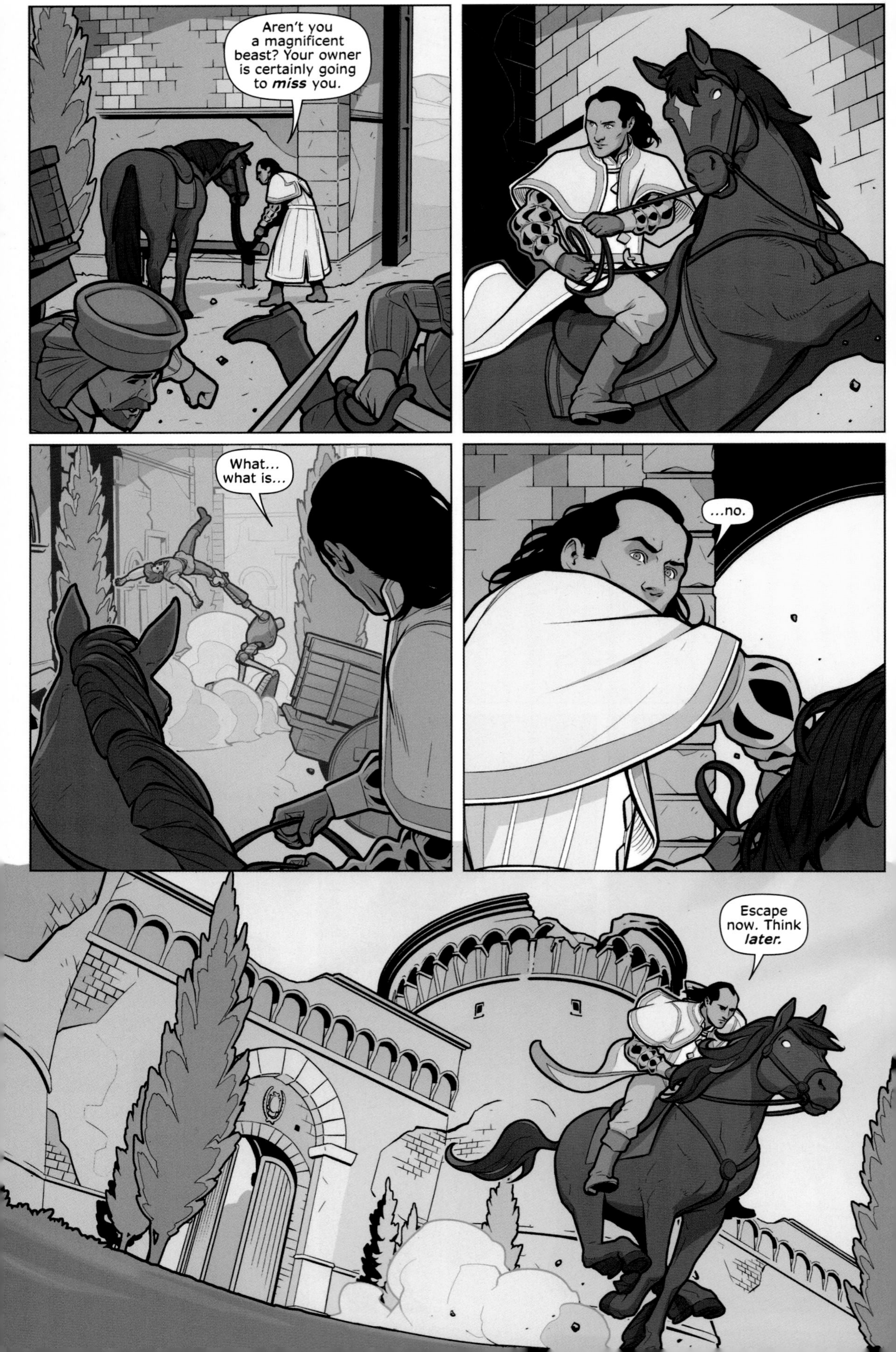
Aren't you a magnificent beast? Your owner is certainly going to *miss* you.
What... what is...
...no.
Escape now. Think *later.*

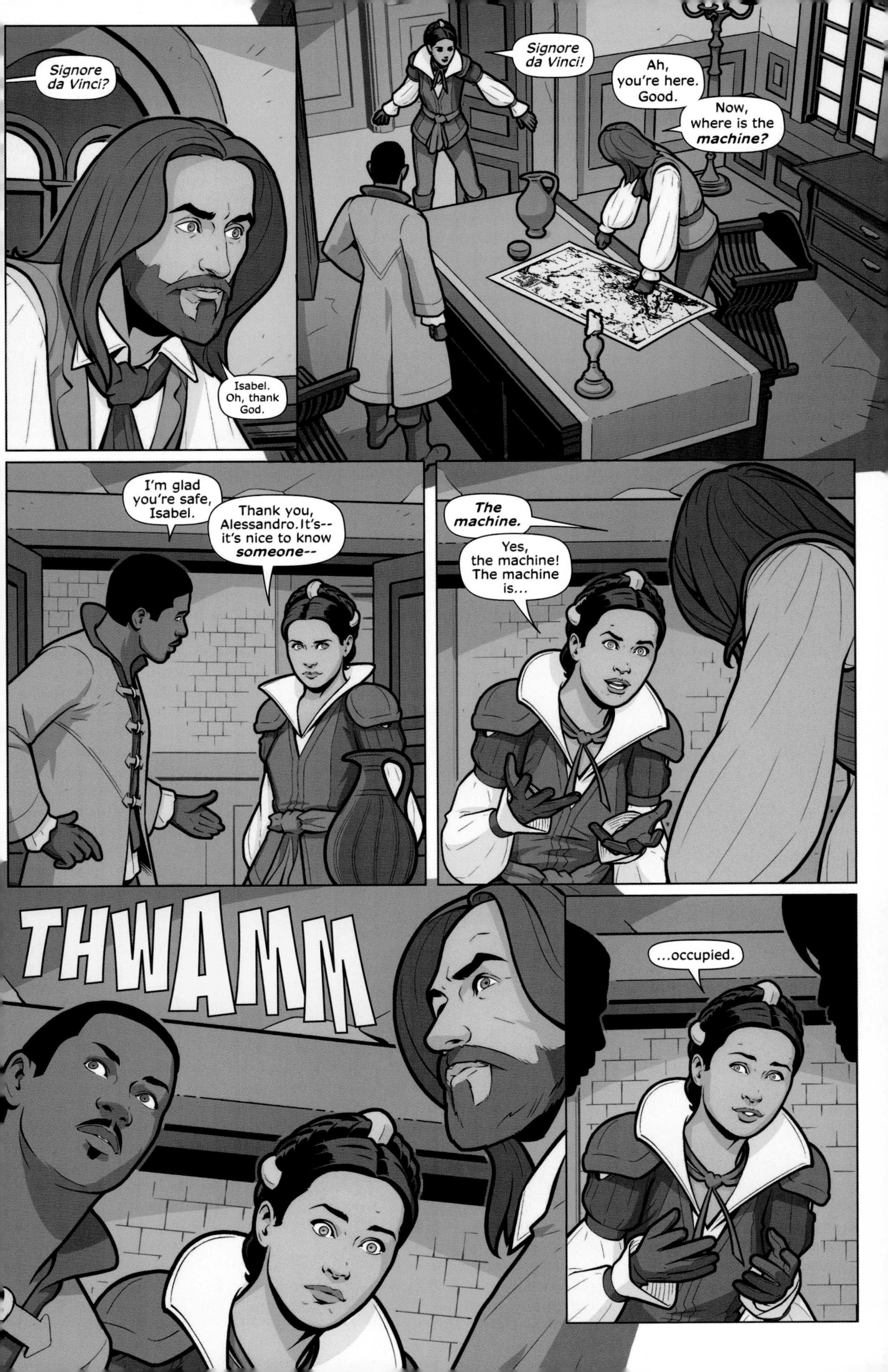
Signore da Vinci?
Isabel. Oh, thank God.
Signore da Vinci!
Ah, you're here. Good.
Now, where is the *machine?*
I'm glad you're safe, Isabel.
Thank you, Alessandro. It's-- it's nice to know *someone--*
The machine.
Yes, the machine! The machine is...
THWAMM
...occupied.

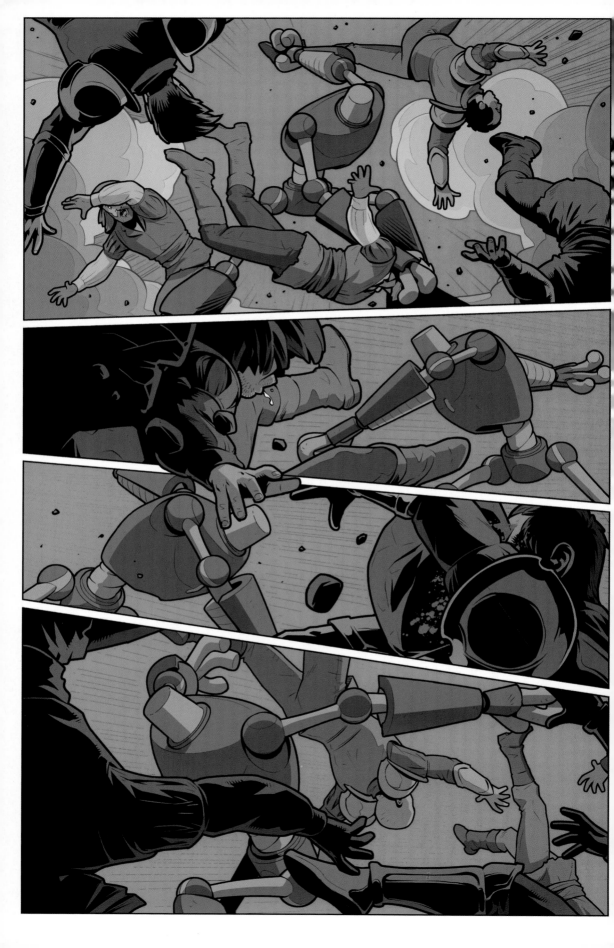

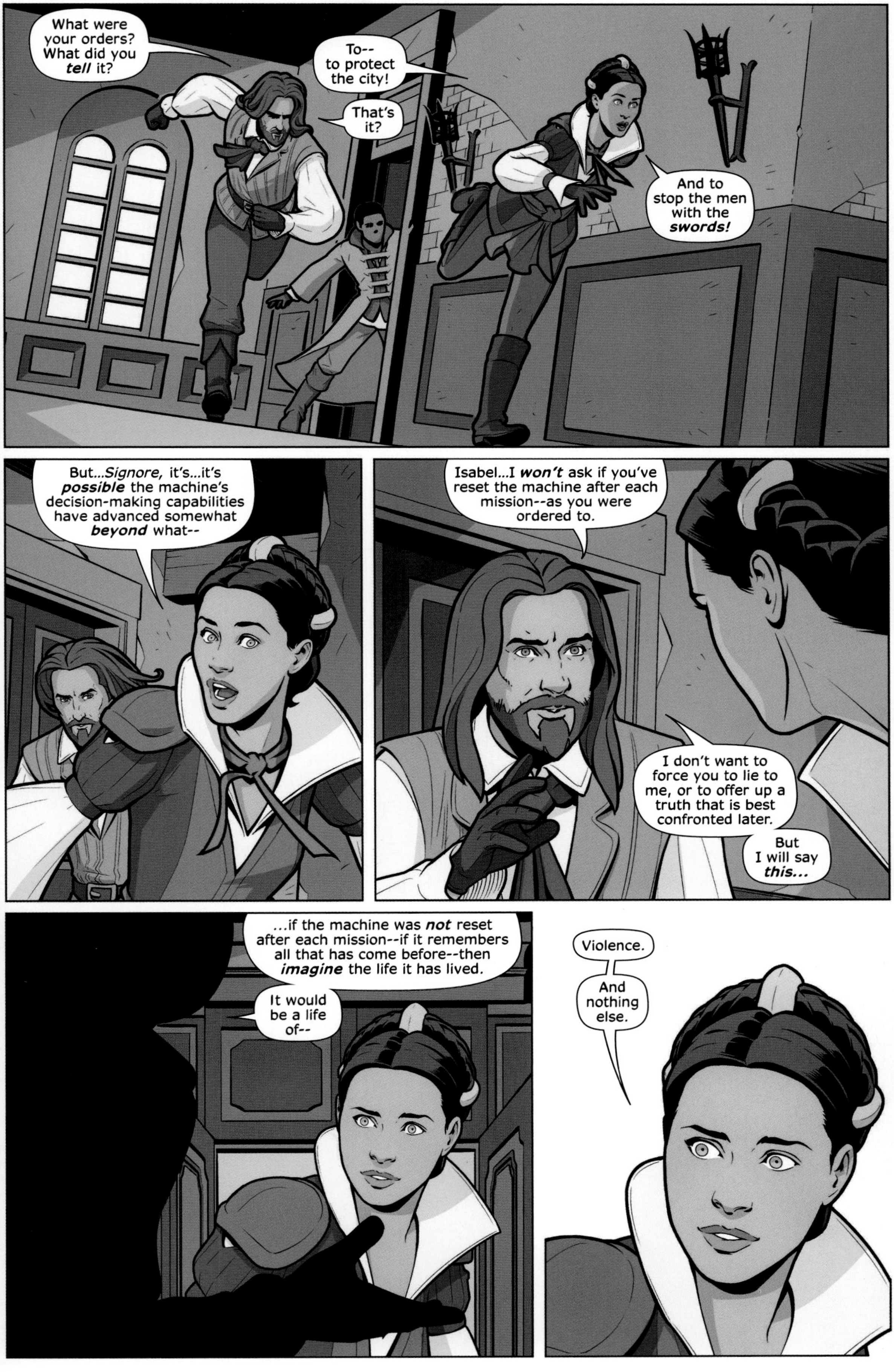
What were your orders? What did you *tell* it?
To-- to protect the city!
That's it?
And to stop the men with the *swords!*
But...*Signore,* it's...it's *possible* the machine's decision-making capabilities have advanced somewhat *beyond* what--
Isabel...I *won't* ask if you've reset the machine after each mission--as you were ordered to.
I don't want to force you to lie to me, or to offer up a truth that is best confronted later.
But I will say *this...*
...if the machine was *not* reset after each mission--if it remembers all that has come before--then *imagine* the life it has lived.
It would be a life of--
Violence.
And nothing else.

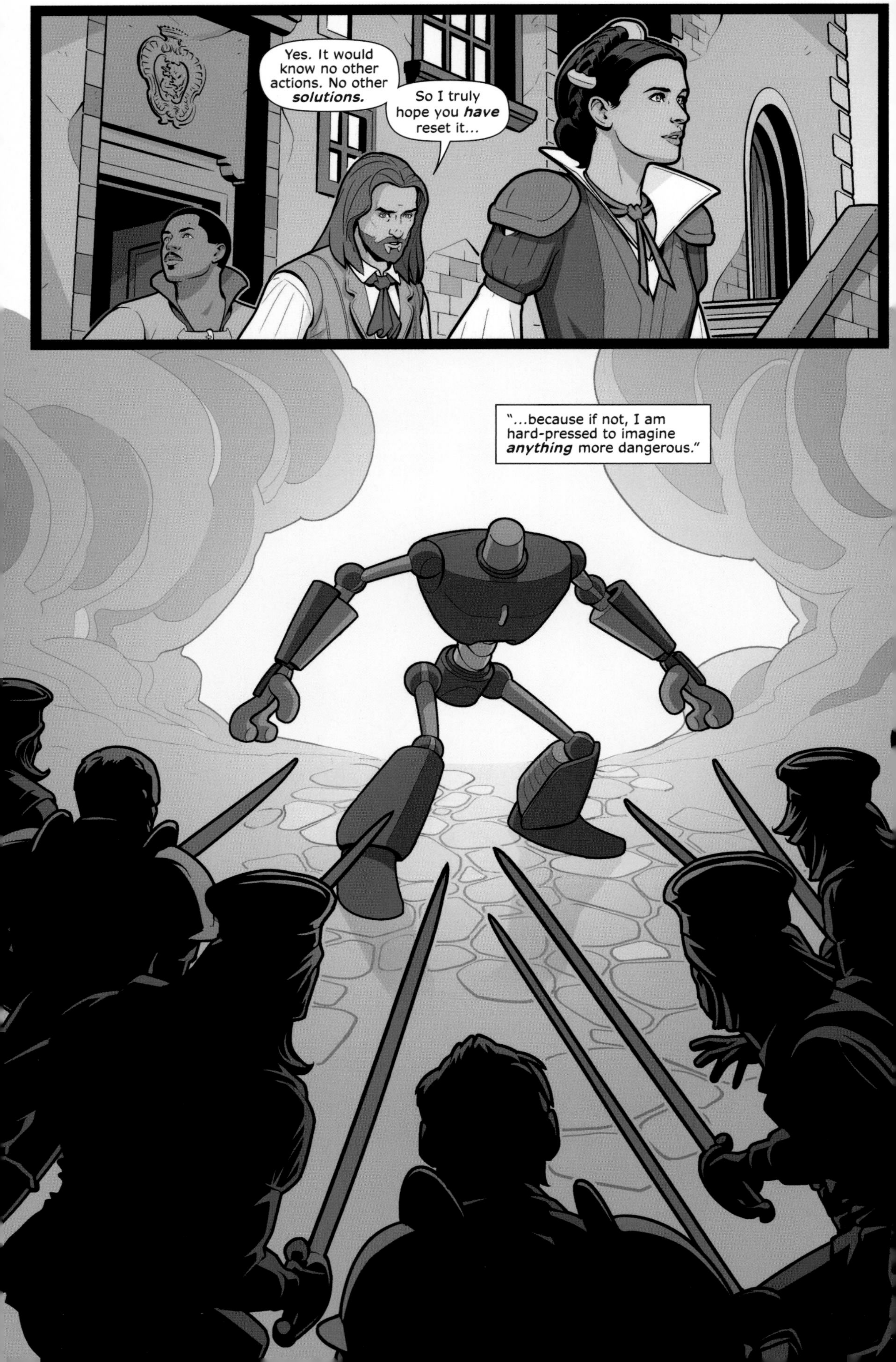
Yes. It would know no other actions. No other *solutions.*
So I truly hope you *have* reset it...
"...because if not, I am hard-pressed to imagine *anything* more dangerous."

4

THE BLOSSOMS ARE FRAGILE AND MOTIONLESS

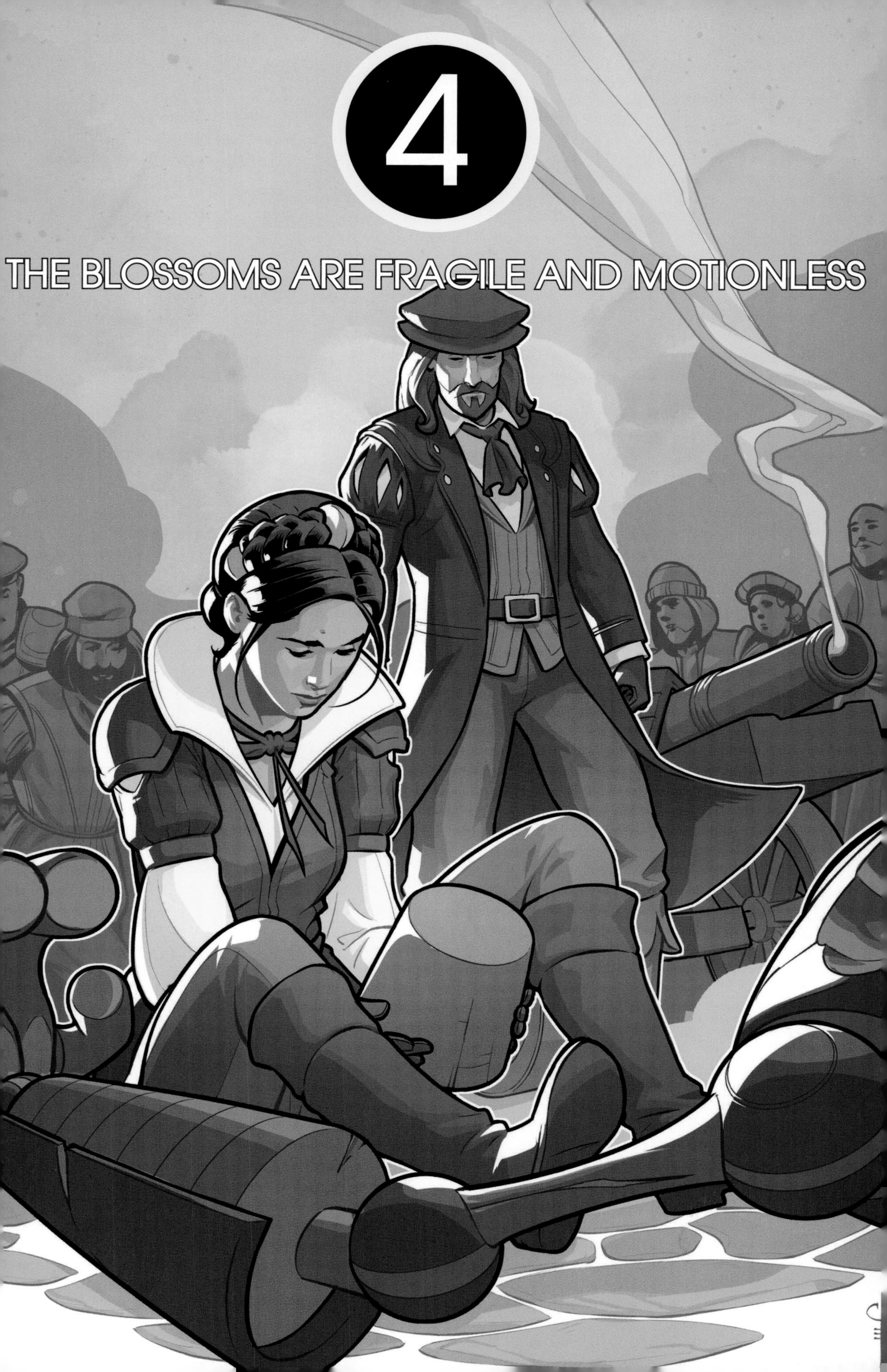

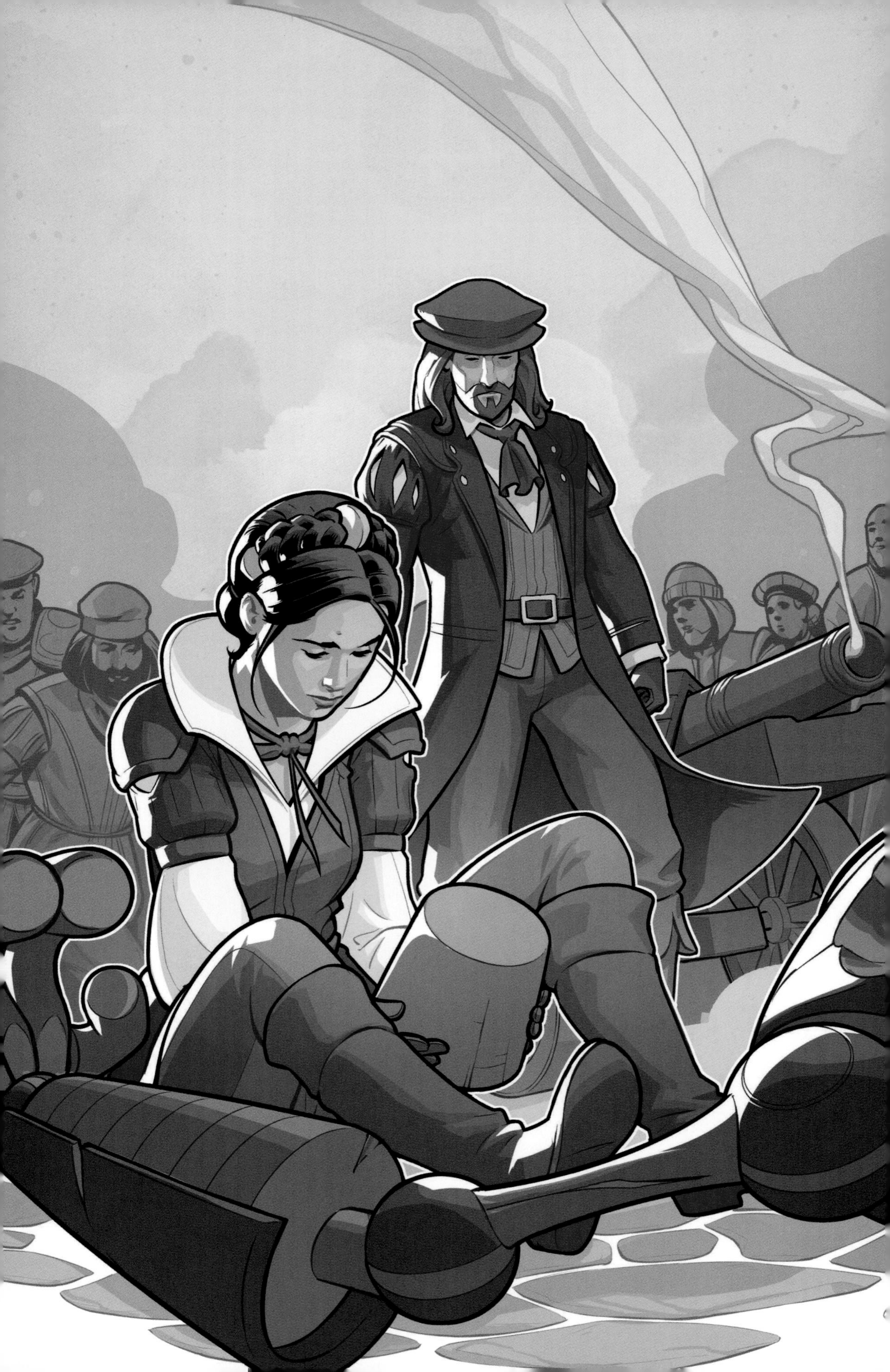

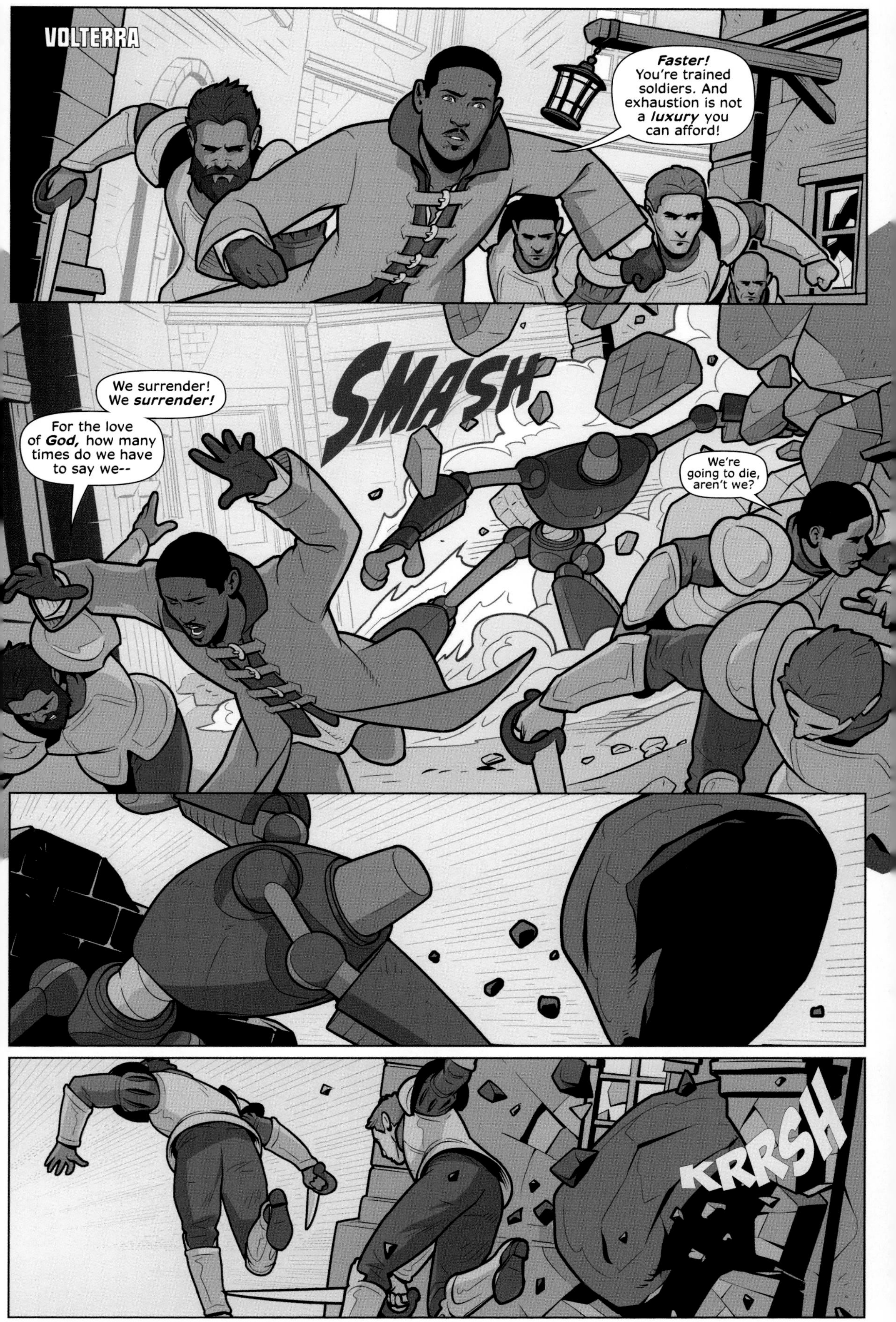

VOLTERRA
Faster! You're trained soldiers. And exhaustion is not a ***luxury*** you can afford!
SMASH
We surrender! We ***surrender!***
For the love of ***God,*** how many times do we have to say we--
We're going to die, aren't we?
KRRSH

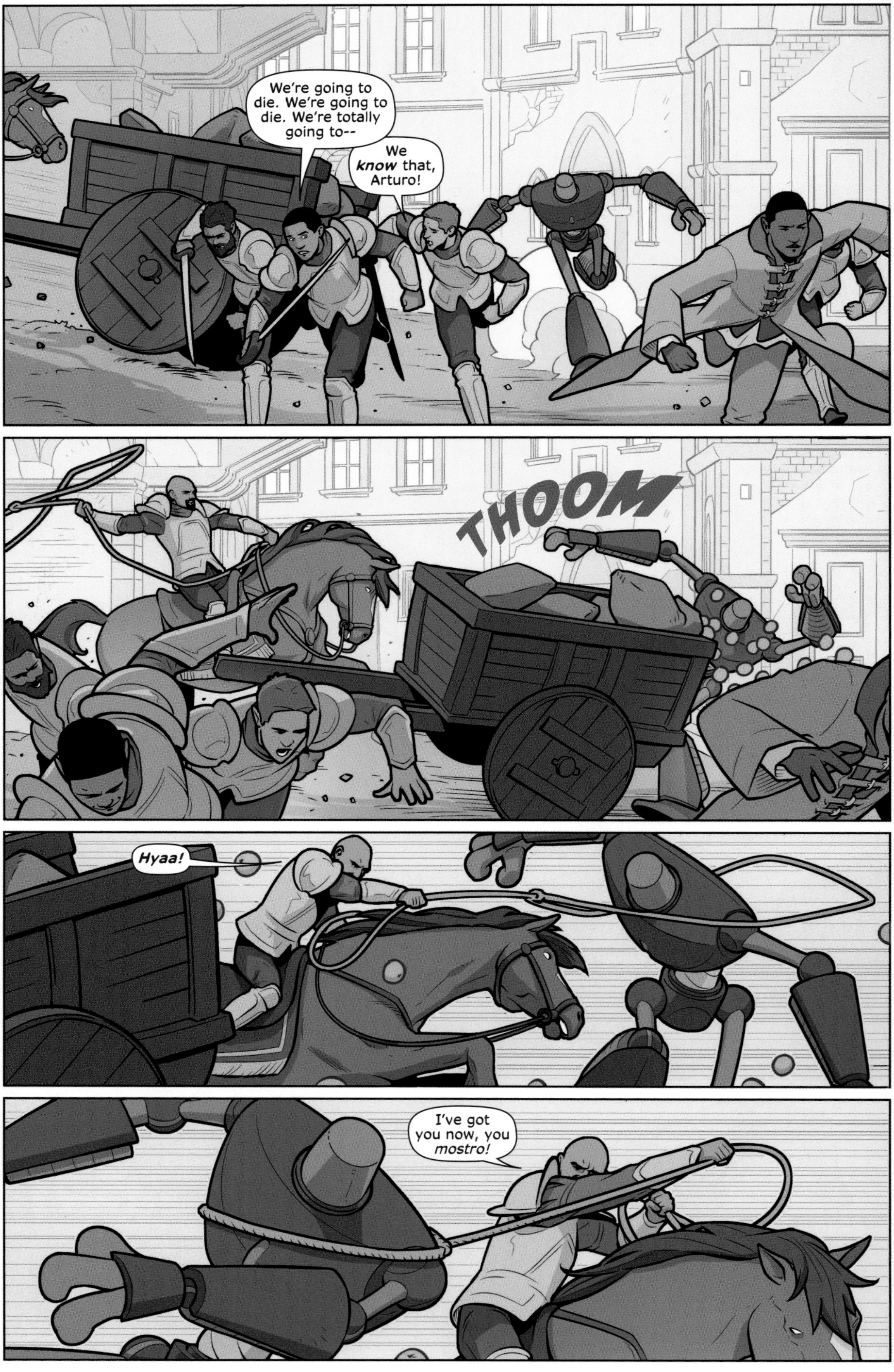
We're going to die. We're going to die. We're totally going to--
We *know* that, Arturo!
THOOM
Hyaa!
I've got you now, you *mostro!*

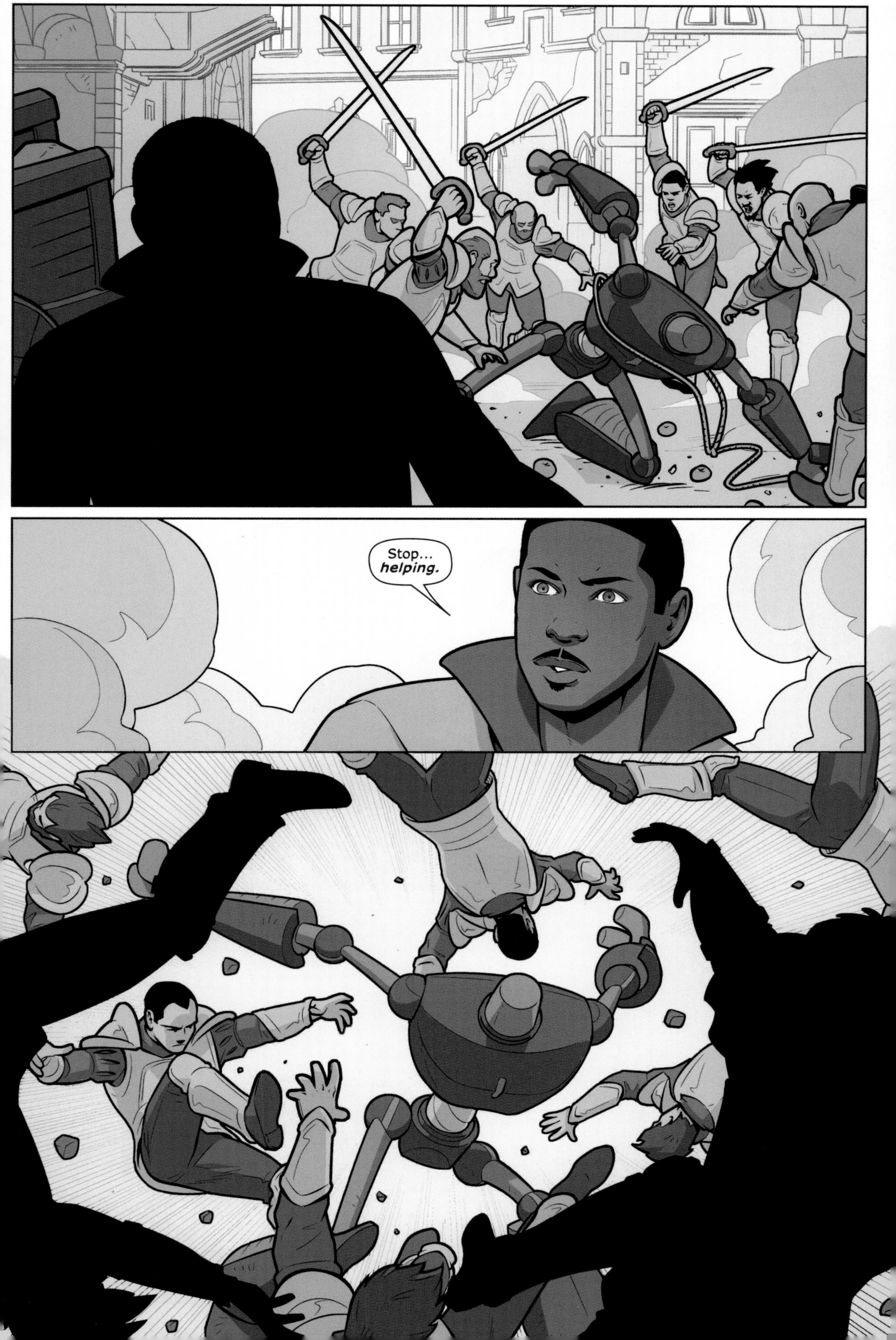
Stop... *helping.*

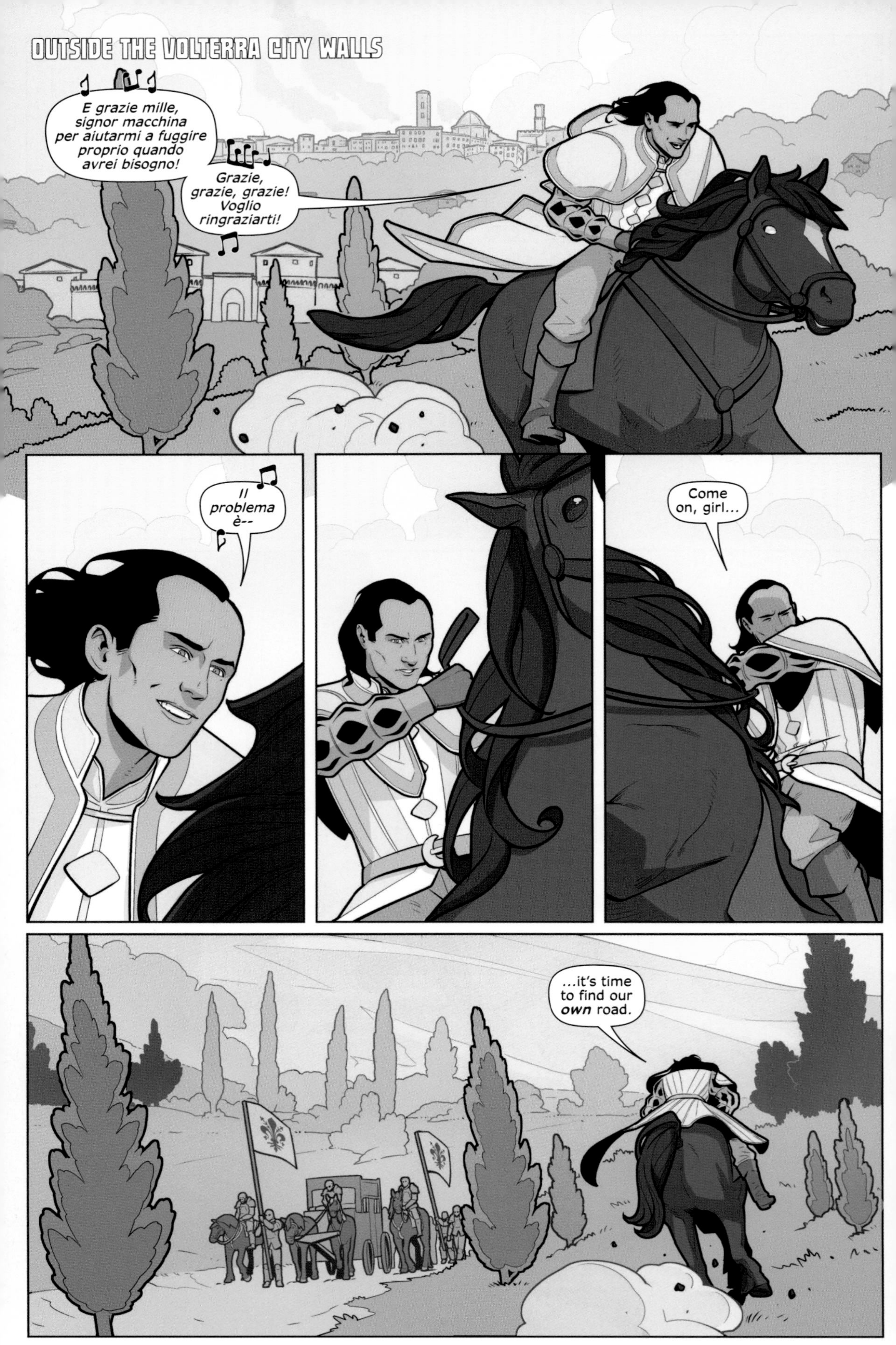
OUTSIDE THE VOLTERRA CITY WALLS
E grazie mille, signor macchina per aiutarmi a fuggire proprio quando avrei bisogno!
Grazie, grazie, grazie! Voglio ringraziarti!
Il problema è--
Come on, girl...
...it's time to find our *own* road.

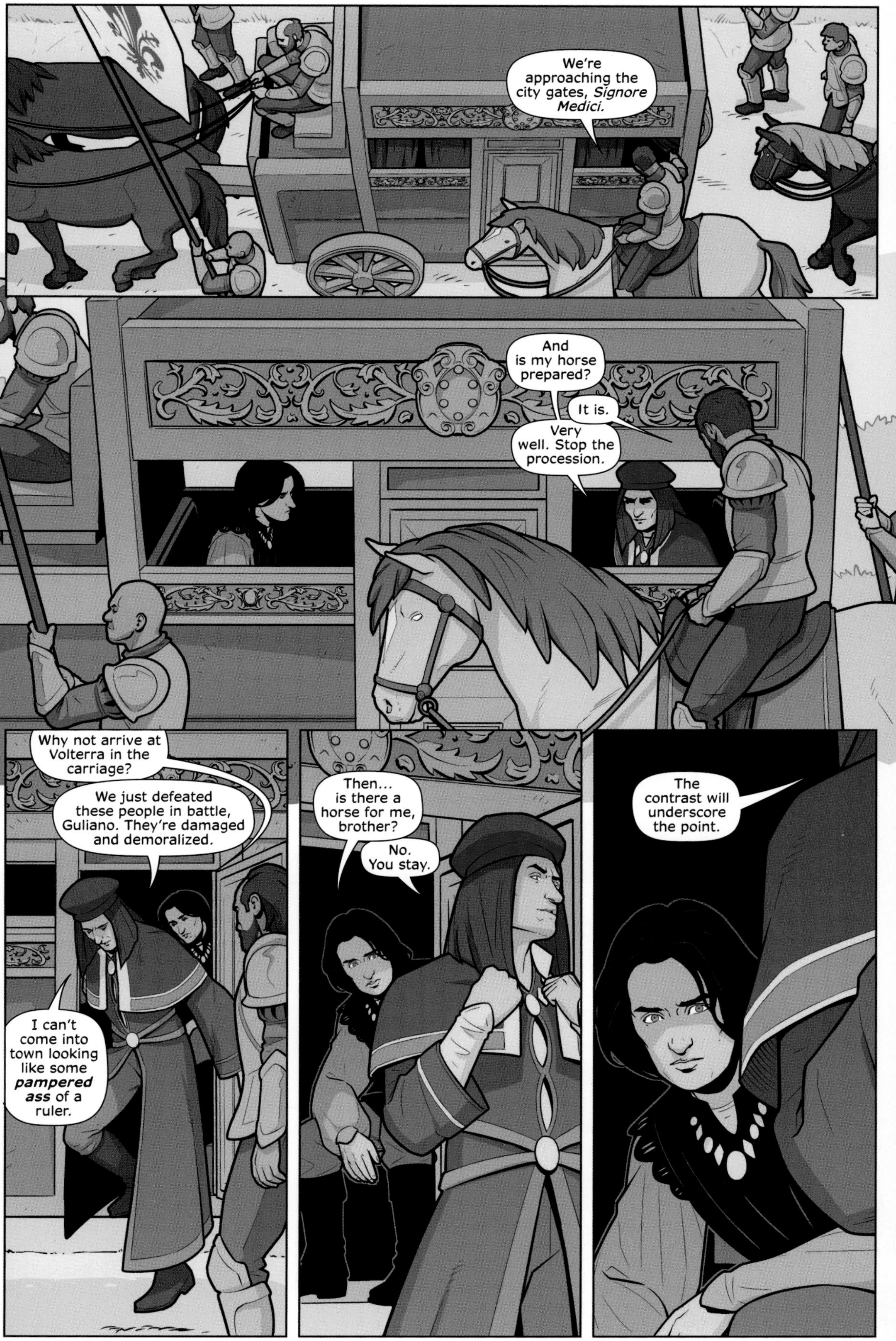

We're approaching the city gates, *Signore Medici.*
And is my horse prepared?
It is.
Very well. Stop the procession.
Why not arrive at Volterra in the carriage?
We just defeated these people in battle, Guliano. They're damaged and demoralized.
I can't come into town looking like some ***pampered ass*** of a ruler.
Then... is there a horse for me, brother?
No. You stay.
The contrast will underscore the point.

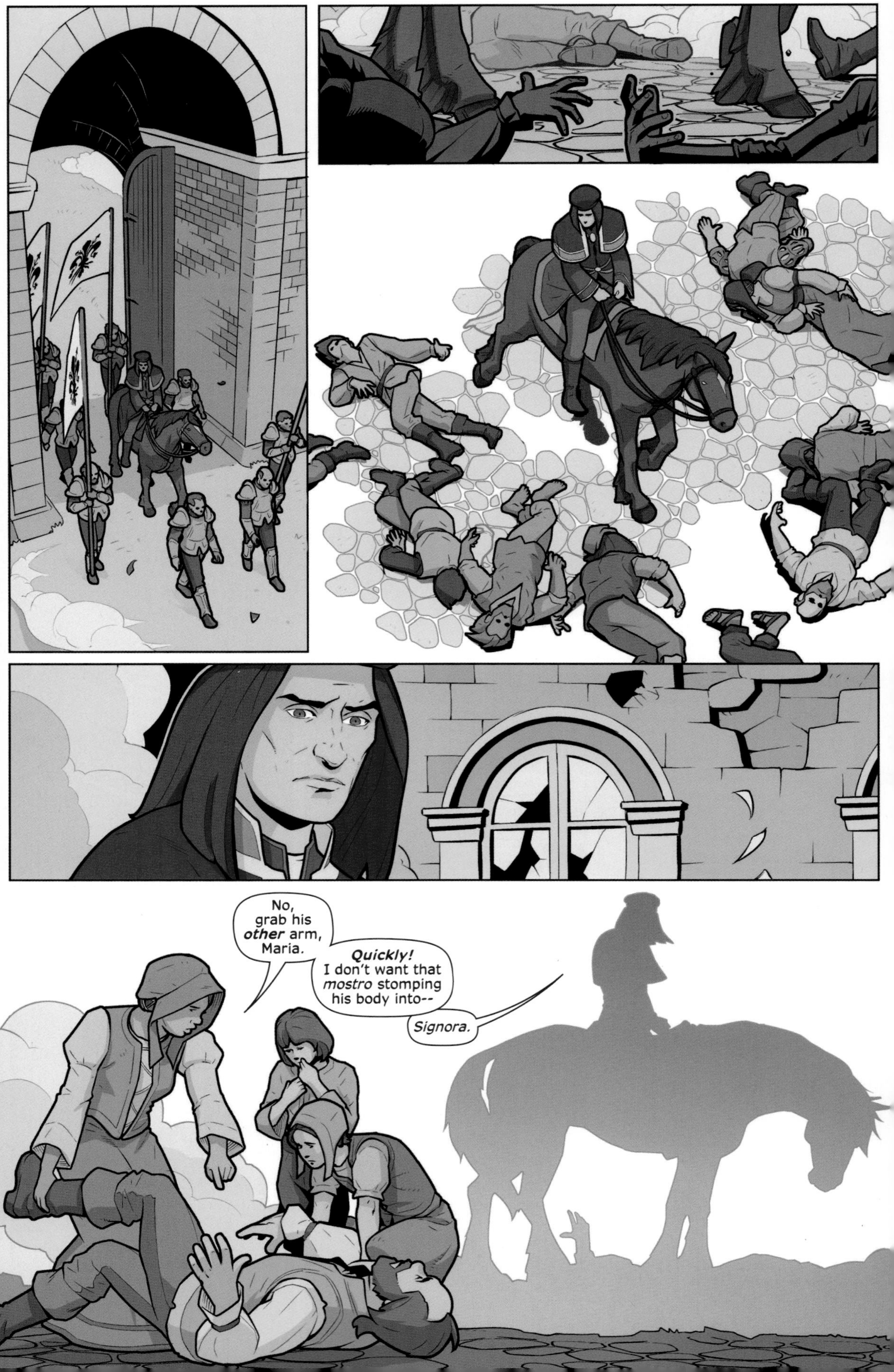
No, grab his *other* arm, Maria.
Quickly! I don't want that *mostro* stomping his body into--
Signora.

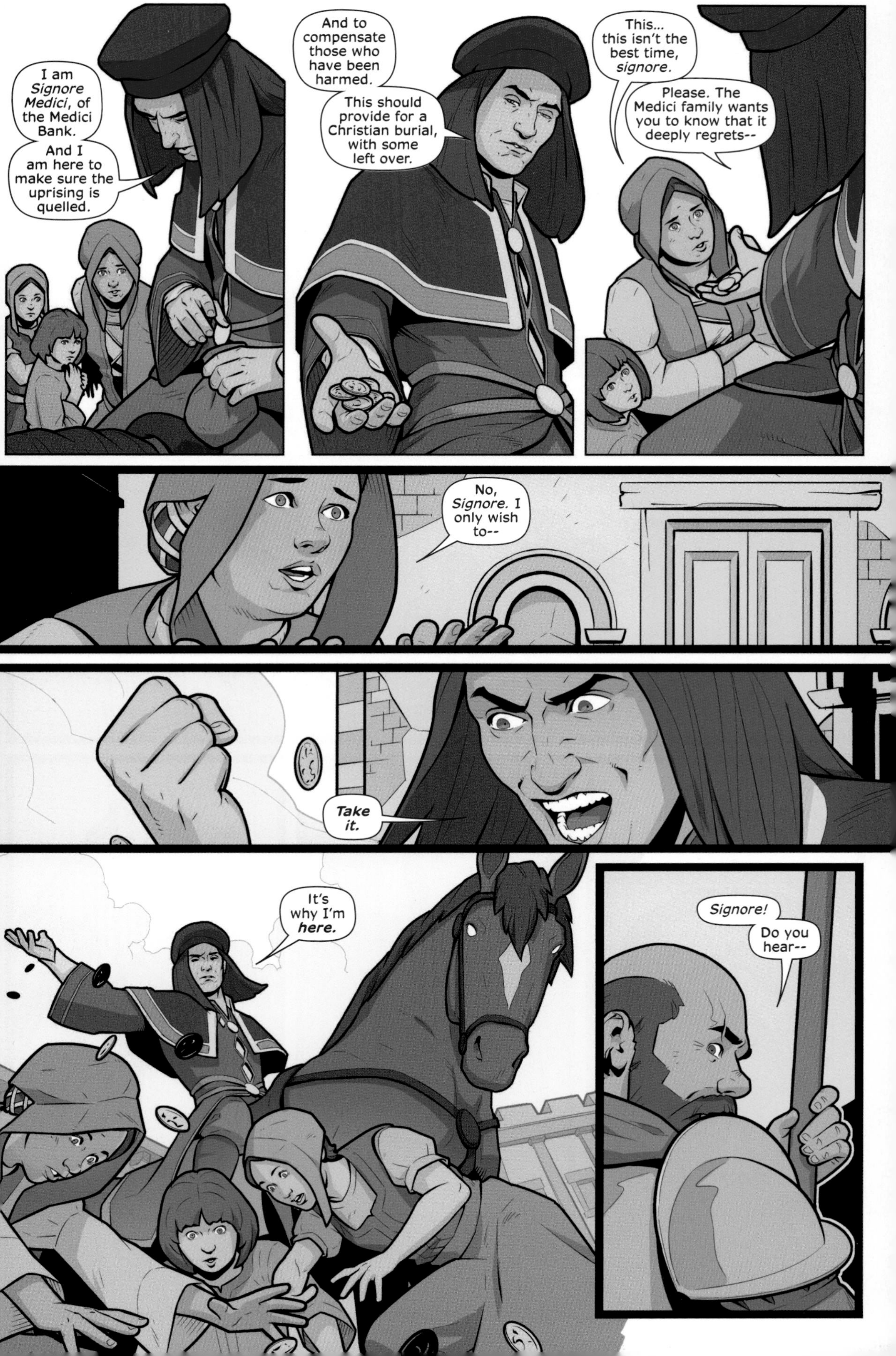
I am *Signore Medici*, of the Medici Bank.
And I am here to make sure the uprising is quelled.
And to compensate those who have been harmed.
This should provide for a Christian burial, with some left over.
This... this isn't the best time, *signore.*
Please. The Medici family wants you to know that it deeply regrets--
No, *Signore.* I only wish to--
Take it.
It's why I'm ***here.***
Signore!
Do you hear--

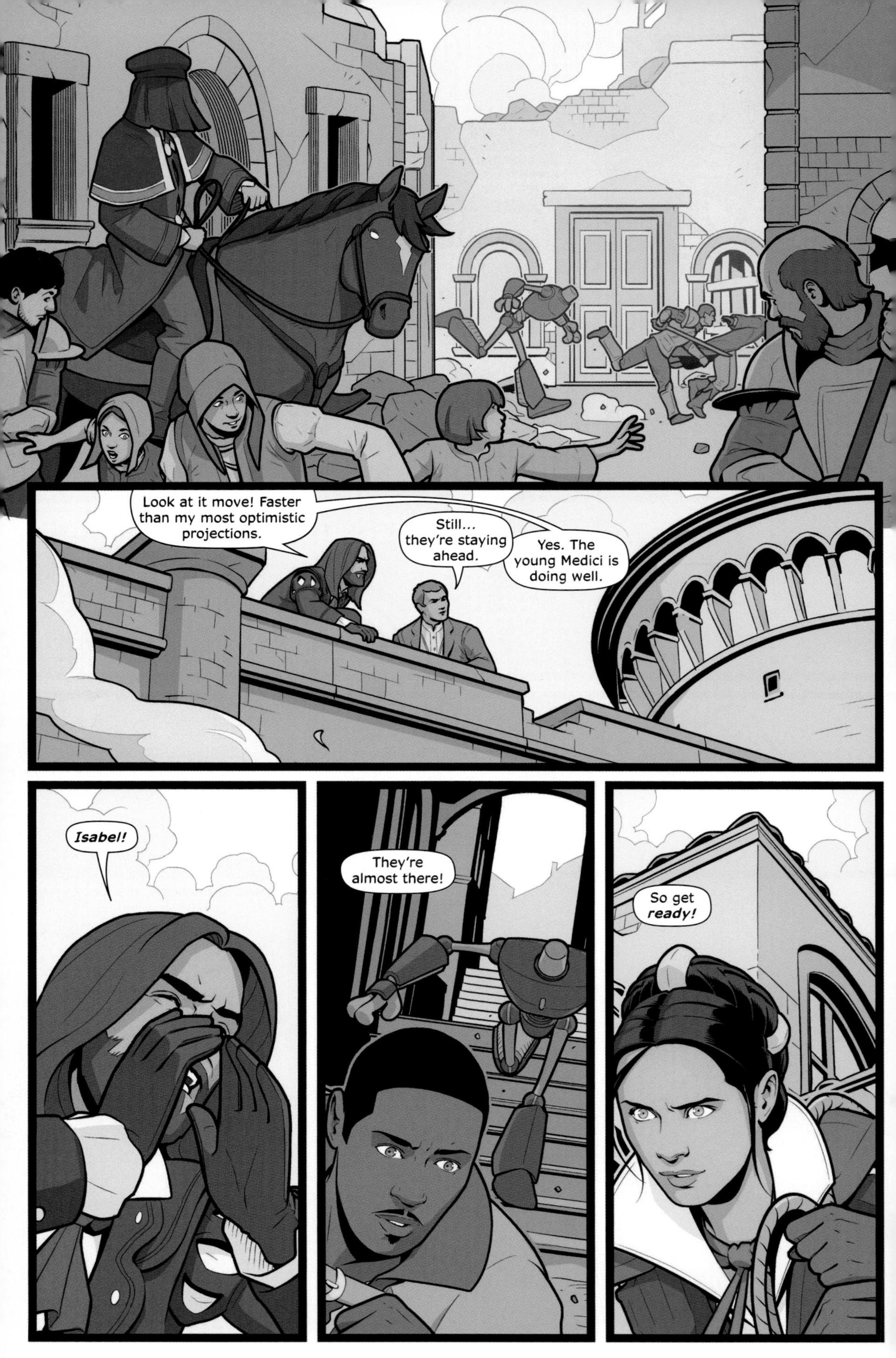
Look at it move! Faster than my most optimistic projections.
Still... they're staying ahead.
Yes. The young Medici is doing well.
Isabel!
They're almost there!
So get *ready!*

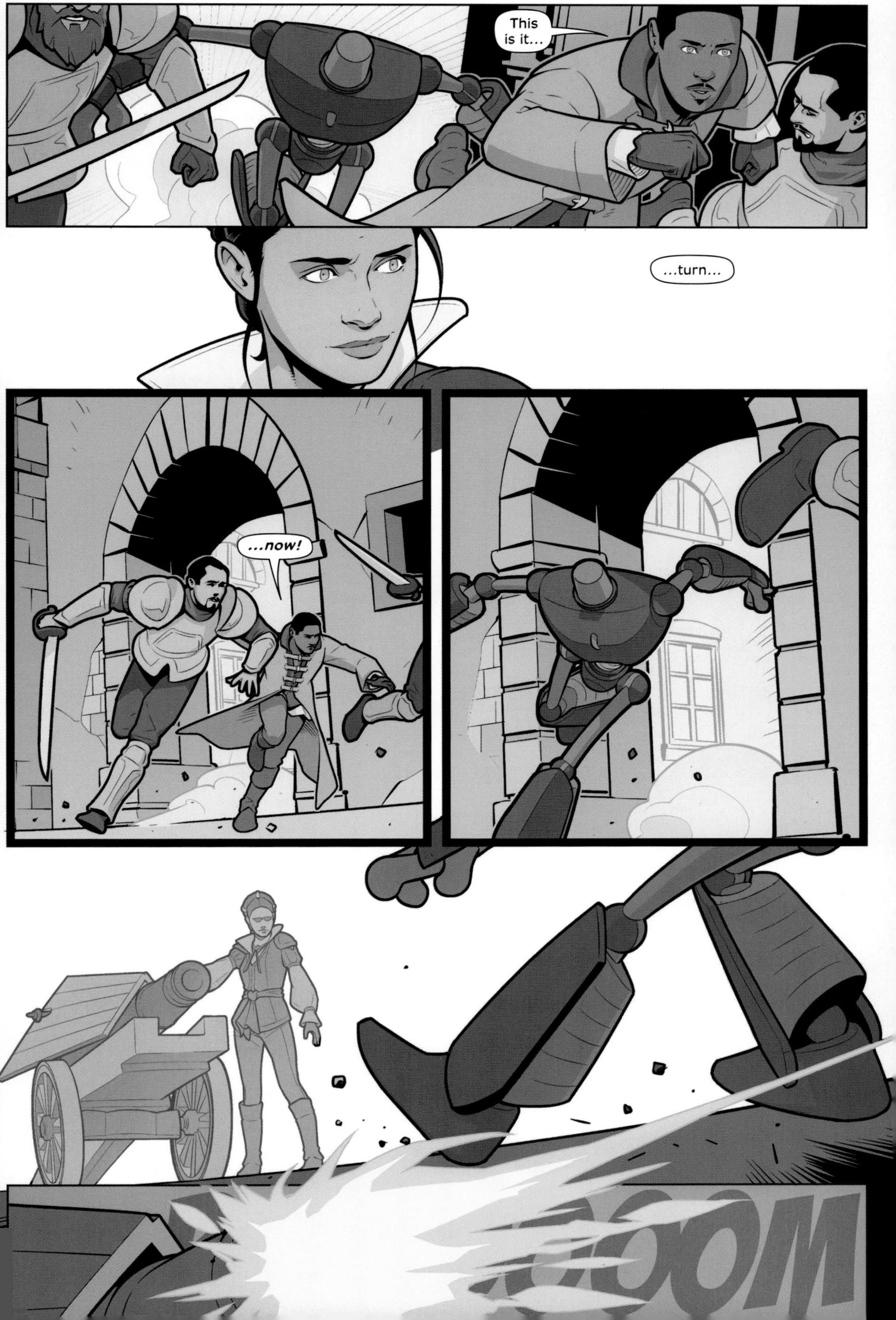
This is it...
...turn...
...now!
OOOM

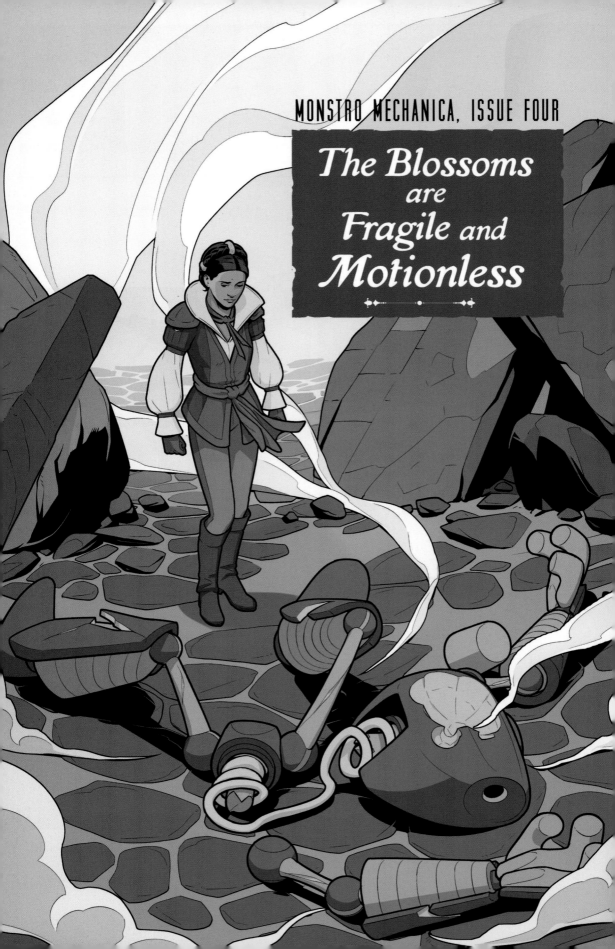

MONSTRO MECHANICA, ISSUE FOUR

The Blossoms are Fragile and Motionless

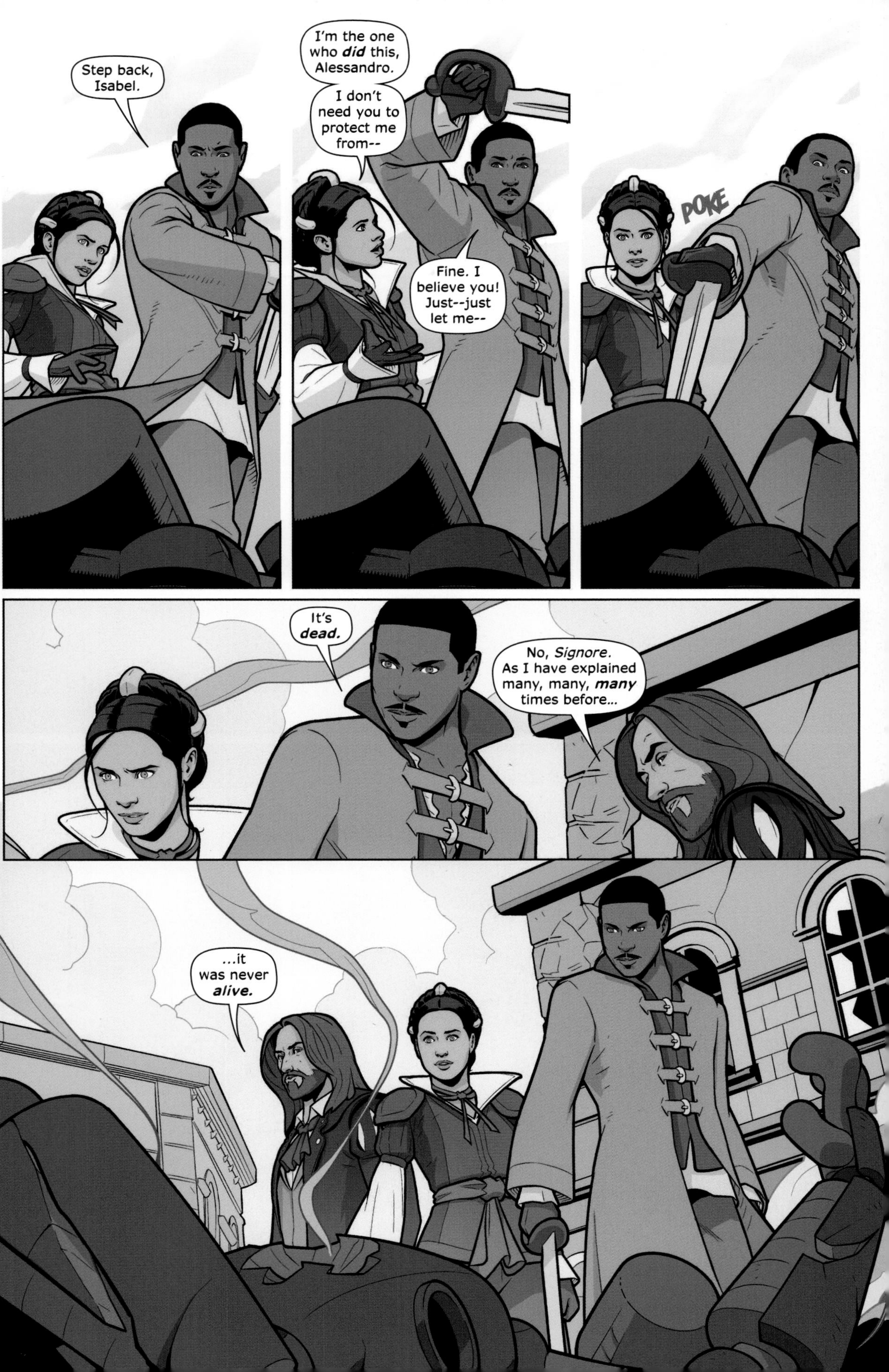
Step back, Isabel.
I'm the one who *did* this, Alessandro.
I don't need you to protect me from--
Fine. I believe you! Just--just let me--
POKE
It's *dead.*
No, *Signore*. As I have explained many, many, *many* times before...
...it was never *alive.*

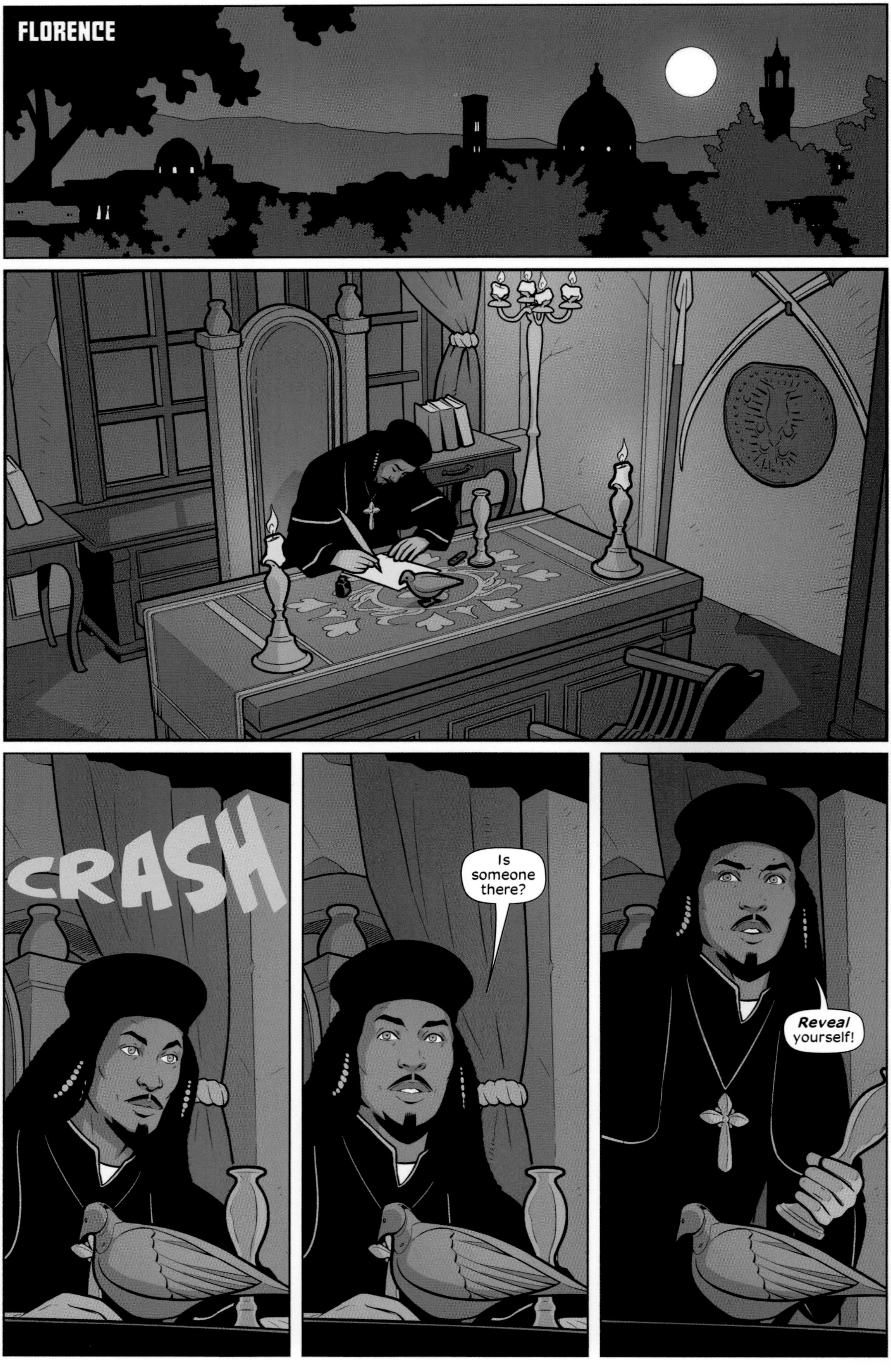
FLORENCE
CRASH
Is someone there?
Reveal yourself!

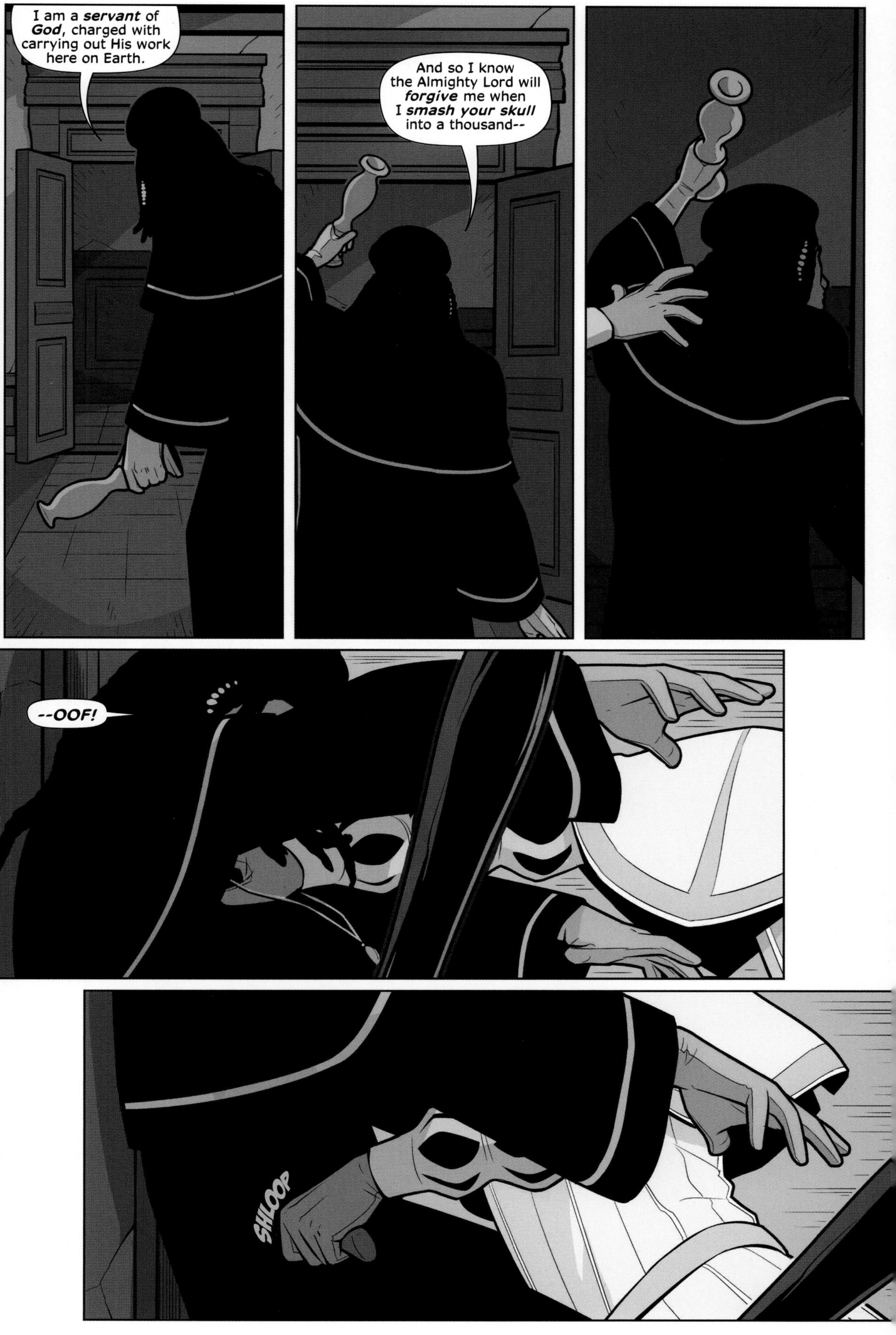
I am a servant of God, charged with carrying out His work here on Earth.
And so I know the Almighty Lord will forgive me when I smash your skull into a thousand--
--OOF!
SHLOOP

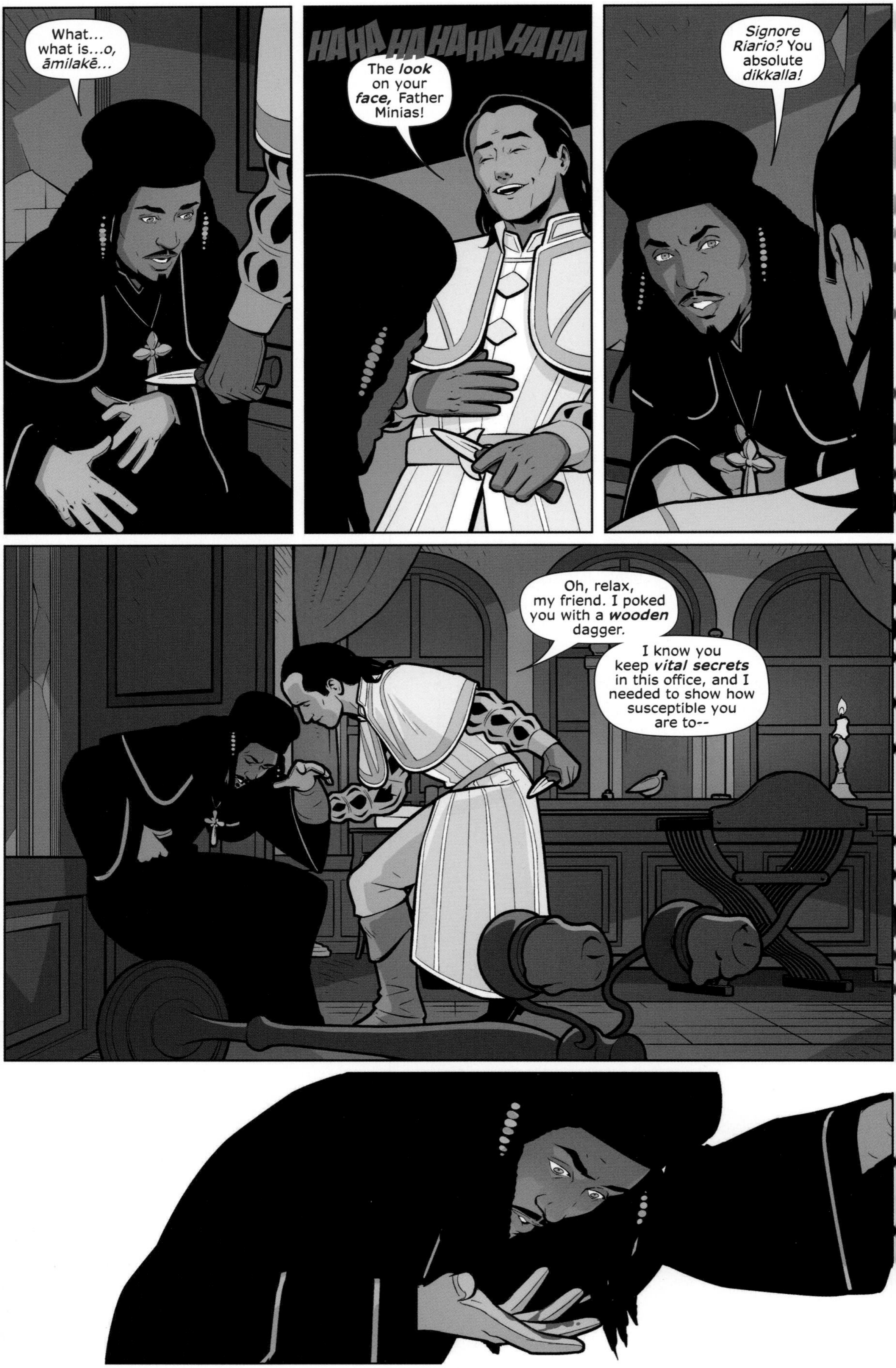

What... what is...o, āmilakē...
HAHAHAHAHAHAHA
The look on your face, Father Minias!
Signore Riario? You absolute dikkalla!
Oh, relax, my friend. I poked you with a wooden dagger.
I know you keep vital secrets in this office, and I needed to show how susceptible you are to--

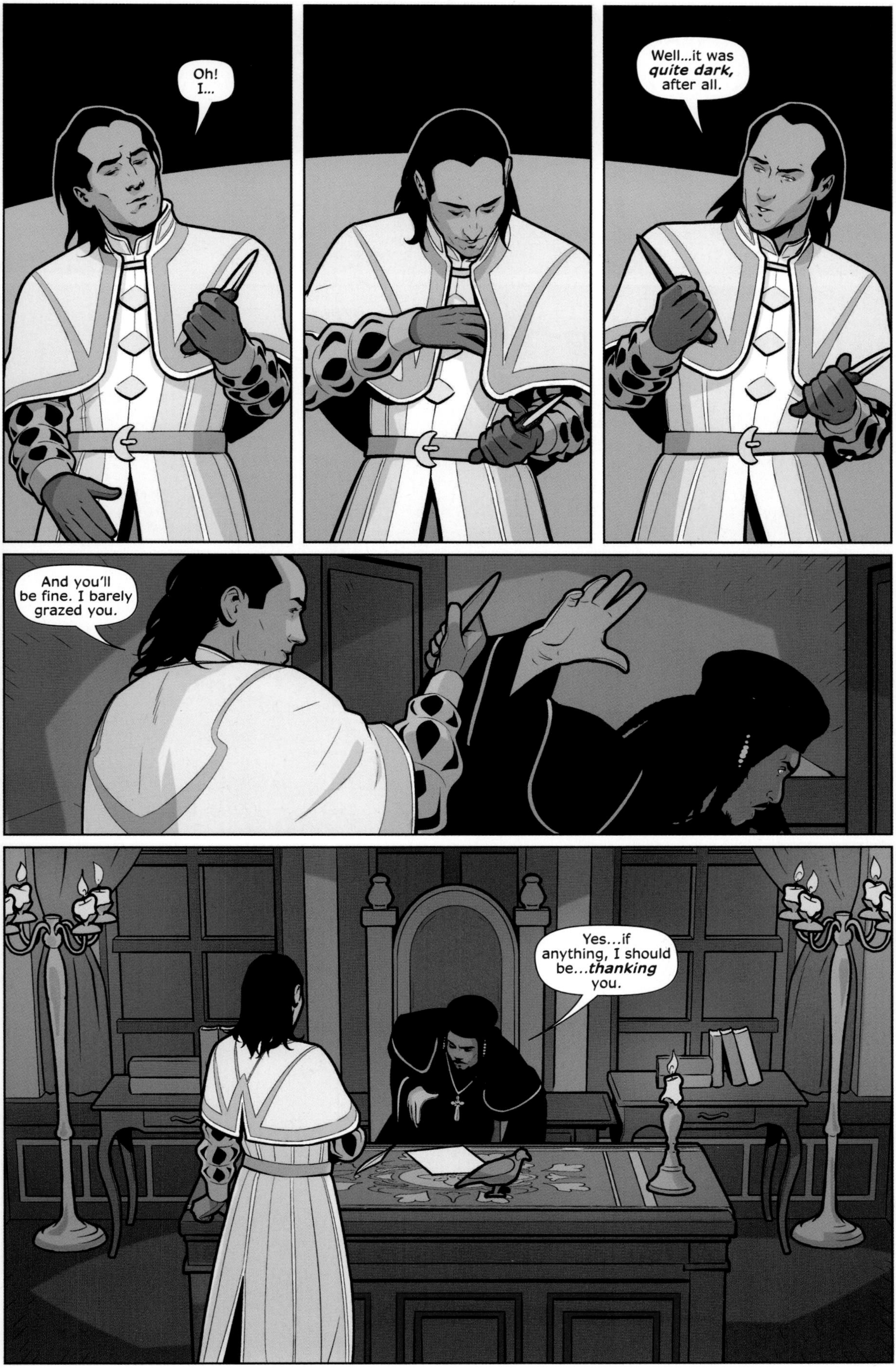
Oh! I...
Well...it was *quite dark,* after all.
And you'll be fine. I barely grazed you.
Yes...if anything, I should be...*thanking* you.

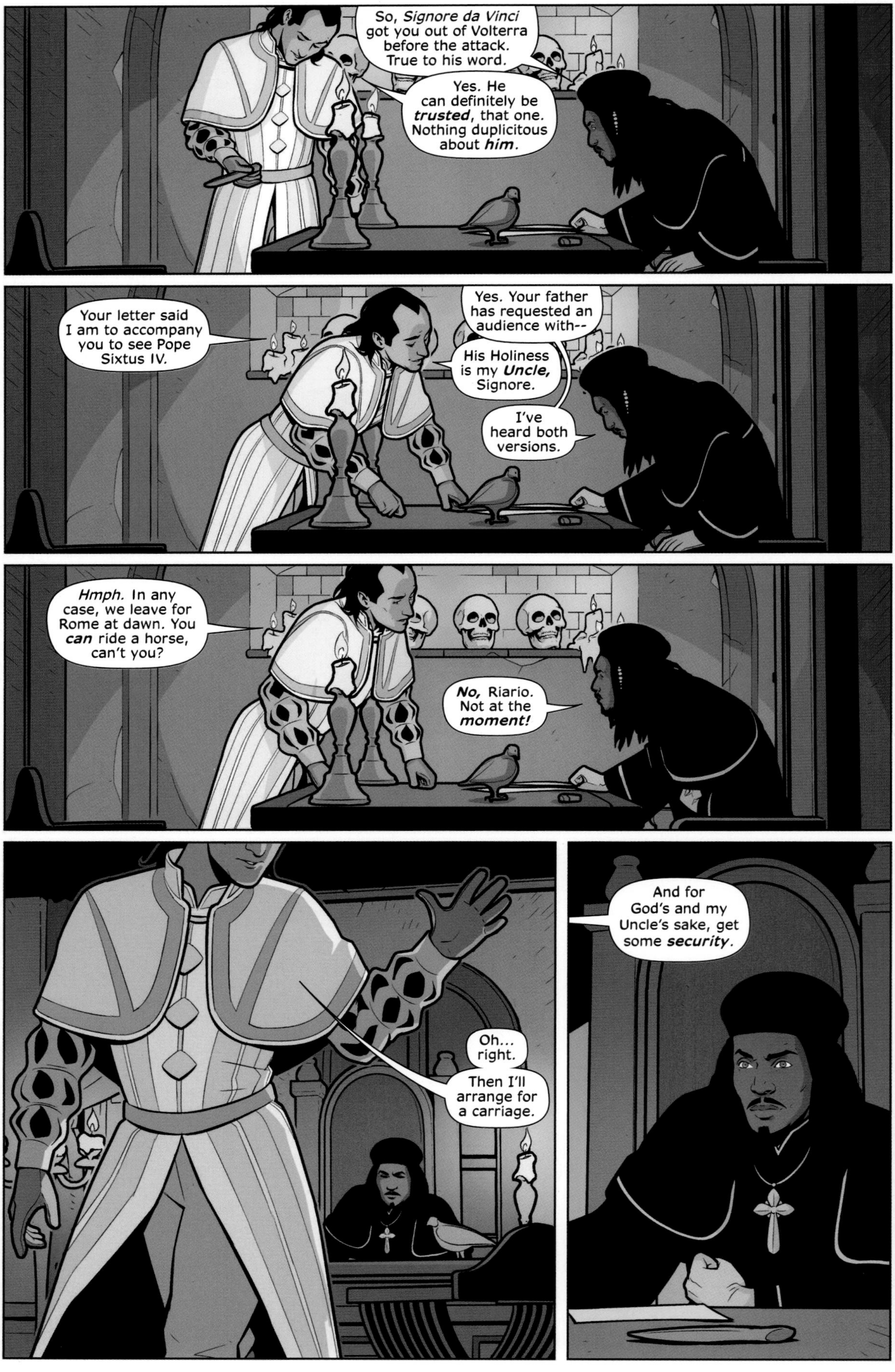
So, *Signore da Vinci* got you out of Volterra before the attack. True to his word.
Yes. He can definitely be ***trusted***, that one. Nothing duplicitous about ***him***.
Your letter said I am to accompany you to see Pope Sixtus IV.
Yes. Your father has requested an audience with--
His Holiness is my ***Uncle,*** Signore.
I've heard both versions.
Hmph. In any case, we leave for Rome at dawn. You ***can*** ride a horse, can't you?
No, Riario. Not at the ***moment!***
Oh... right.
Then I'll arrange for a carriage.
And for God's and my Uncle's sake, get some ***security***.

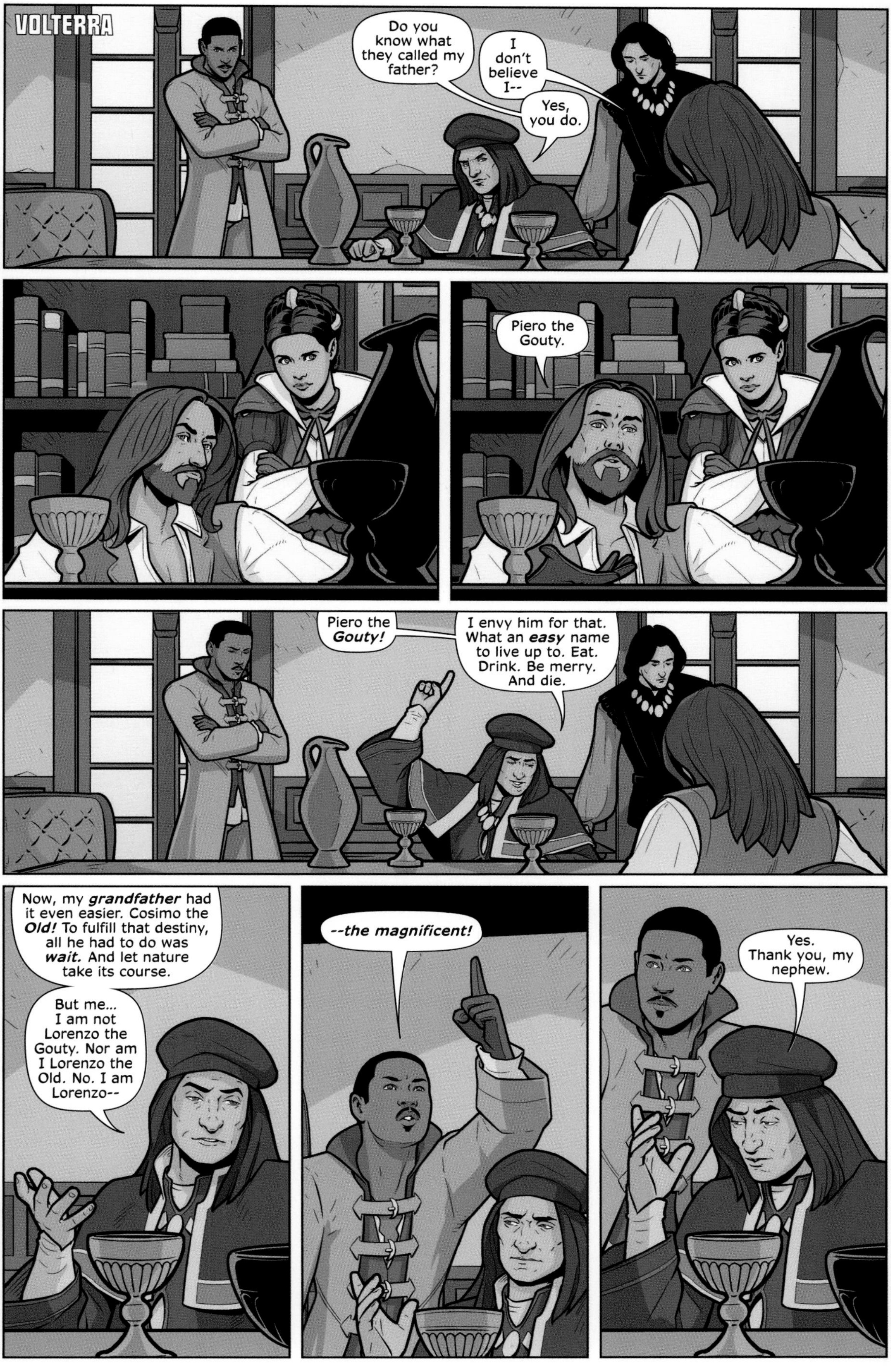
VOLTERRA
Do you know what they called my father?
I don't believe I--
Yes, you do.
Piero the Gouty.
Piero the *Gouty!*
I envy him for that. What an *easy* name to live up to. Eat. Drink. Be merry. And die.
Now, my *grandfather* had it even easier. Cosimo the *Old!* To fulfill that destiny, all he had to do was *wait.* And let nature take its course.
But me... I am not Lorenzo the Gouty. Nor am I Lorenzo the Old. No. I am Lorenzo--
--the magnificent!
Yes. Thank you, my nephew.

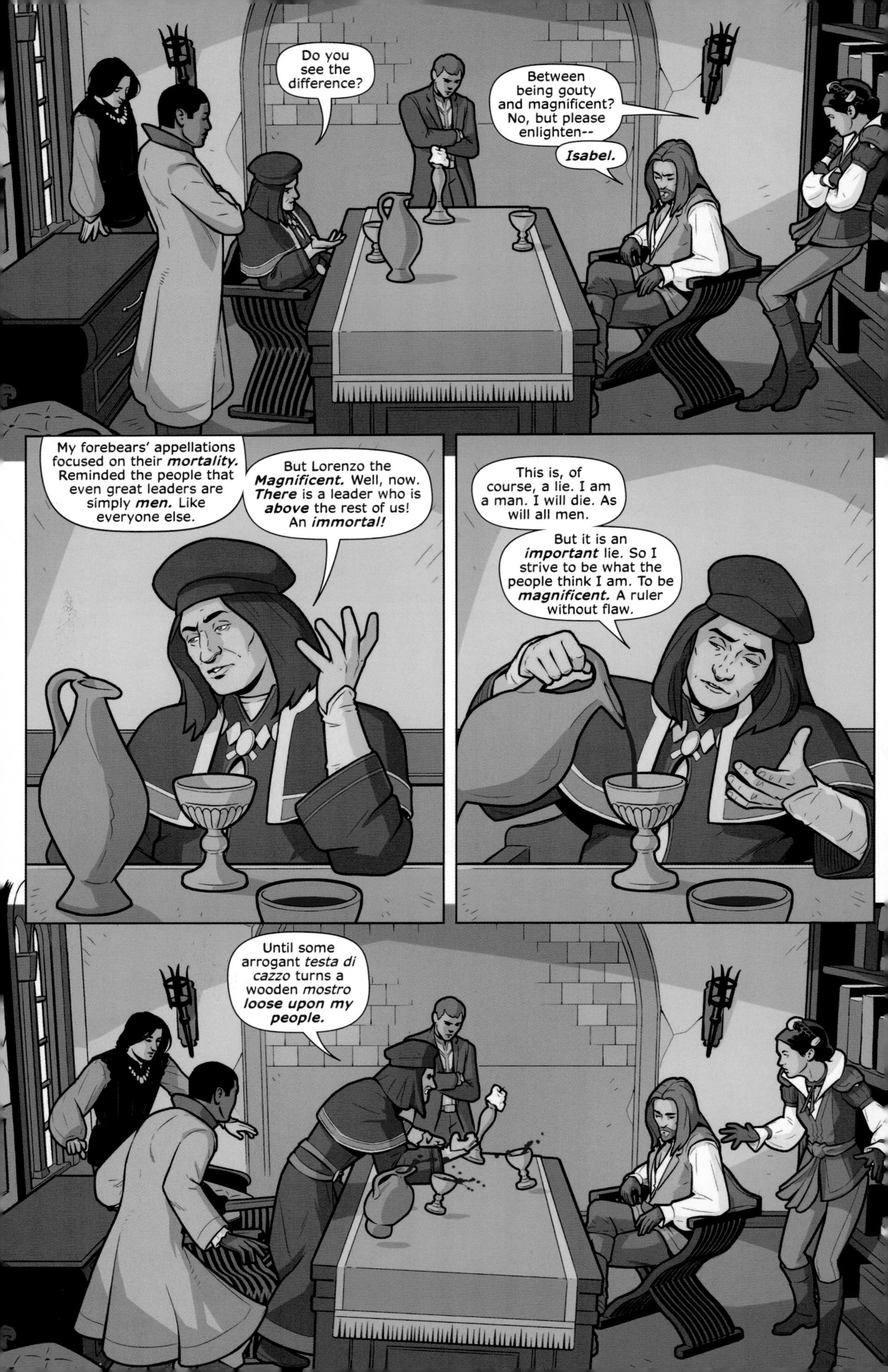
Do you see the difference?
Between being gouty and magnificent? No, but please enlighten--
Isabel.
My forebears' appellations focused on their *mortality.* Reminded the people that even great leaders are simply *men.* Like everyone else.
But Lorenzo the *Magnificent.* Well, now. *There* is a leader who is *above* the rest of us! An *immortal!*
This is, of course, a lie. I am a man. I will die. As will all men.
But it is an *important* lie. So I strive to be what the people think I am. To be *magnificent.* A ruler without flaw.
Until some arrogant *testa di cazzo* turns a wooden *mostro* **loose upon my people.**

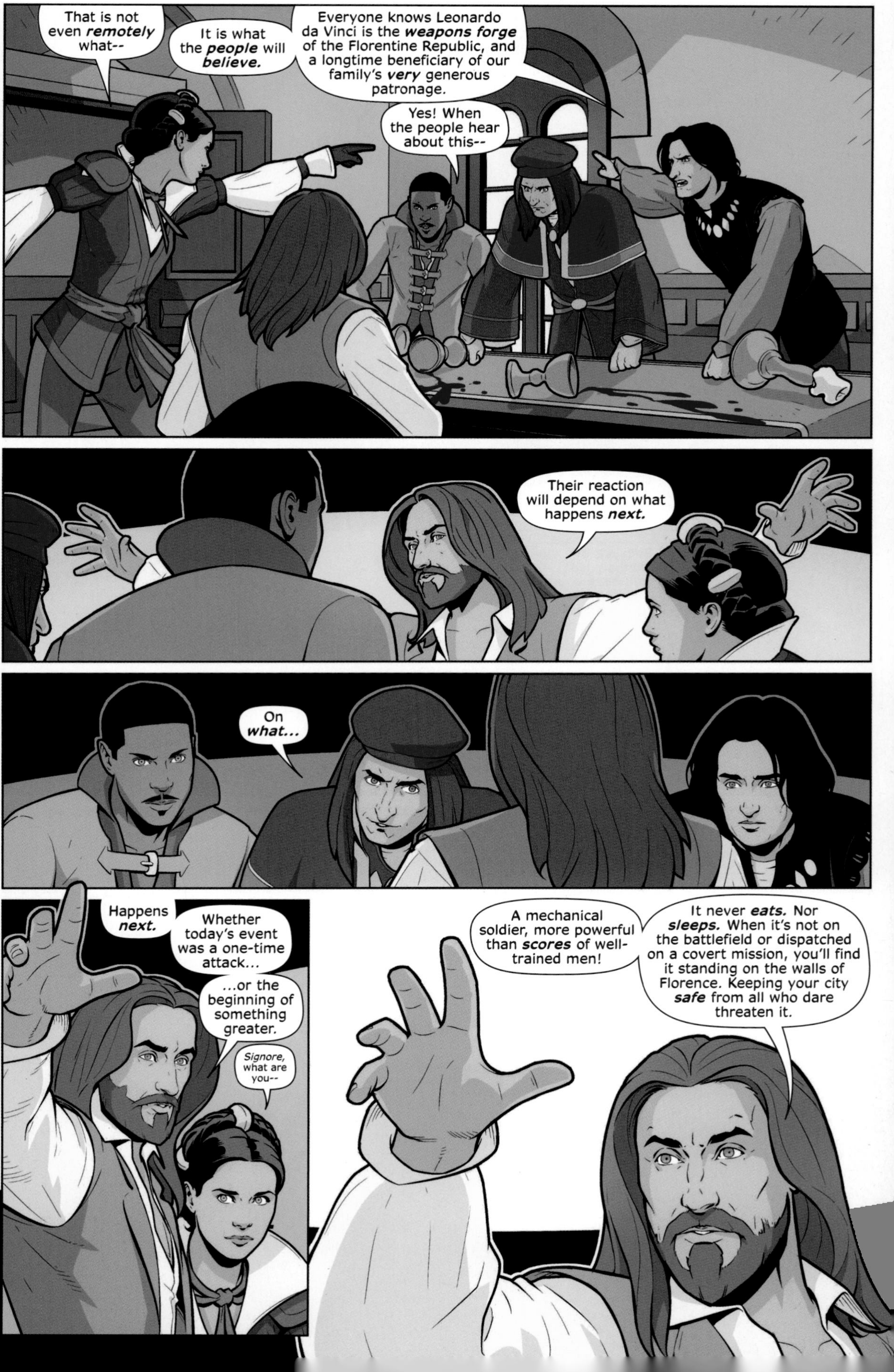
That is not even *remotely* what--
It is what the *people* will *believe.*
Everyone knows Leonardo da Vinci is the ***weapons forge*** of the Florentine Republic, and a longtime beneficiary of our family's ***very*** generous patronage.
Yes! When the people hear about this--
Their reaction will depend on what happens ***next.***
On ***what...***
Happens ***next.***
Whether today's event was a one-time attack...
...or the beginning of something greater.
Signore, what are you--
A mechanical soldier, more powerful than ***scores*** of well-trained men!
It never ***eats.*** Nor ***sleeps.*** When it's not on the battlefield or dispatched on a covert mission, you'll find it standing on the walls of Florence. Keeping your city ***safe*** from all who dare threaten it.

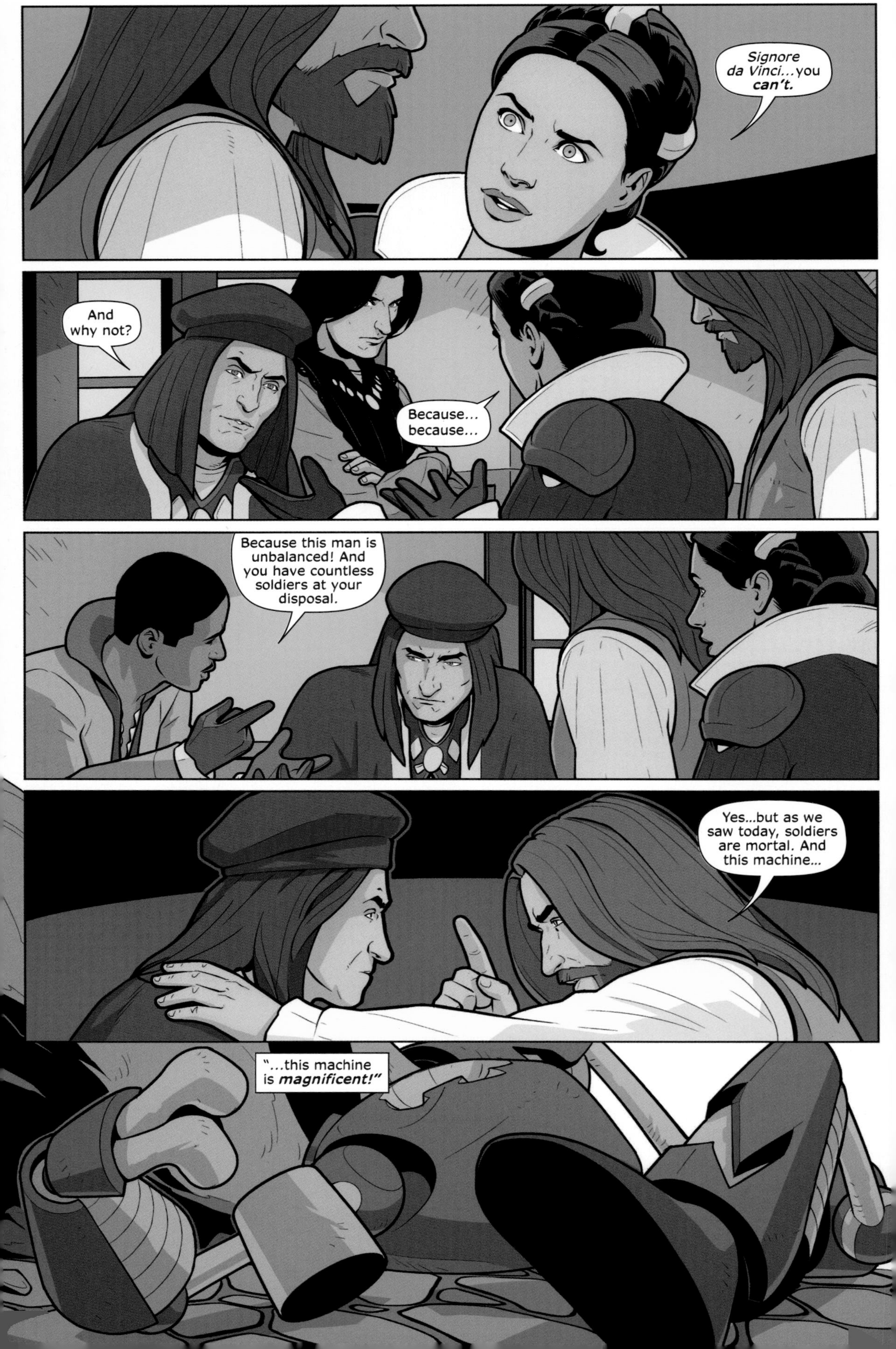
Signore da Vinci...you *can't.*
And why not?
Because... because...
Because this man is unbalanced! And you have countless soldiers at your disposal.
Yes...but as we saw today, soldiers are mortal. And this machine...
"...this machine is *magnificent!*"

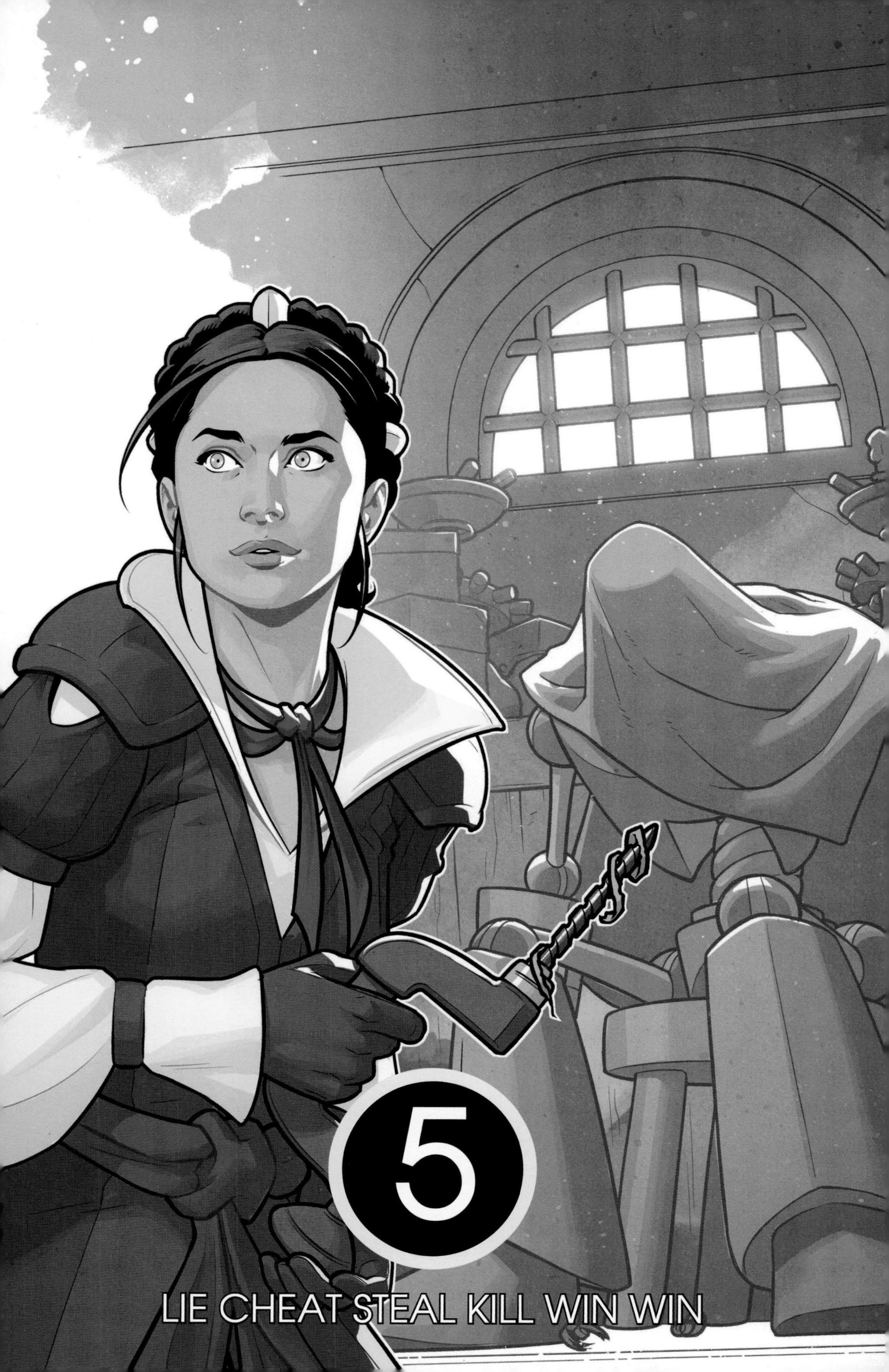
5
LIE CHEAT STEAL KILL WIN WIN

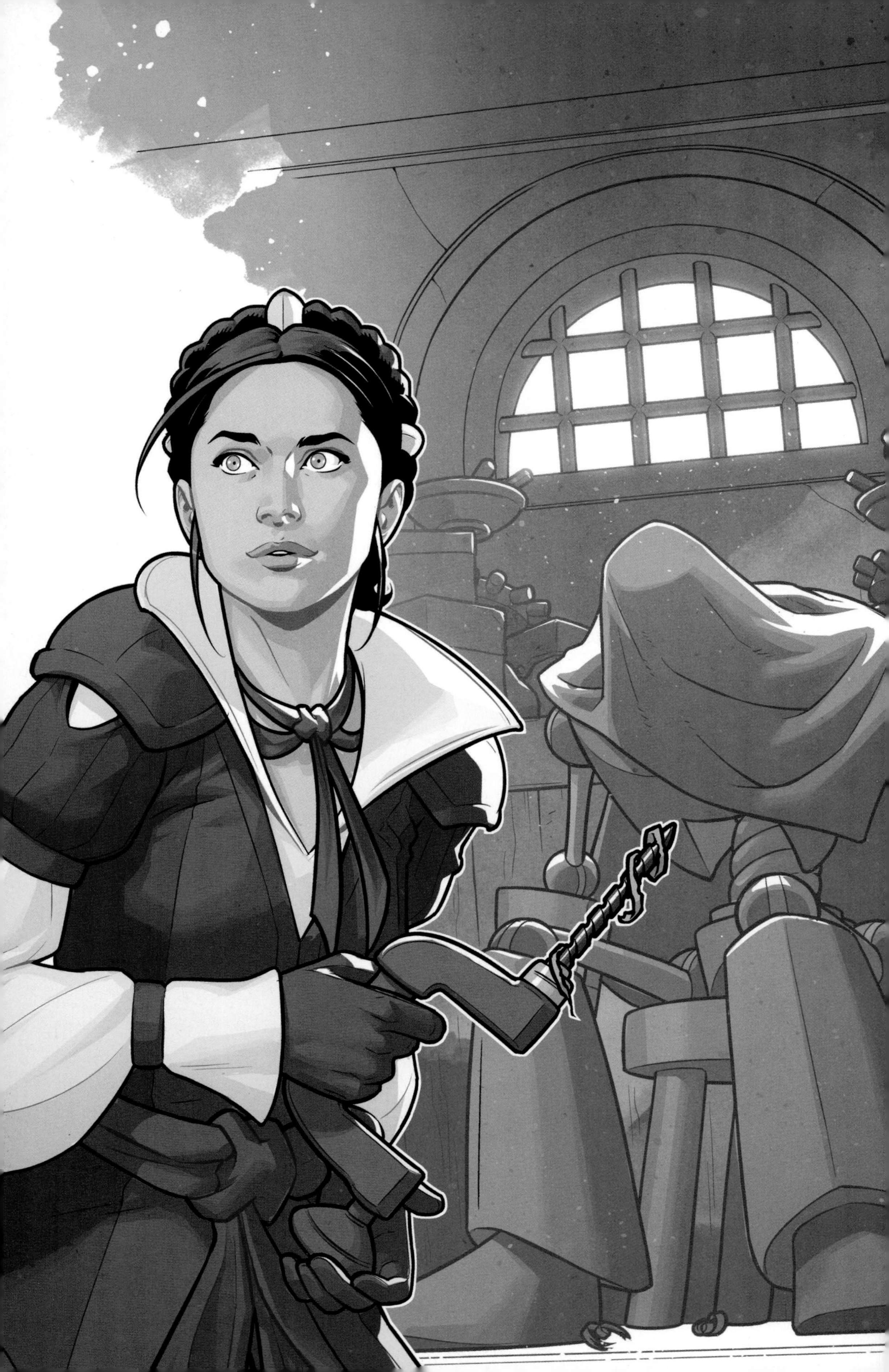

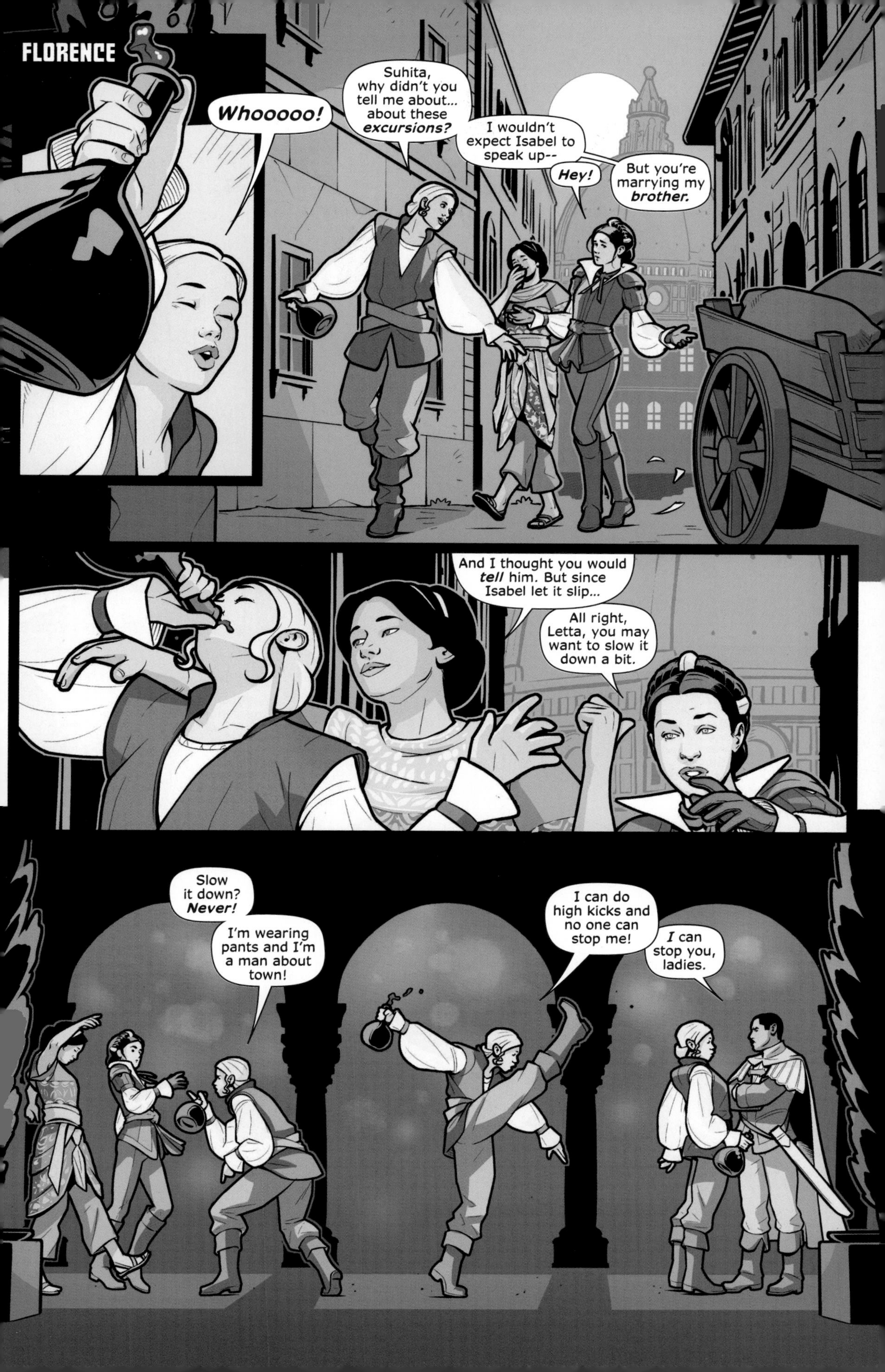

FLORENCE
Whoooooo!
Suhita, why didn't you tell me about... about these *excursions?*
I wouldn't expect Isabel to speak up--
Hey!
But you're marrying my *brother.*
And I thought you would *tell* him. But since Isabel let it slip...
All right, Letta, you may want to slow it down a bit.
Slow it down? *Never!*
I'm wearing pants and I'm a man about town!
I can do high kicks and no one can stop me!
I can stop you, ladies.

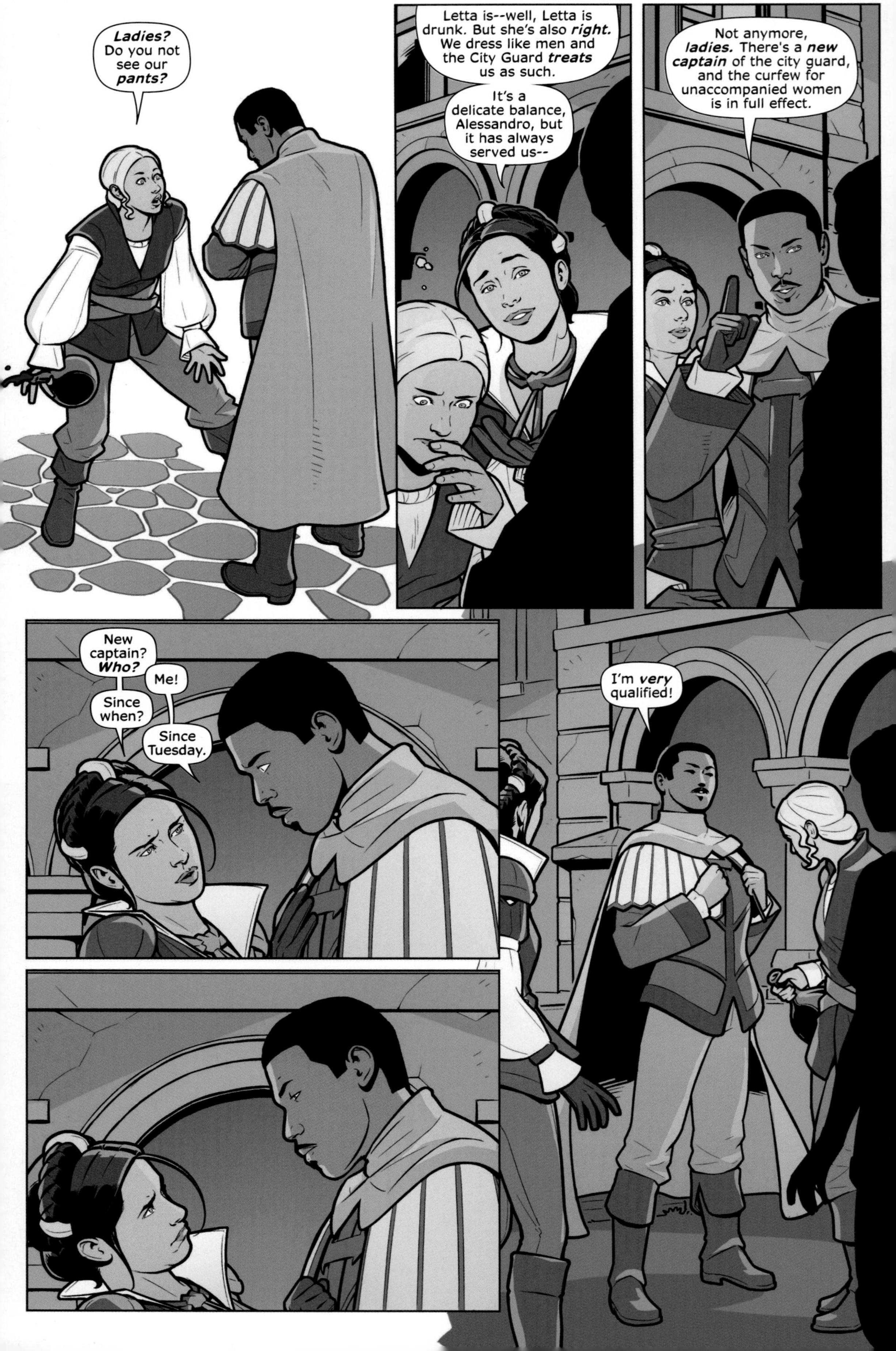

Ladies? Do you not see our pants?
Letta is--well, Letta is drunk. But she's also right. We dress like men and the City Guard treats us as such.
It's a delicate balance, Alessandro, but it has always served us--
Not anymore, ladies. There's a new captain of the city guard, and the curfew for unaccompanied women is in full effect.
New captain? Who?
Me!
Since when?
Since Tuesday.
I'm very qualified!

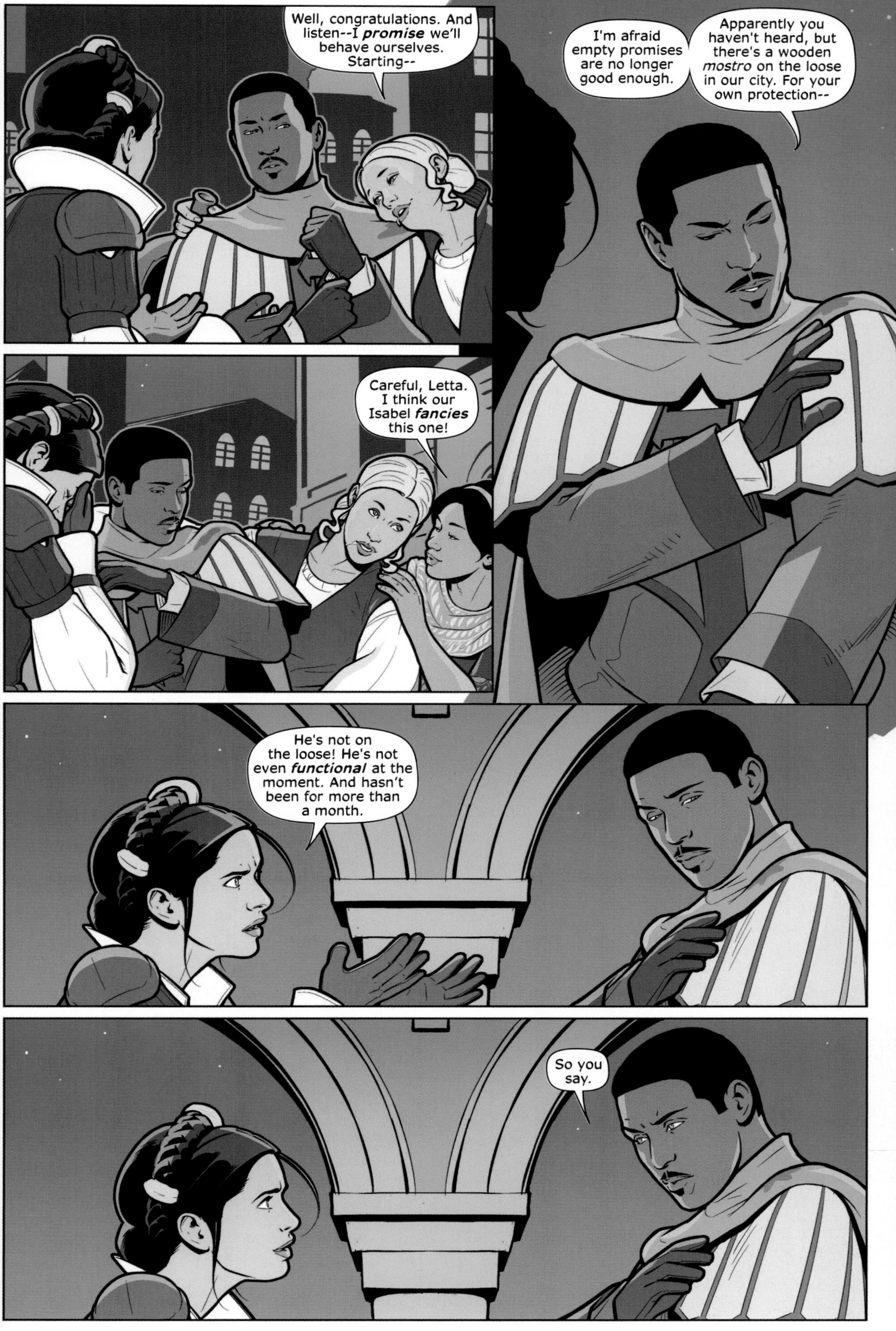
Well, congratulations. And listen--I *promise* we'll behave ourselves. Starting--
Careful, Letta. I think our Isabel *fancies* this one!
I'm afraid empty promises are no longer good enough.
Apparently you haven't heard, but there's a wooden *mostro* on the loose in our city. For your own protection--
He's not on the loose! He's not even *functional* at the moment. And hasn't been for more than a month.
So you say.

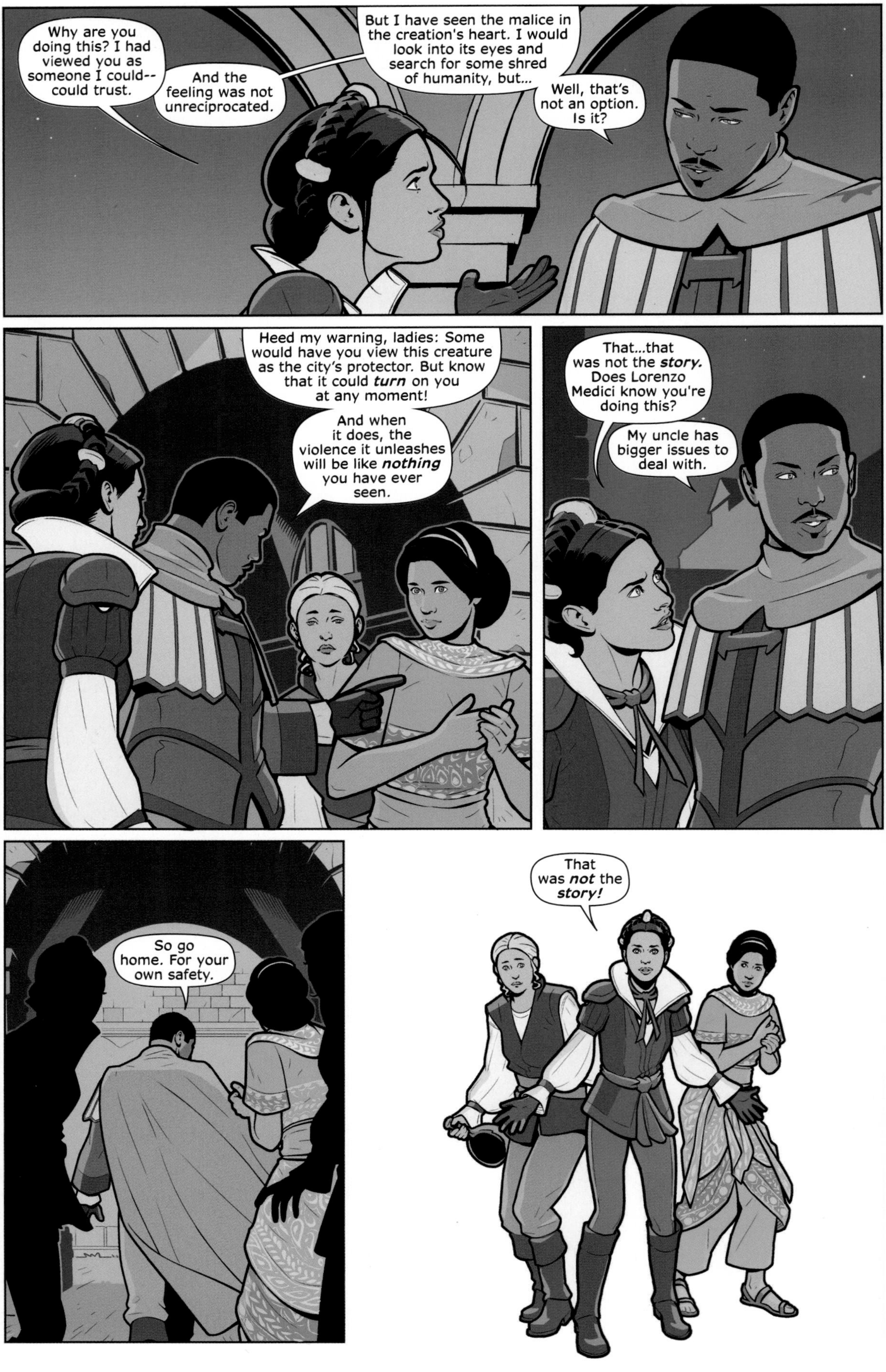
Why are you doing this? I had viewed you as someone I could--could trust.
And the feeling was not unreciprocated.
But I have seen the malice in the creation's heart. I would look into its eyes and search for some shred of humanity, but...
Well, that's not an option. Is it?
Heed my warning, ladies: Some would have you view this creature as the city's protector. But know that it could *turn* on you at any moment!
And when it does, the violence it unleashes will be like ***nothing*** you have ever seen.
That...that was not the ***story.*** Does Lorenzo Medici know you're doing this?
My uncle has bigger issues to deal with.
So go home. For your own safety.
That was ***not*** the ***story!***

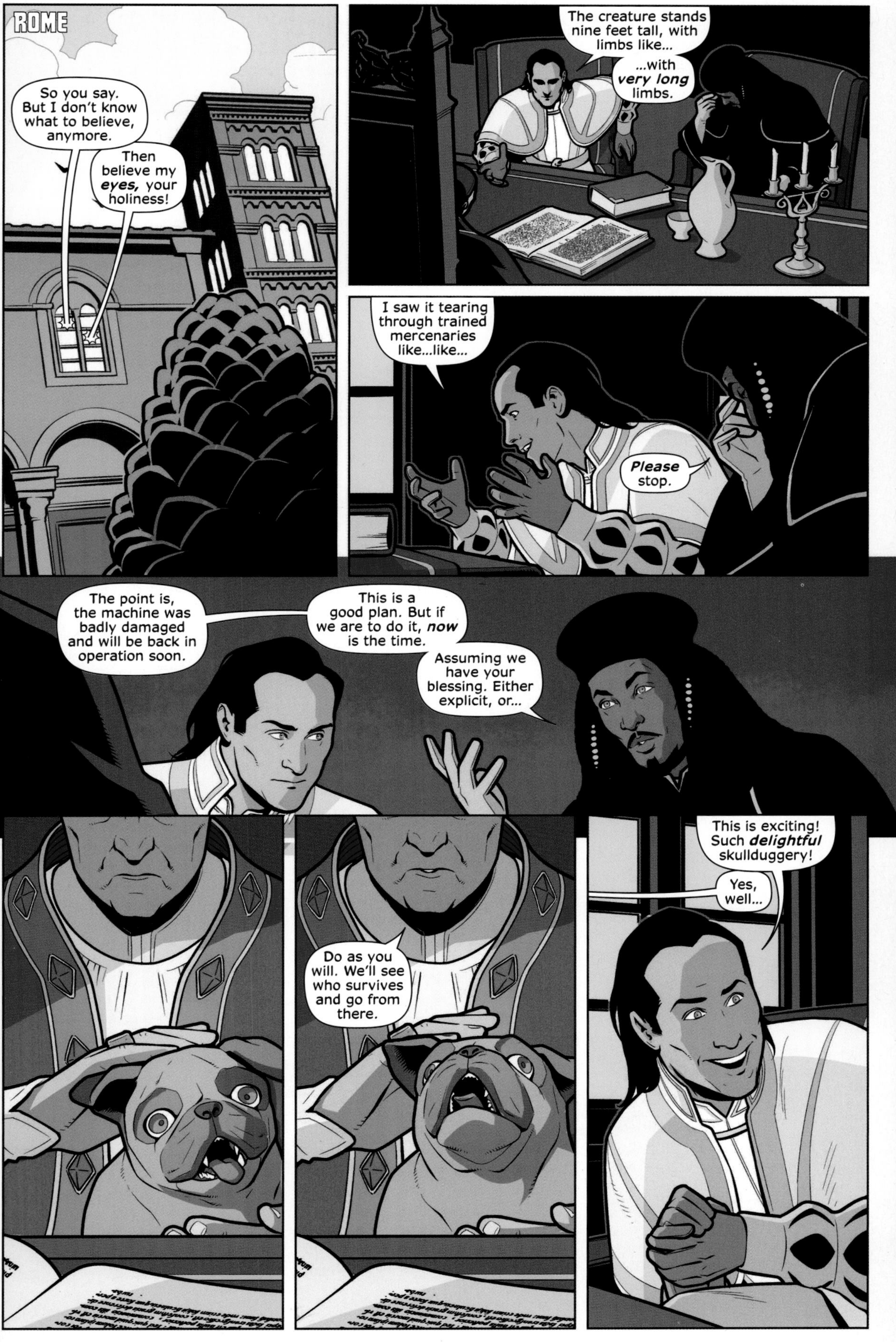
ROME
So you say. But I don't know what to believe, anymore.
Then believe my *eyes,* your holiness!
The creature stands nine feet tall, with limbs like...
...with *very long* limbs.
I saw it tearing through trained mercenaries like...like...
Please stop.
The point is, the machine was badly damaged and will be back in operation soon.
This is a good plan. But if we are to do it, *now* is the time.
Assuming we have your blessing. Either explicit, or...
Do as you will. We'll see who survives and go from there.
This is exciting! Such *delightful* skullduggery!
Yes, well...

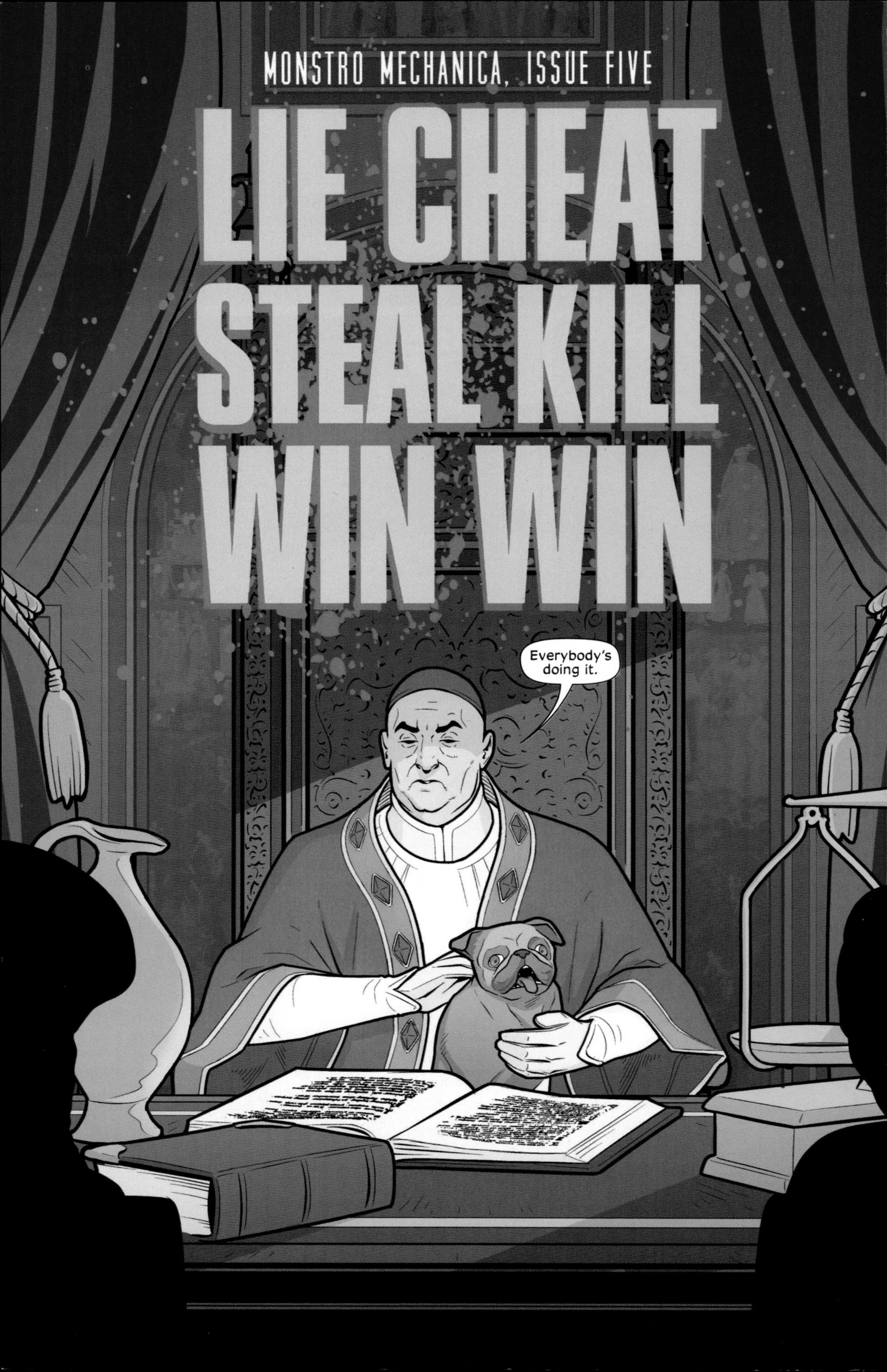
MONSTRO MECHANICA, ISSUE FIVE
LIE CHEAT
STEAL KILL
WIN WIN
Everybody's doing it.

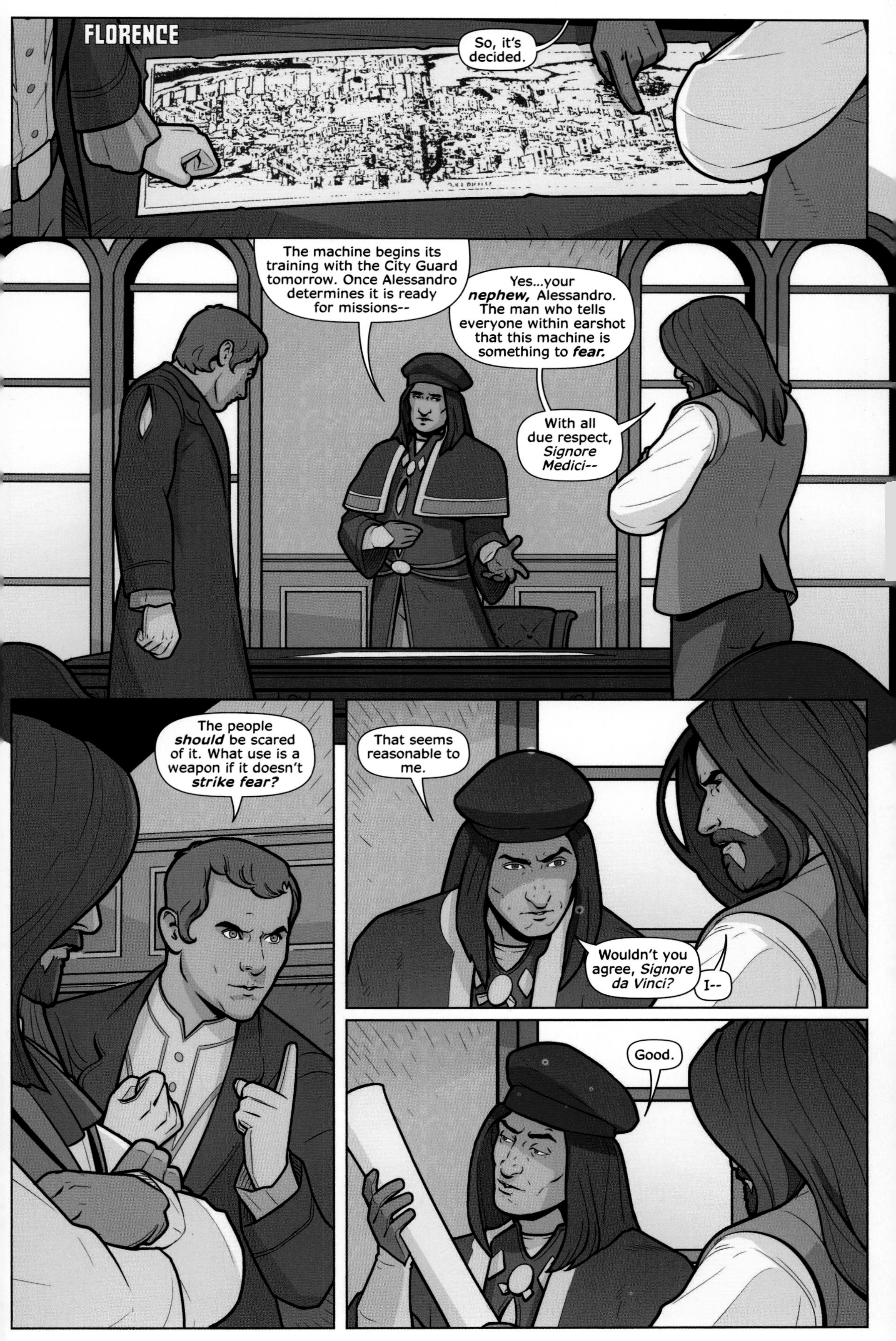
FLORENCE
So, it's decided.
The machine begins its training with the City Guard tomorrow. Once Alessandro determines it is ready for missions--
Yes...your *nephew,* Alessandro. The man who tells everyone within earshot that this machine is something to *fear.*
With all due respect, *Signore Medici--*
The people *should* be scared of it. What use is a weapon if it doesn't *strike fear?*
That seems reasonable to me.
Wouldn't you agree, *Signore da Vinci?*
I--
Good.

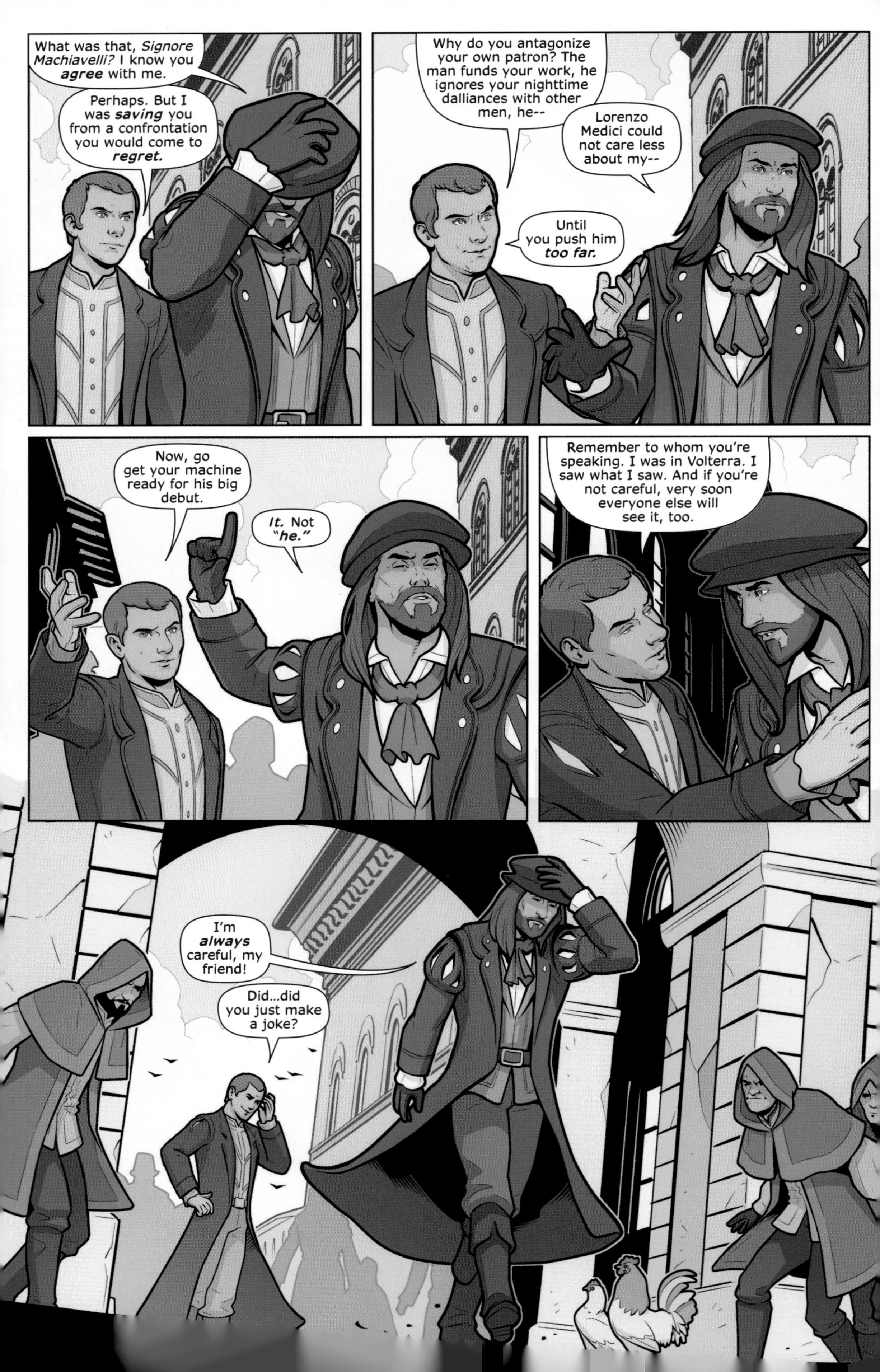
What was that, *Signore Machiavelli?* I know you ***agree*** with me.
Perhaps. But I was ***saving*** you from a confrontation you would come to ***regret.***
Why do you antagonize your own patron? The man funds your work, he ignores your nighttime dalliances with other men, he--
Lorenzo Medici could not care less about my--
Until you push him ***too far.***
Now, go get your machine ready for his big debut.
It. Not "***he.***"
Remember to whom you're speaking. I was in Volterra. I saw what I saw. And if you're not careful, very soon everyone else will see it, too.
I'm ***always*** careful, my friend!
Did...did you just make a joke?

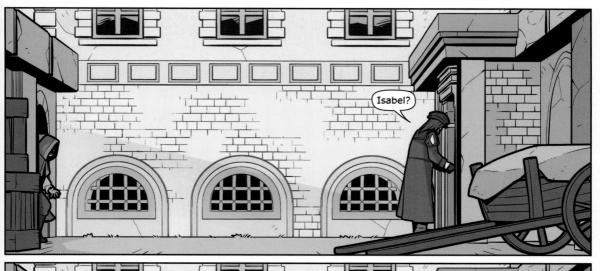

Isabel?

Isabel, are you here?

I just came out of the most *idiotic* meeting.

Where are the figure sketches I was working on yesterday?

I need to *burn* some terrible art. It will make me feel better.

I just... I just want to study. And create. Add some beauty to this world.

Is that so much to ask?

Yes.

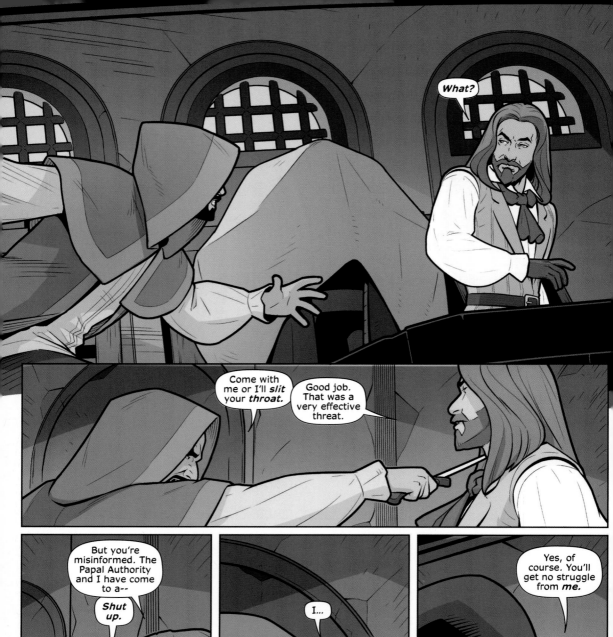

What?

Come with me or I'll *slit* your *throat.*

Good job. That was a very effective threat.

But you're misinformed. The Papal Authority and I have come to a--

Shut up.

I...

Yes, of course. You'll get no struggle from *me.*

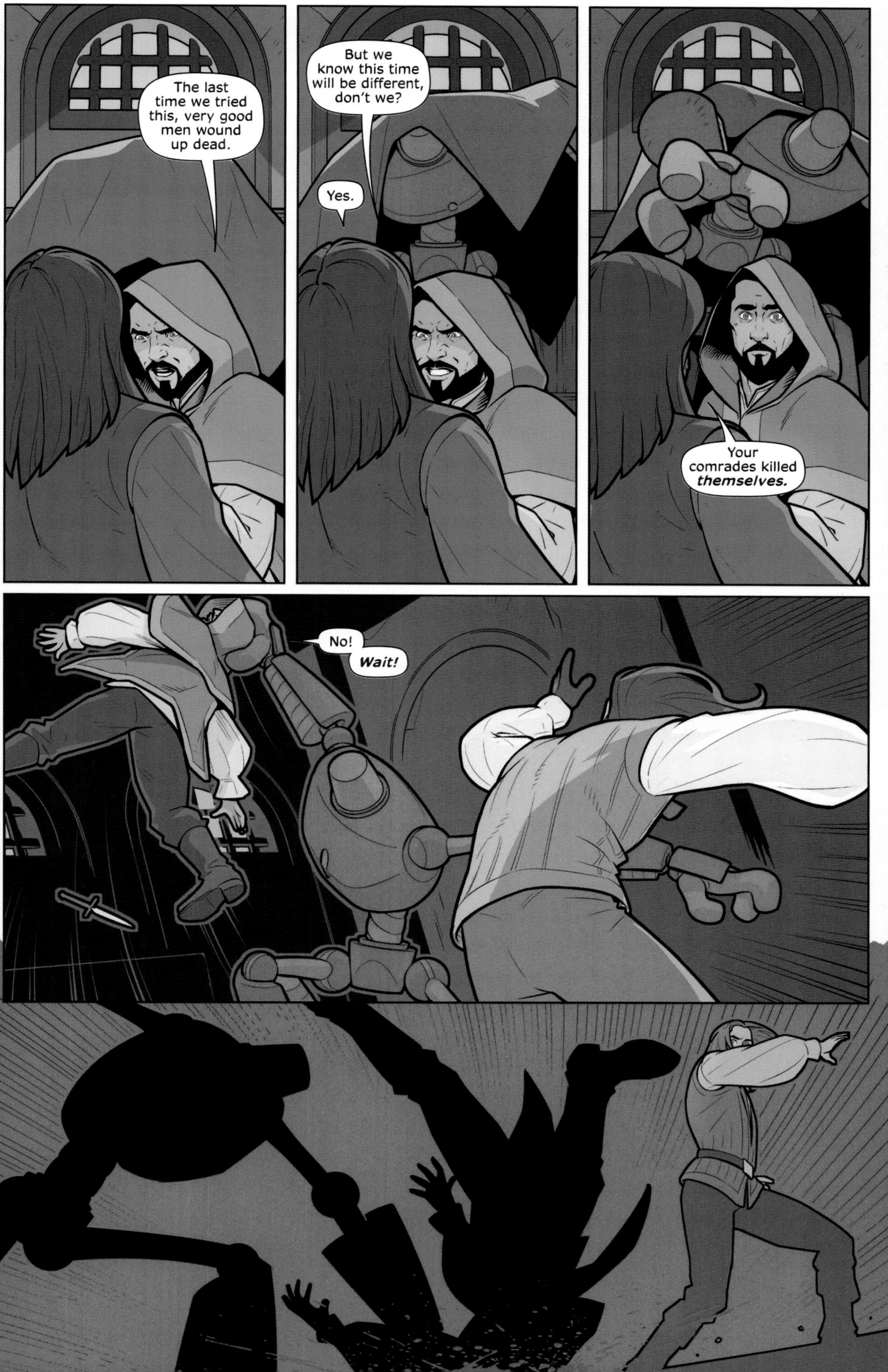
The last time we tried this, very good men wound up dead.
But we know this time will be different, don't we?
Yes.
Your comrades killed *themselves.*
No!
Wait!

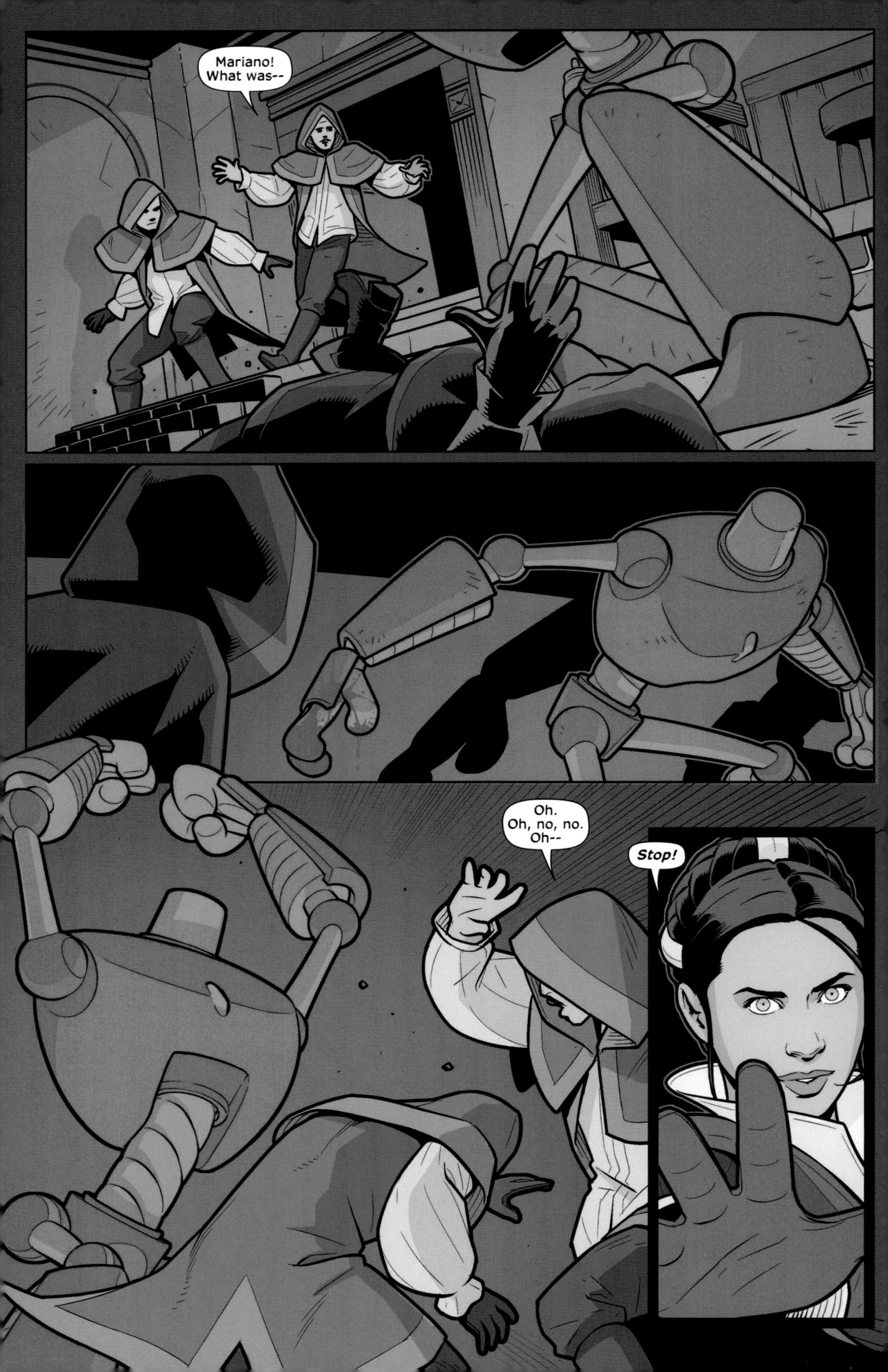
Mariano! What was--
Oh. Oh, no, no. Oh--
Stop!

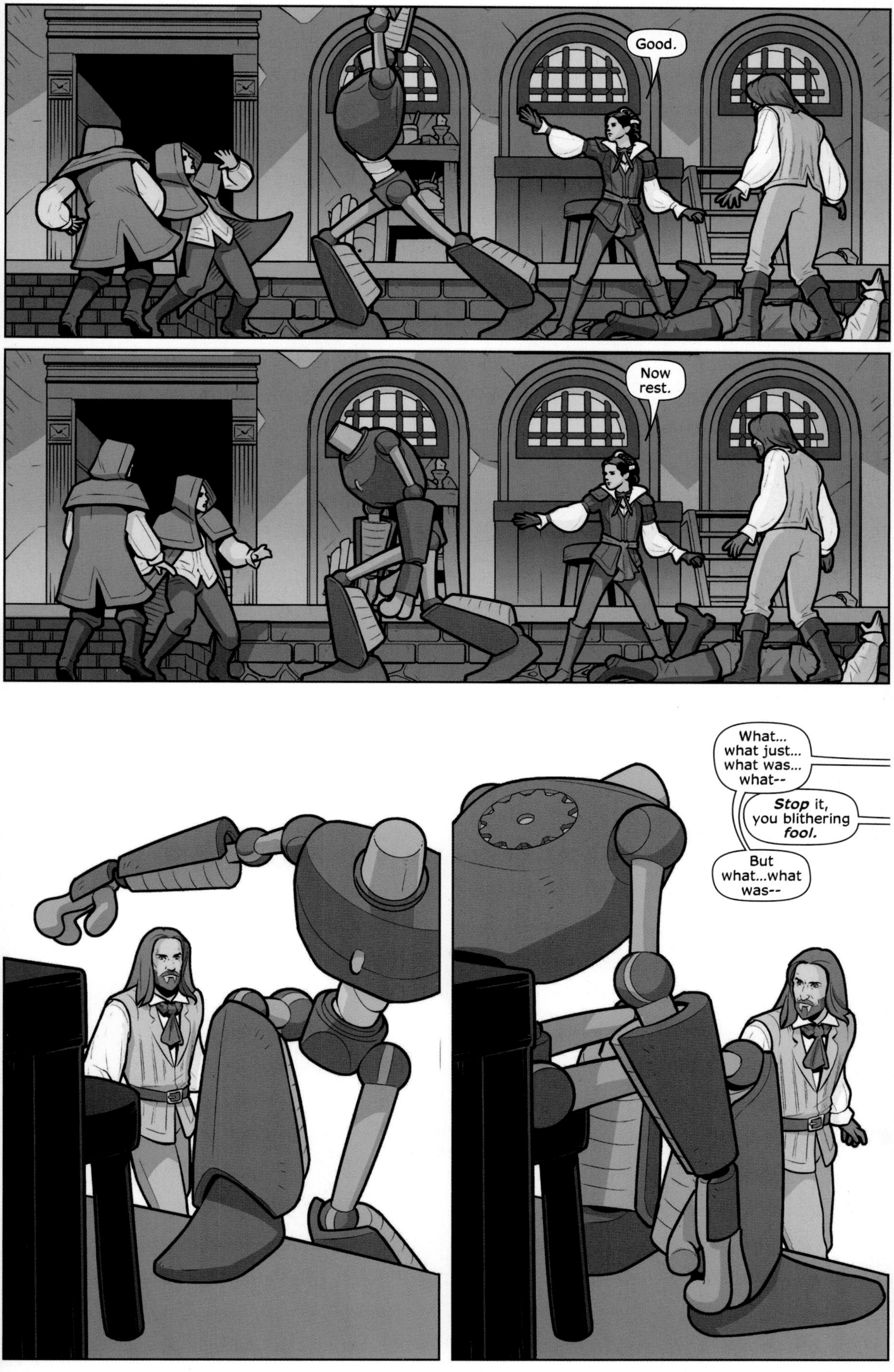
Good.
Now rest.
What... what just... what was... what--
Stop it, you blithering fool.
But what...what was--

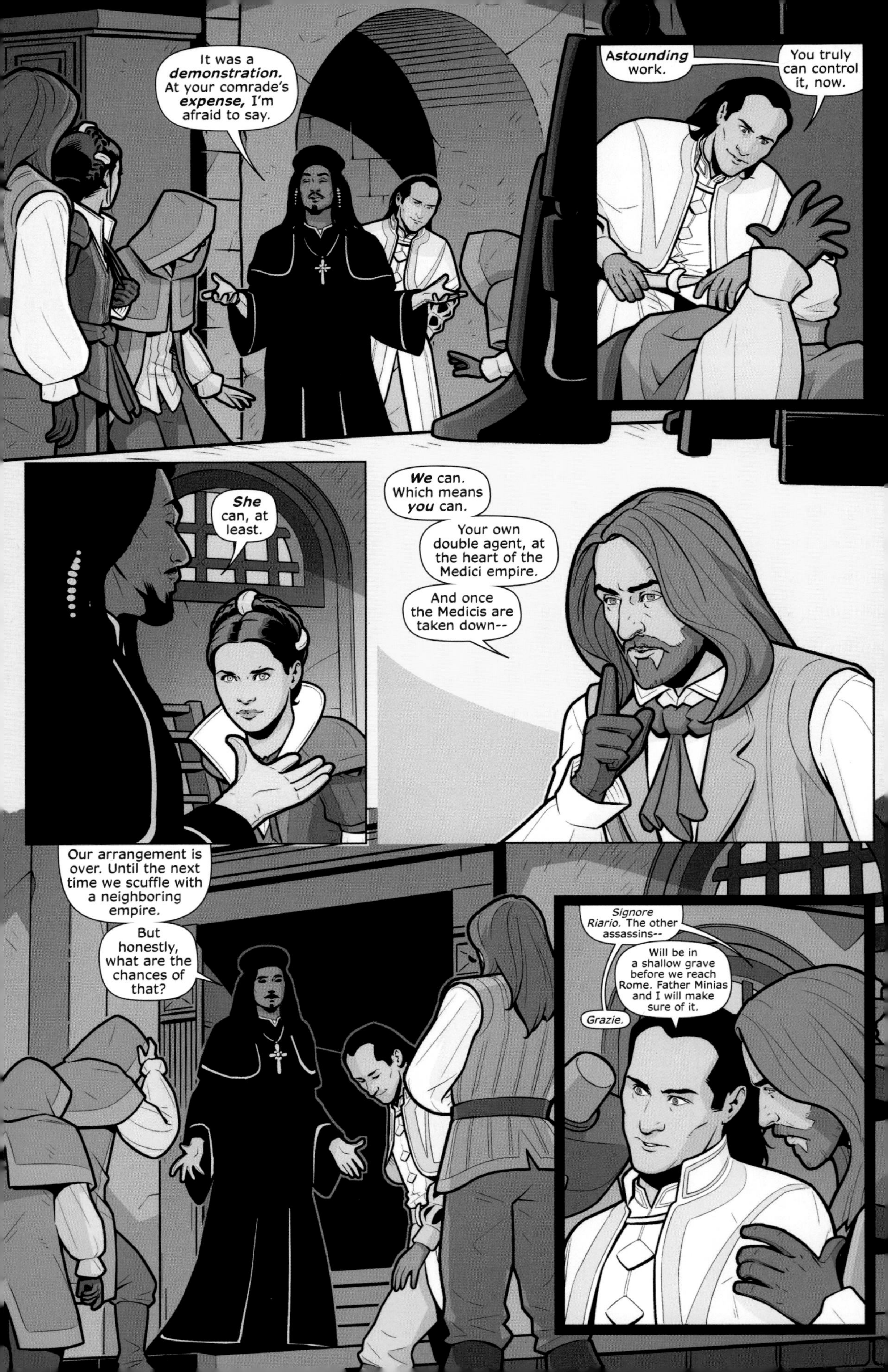
It was a *demonstration.* At your comrade's *expense,* I'm afraid to say.
A*stounding* work.
You truly can control it, now.
She can, at least.
We can. Which means *you* can.
Your own double agent, at the heart of the Medici empire.
And once the Medicis are taken down--
Our arrangement is over. Until the next time we scuffle with a neighboring empire.
But honestly, what are the chances of that?
Signore Riario. The other assassins--
Will be in a shallow grave before we reach Rome. Father Minias and I will make sure of it.
Grazie.

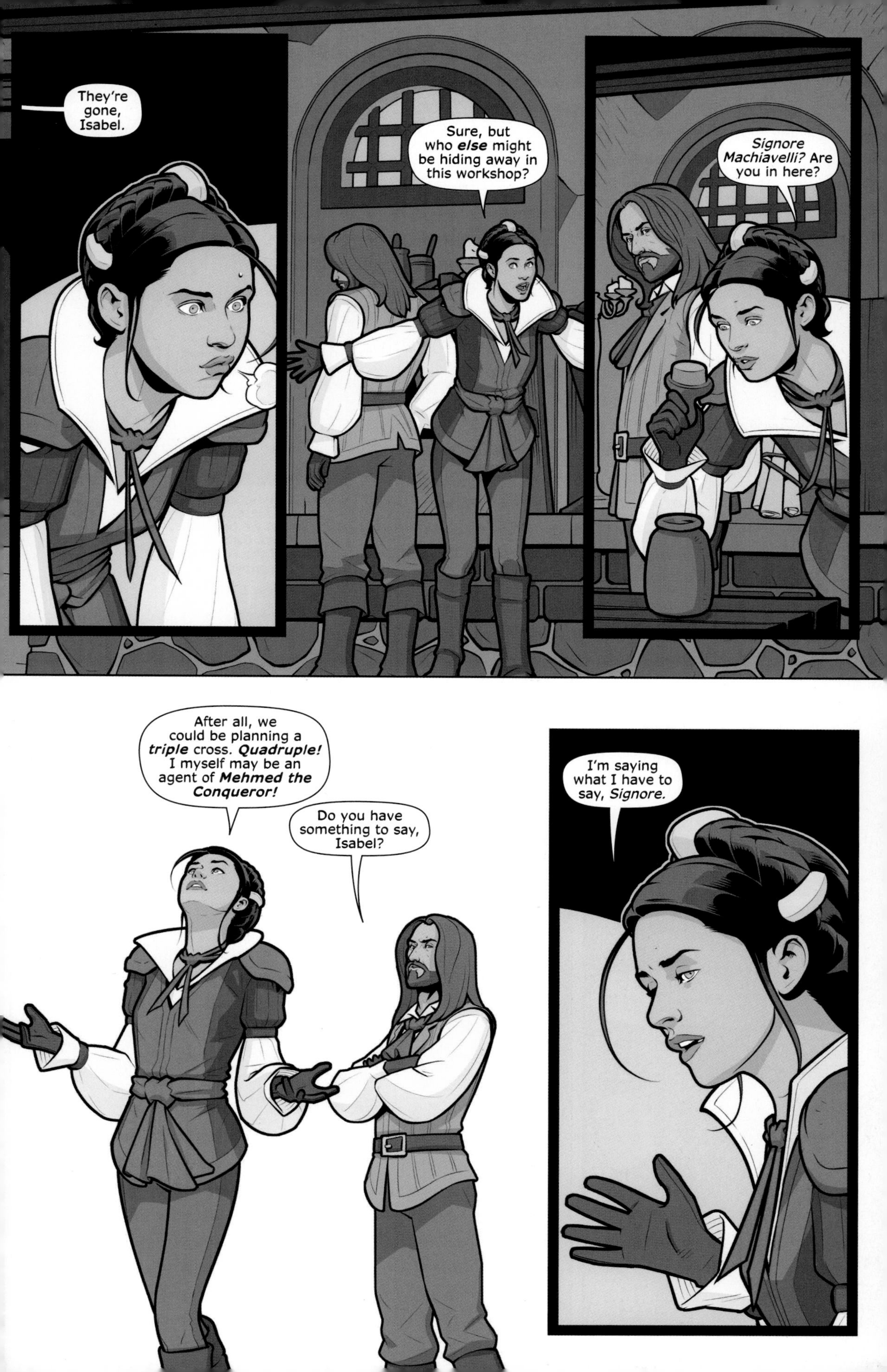

They're gone, Isabel.
Sure, but who *else* might be hiding away in this workshop?
Signore Machiavelli? Are you in here?
After all, we could be planning a ***triple*** cross. ***Quadruple!*** I myself may be an agent of ***Mehmed the Conqueror!***
Do you have something to say, Isabel?
I'm saying what I have to say, *Signore.*

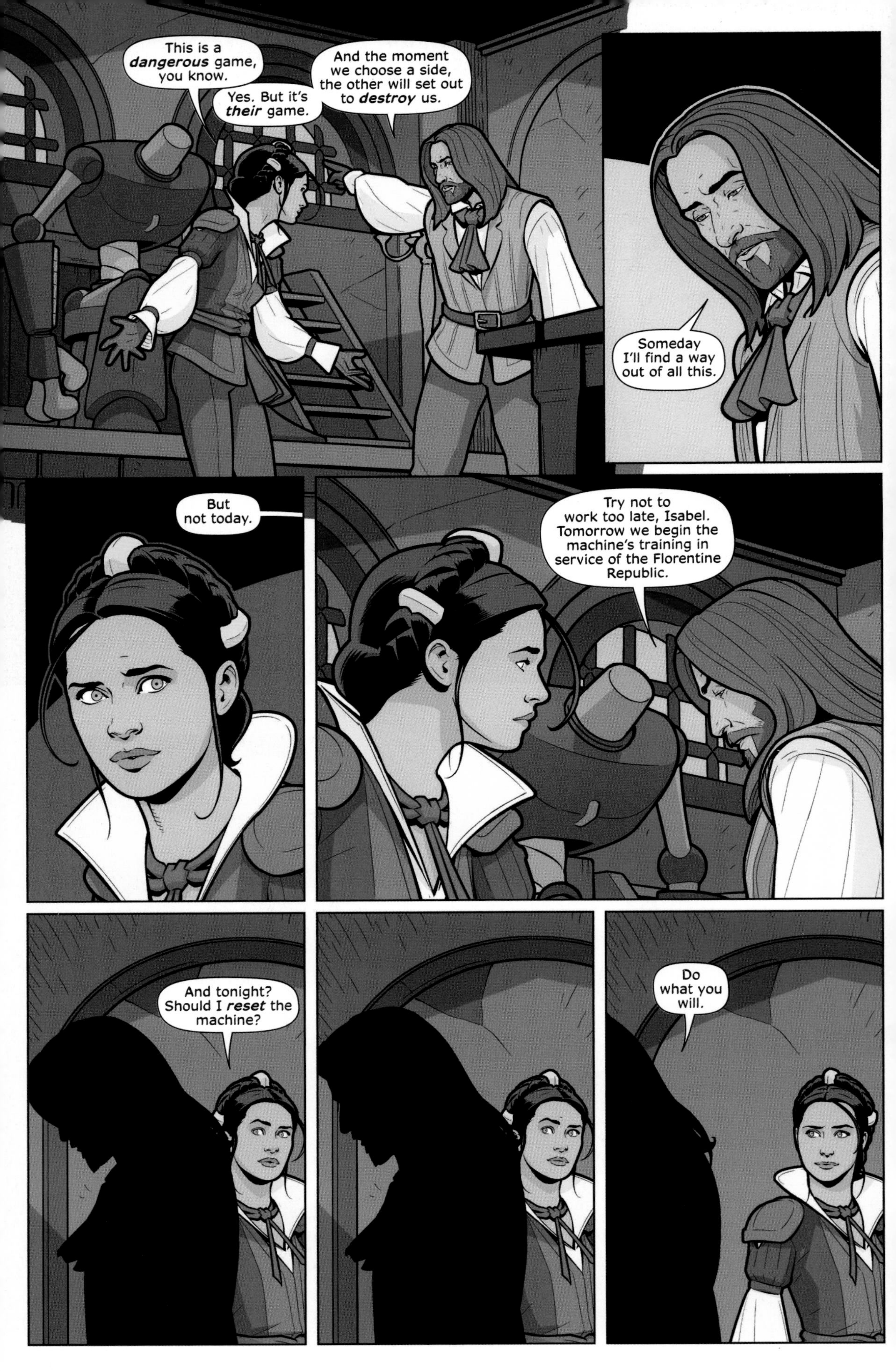
This is a *dangerous* game, you know.
Yes. But it's *their* game.
And the moment we choose a side, the other will set out to *destroy* us.
Someday I'll find a way out of all this.
But not today.
Try not to work too late, Isabel. Tomorrow we begin the machine's training in service of the Florentine Republic.
And tonight? Should I *reset* the machine?
Do what you will.

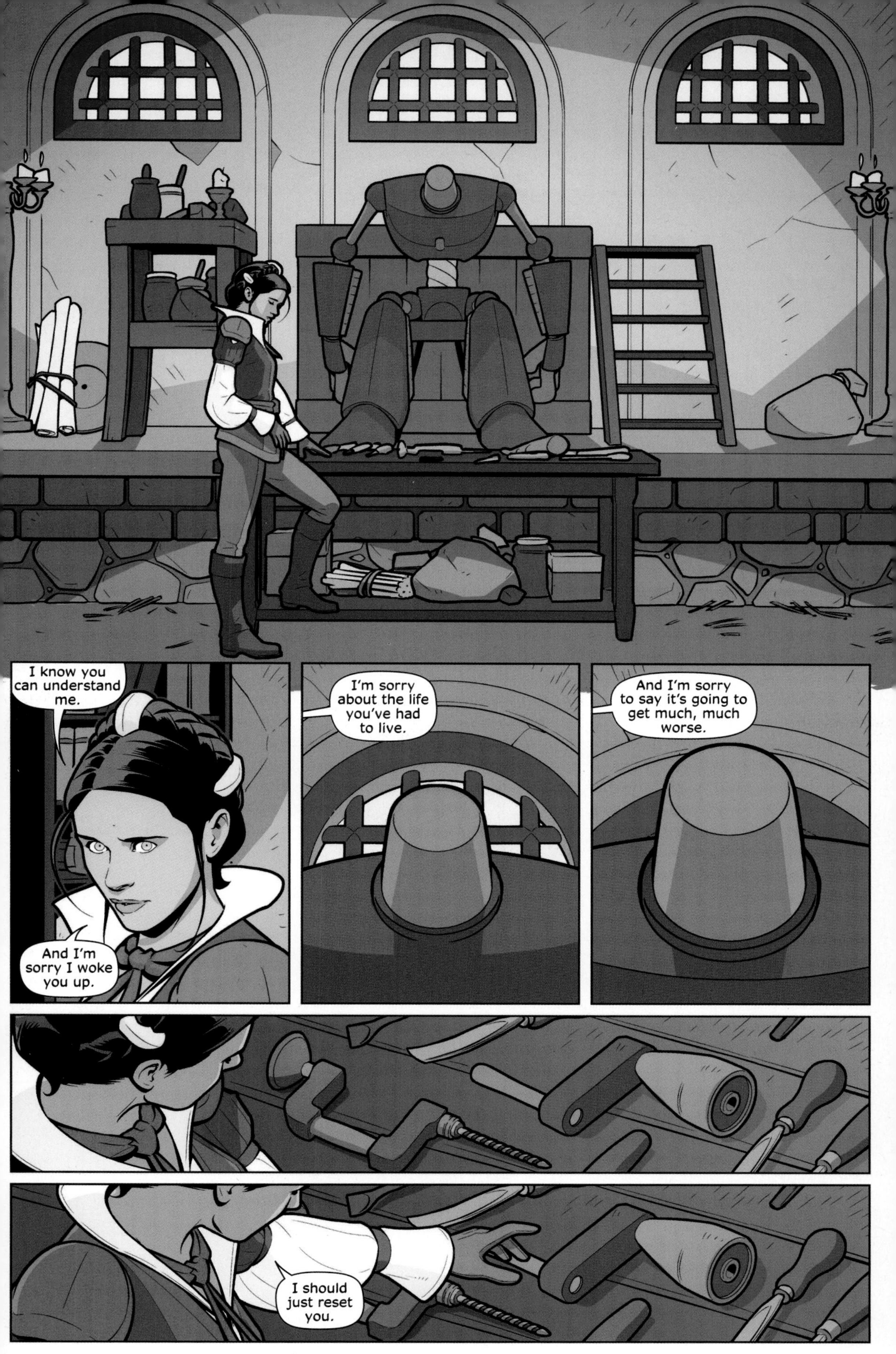

I know you can understand me.
And I'm sorry I woke you up.
I'm sorry about the life you've had to live.
And I'm sorry to say it's going to get much, much worse.
I should just reset you.

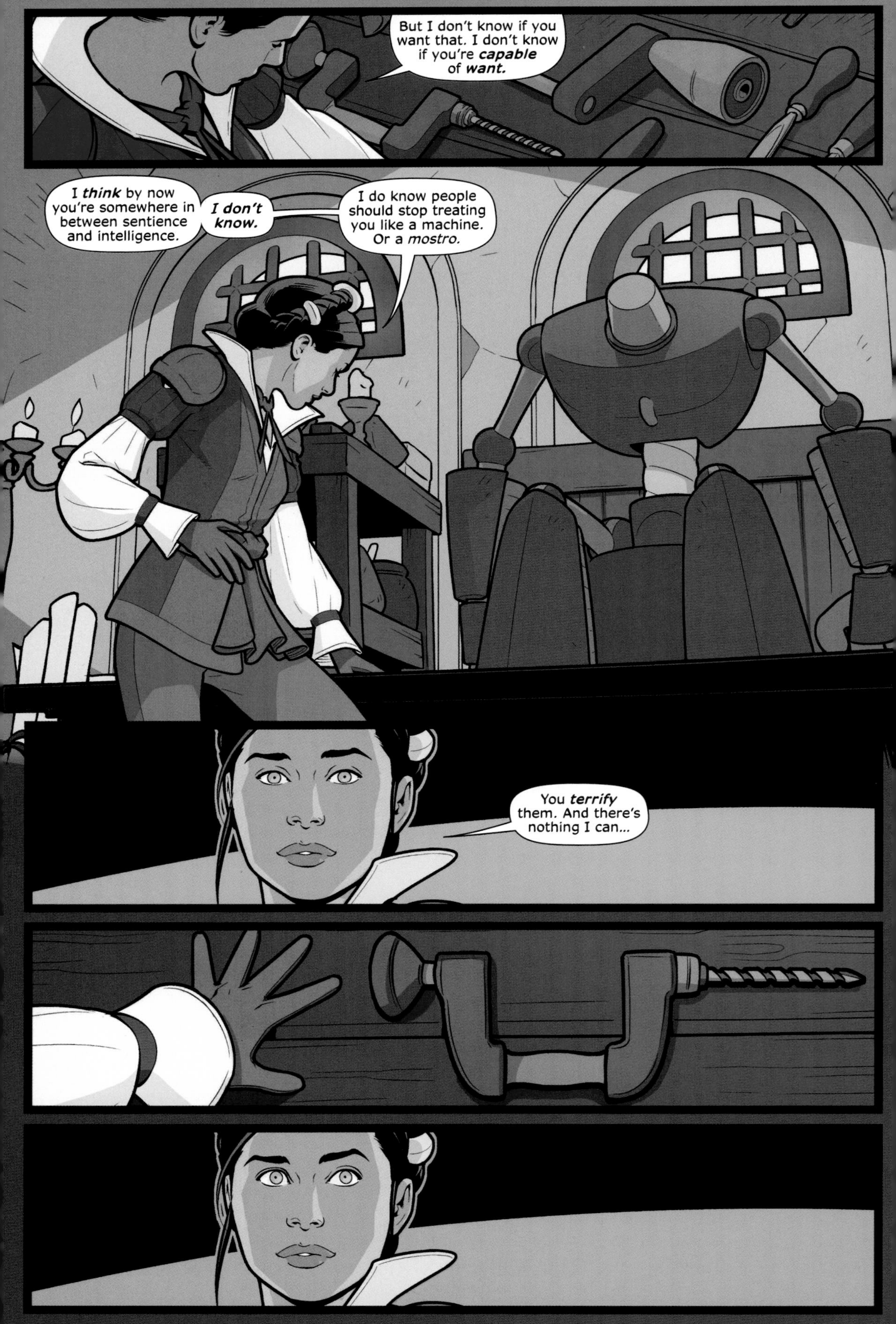
But I don't know if you want that. I don't know if you're ***capable*** of ***want.***
I ***think*** by now you're somewhere in between sentience and intelligence.
I don't know.
I do know people should stop treating you like a machine. Or a *mostro.*
You ***terrify*** them. And there's nothing I can...

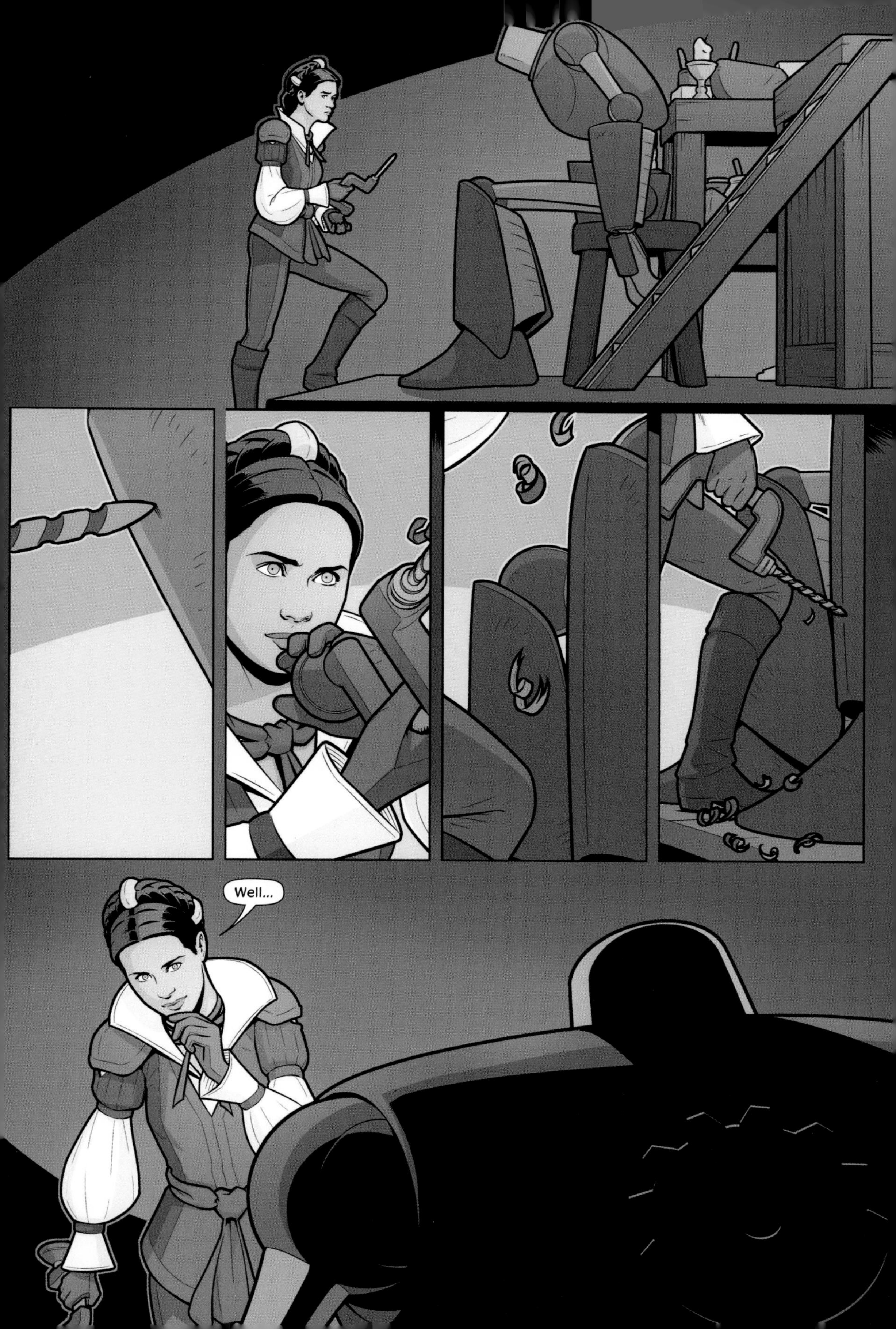
Well...

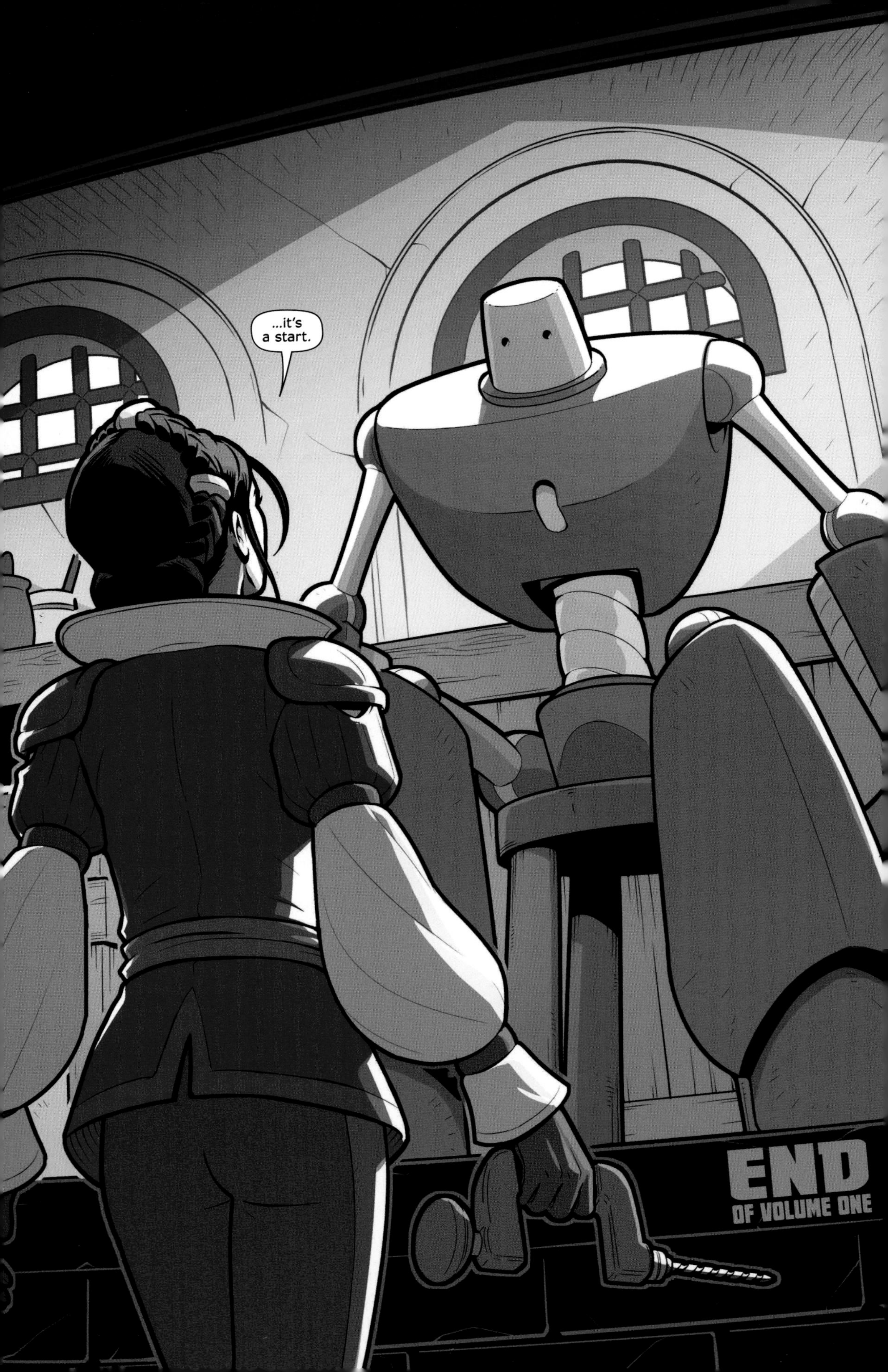
...it's a start.
END
OF VOLUME ONE

COVER GALLERY

Issue 1
ARIELA KRISTANTINA w/ ANDRE SZYMANOWICZ
cover B

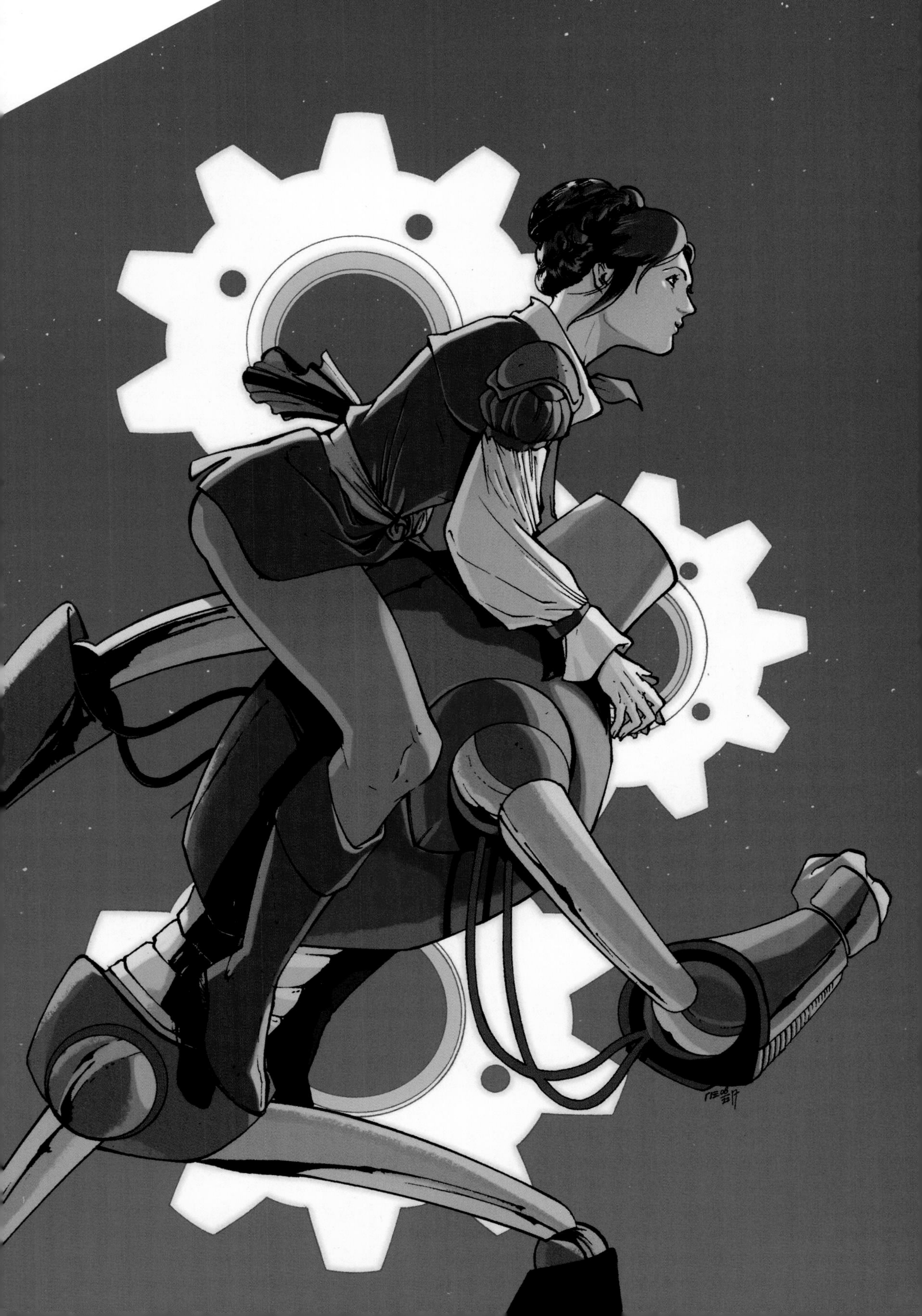

SKETCHBOOK

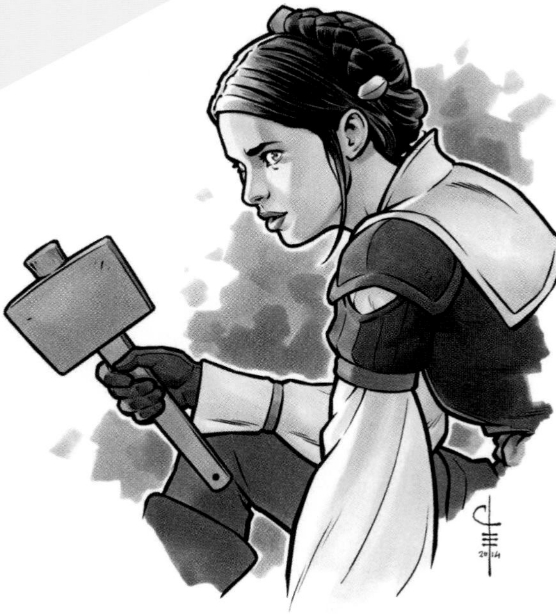

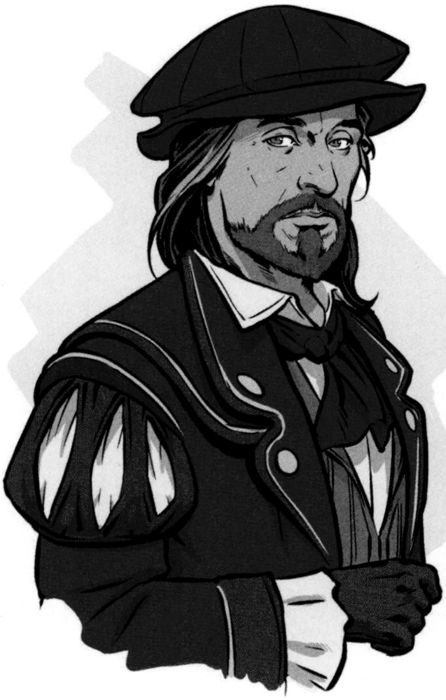

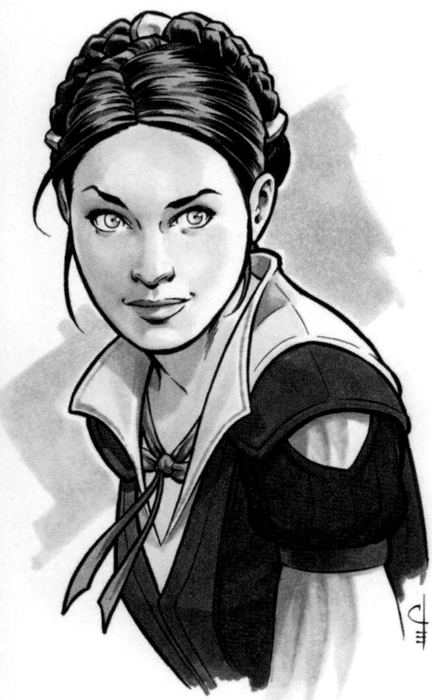

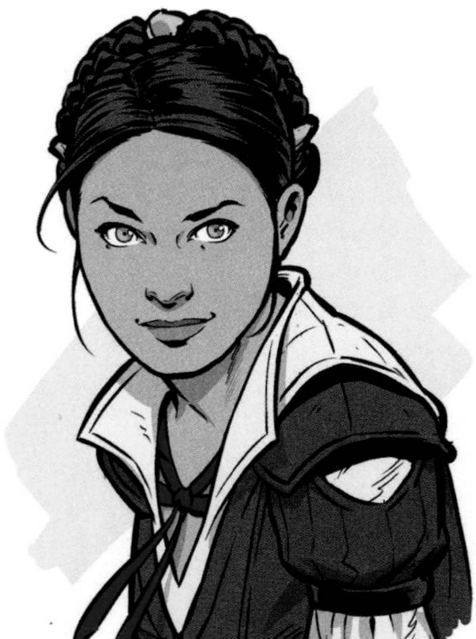

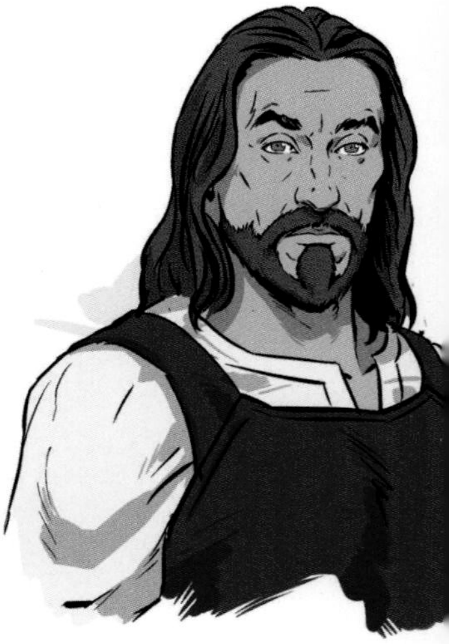

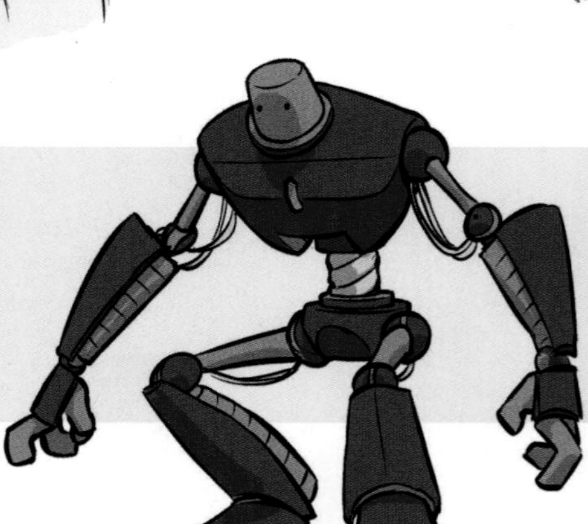

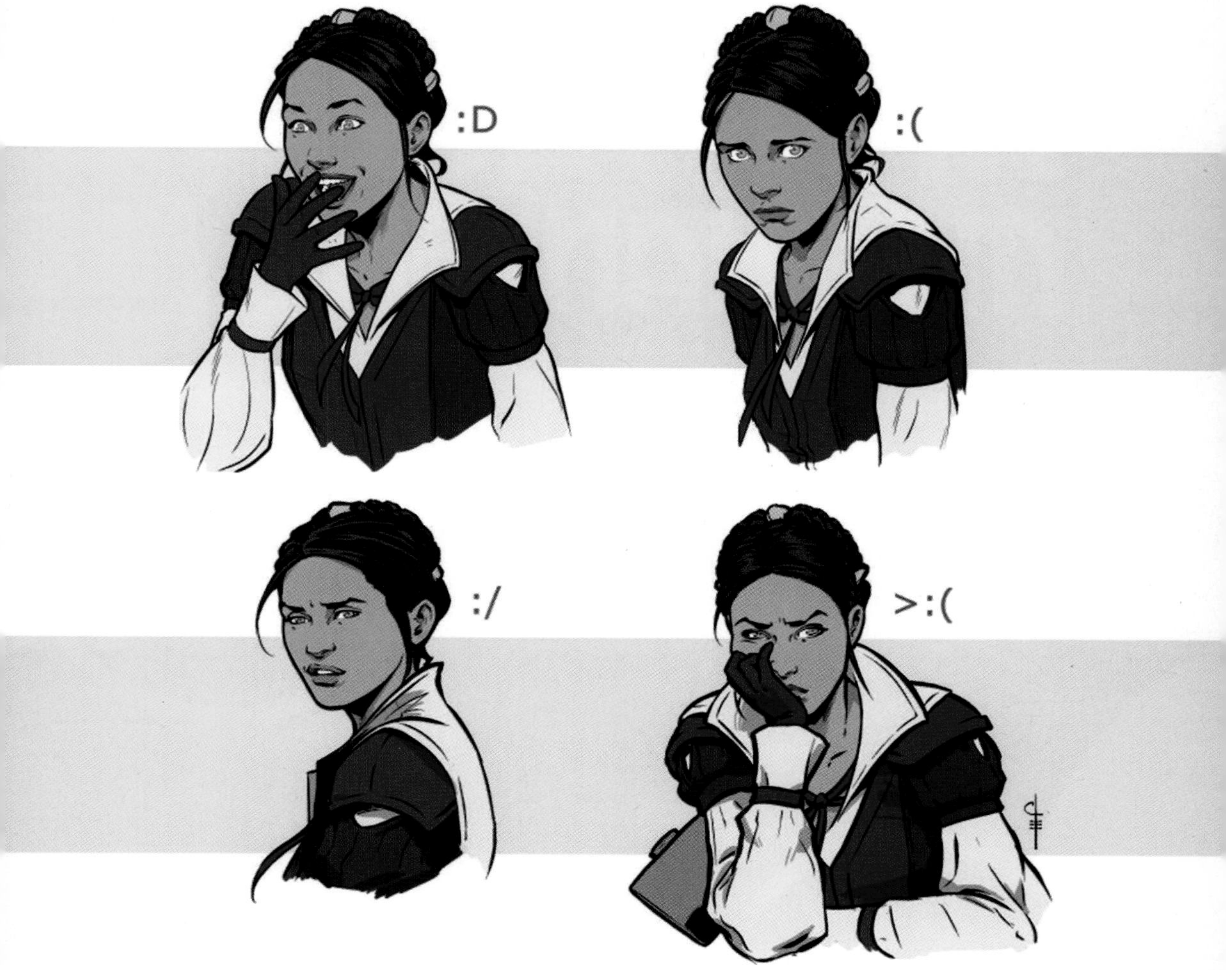
:D
:(
:/
>:(

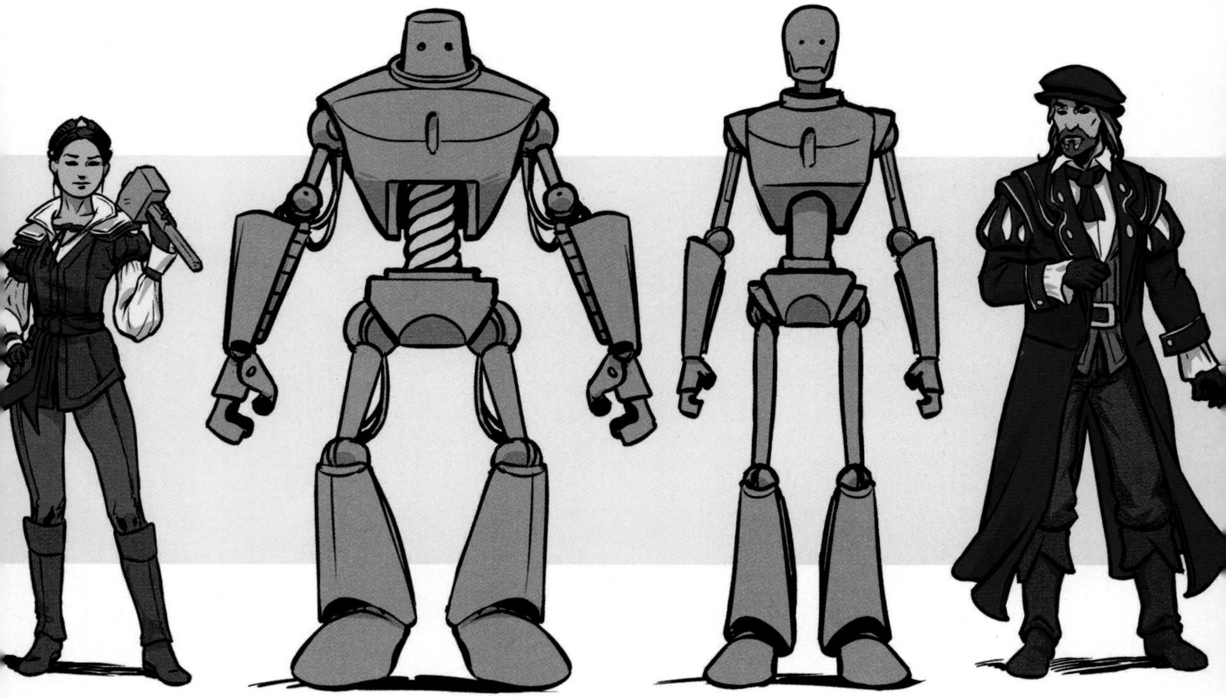

ABOUT THE CREATORS OF

MONSTRO MECHANICA™

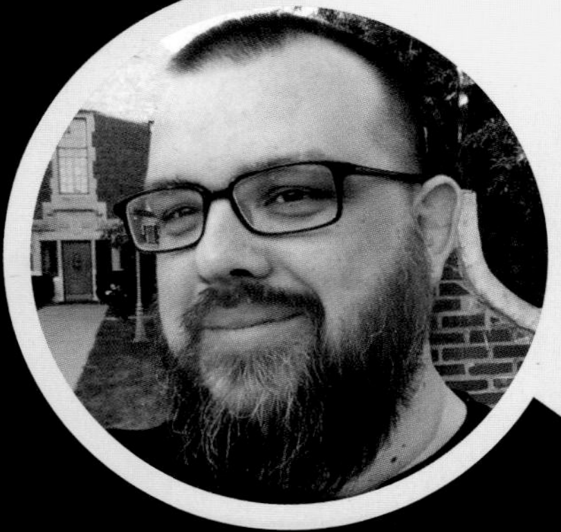

PAUL ALLOR
writer

@PaulAllor

Paul is a comic-book writer, editor and letterer based in north-central Indiana. He has worked on *Teenage Mutant Ninja Turtles, Clue* and *Uncanny Inhumans*, as well as creator-owned comics such as *Tet, Strange Nation* and *Past the Last Mountain*. He is also an instructor and the operations manager at Comics Experience. You can find him at www.paulallor.com.

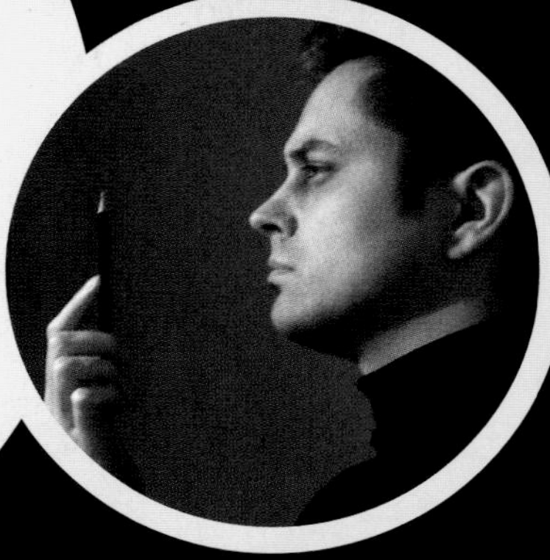

CHRIS EVENHUIS
artist

@ChrisEvenhuis

Chris is a freelance artist and illustrator based in The Netherlands. He has worked on *Wynonna Earp, Magic: The Gathering, Shadow Show: Stories In Celebration of Ray Bradbury, Action Man* and *G.I.Joe*, as well as European comics like *Killing Time* and *Notorious Circus*. Now, Chris lends his full-time talents to MONSTRO MECHANICA!

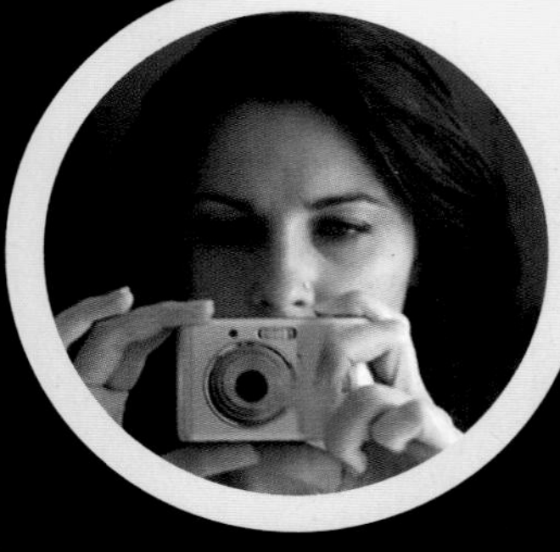

SJAN WEIJERS
colorist

Sjan is a freelance artist based in The Netherlands. She works in animation and video games, providing style guides, character design and art direction for various projects. She also performs toy design in Amsterdam. As a comic artist, her main focus is on color and atmosphere. Sjan has previously worked with Sony Video Entertainment and Dreamworks Animation. MONSTRO MECHANICA is her first AfterShock project!